The Tyranny of the Experts

The Tyranny of the Experts

How Professionals Are
Closing the Open Society

JETHRO K. LIEBERMAN

Walker and Company ☀ New York

301.44
L 71 t

MN

Table of Contents

For Jessica

1
Experts Take Over

1

War is much too serious a matter to be entrusted to the military.
— GEORGES CLEMENCEAU

The C–5A program, once regarded as a brilliant achievement in defense management, is now in disrepute. . . . Not the least important of the lessons learned is that contracts with incentive clauses are too important to be left to lawyers.
— *Armed Forces Journal* (May 10, 1969)

In the original American populistic dream, the omnicompetence of the common man was fundamental and indispensable. It was believed that he could, without much special preparation, pursue the professions and run the government. Today he knows that he cannot even make his breakfast without using devices, more or less mysterious to him, which expertise has put at his disposal; and when he sits down to breakfast and looks at his morning newspaper, he reads about a whole range of vital and intricate issues and acknowledges, if he is candid with himself, that he has not acquired competence to judge most of them.
— RICHARD HOFSTADTER, *Anti-intellectualism in American Life*

1

Professional photographers in Georgia were once required by law to react properly to Wassermann tests before they were permitted to roam the streets with cameras.[1] In times worried by far more awesome issues, this seems laughable. Yet that kind of control is no laughing matter when it is applied to man's most critical problems. For regulations that say what qualifications an expert must possess before he will be permitted to exercise his skills stand directly in the way of those who must solve pressing social problems.

Suppose, to avoid trouble, the experts (with an economic and social stake in things the way they are) write these regulations themselves? For years private bar associations successfully deterred judges from permitting television and still cameras in courtrooms, not because the practice was illegal but because it was "unethical."[2] Members of the North Carolina Dental Board, a state agency charged with selection and discipline of the profession, are elected by a statewide referendum — of dentists.

People might be seriously injured, the professionals argue, if the public were left to the mercies of unscrupulous practitioners. To perform brain surgery obviously requires training. An unknowing litigant may be financially gouged by a lawyer with a penchant for high fees. Incompetent, unethical, and unprofessional conduct must therefore be kept to a minimum. It follows that some form of regulation is necessary. Since professionalism springs from the exercise of specialist skills, judgments relating to competence or proper professional conduct may be exercised only by the professionals themselves. So runs the argument.

Although the professions have been effective in improving the

---

[1] Walter Gellhorn, *Individual Freedom and Governmental Restraints* (1956), p. 125.

[2] Canon 35 of the Code of Judicial Ethics, the provision in question, is not law and became partially moot in favor of the bar in 1965, when the Supreme Court ruled in Estes v. Texas, 381 U.S. 532, that it is unconstitutional to permit cameras in felony courtrooms.

general tone of professional conduct, the fact that experts often sit in judgment of themselves — conferring, suspending, and revoking licenses — raises the question to what degree they have considered the public interest in their management of the professions. A nation which honors a system of checks and balances should surely be wary of the growth of powerful, self-regulating bodies. The medieval guild system would not be consciously tolerated in the United States today; yet to a degree greater than most people realize, America is returning to that presumably long-dead institution, as scores of occupations rush to achieve professional status.

Professionals are dividing the world into spheres of influence and erecting large signs saying "experts at work here, do not proceed further." The public respects the signs and consequently misses the fact that what goes on behind them does not always bear much relation to the professed goals and activities of those who put them up. Professionals frequently say one thing and do another and assert that the layman's inability to find consistency between talk and action is caused by his inherent lack of insight into the professional mysteries. But the gap exists, and it has important political, economic, and social consequences: the public is losing the power to shape its destiny.

It is more than sociologically interesting to note that the development of the professional class and the problem it poses have gone virtually unrecognized. To be sure, there have been a few serious discussions[3] — too serious for wide dissemination. Furthermore, a subgroup of sociology has laid claim to academic discussion of "work" and "professionalization," and the curious ethic that

---

[3] For instance, Gellhorn, *supra* note 1; Henry S. Kariel, *The Decline of American Pluralism* (1961); "The Professions," 92 *Daedalus* (Fall, 1963); Corinne Lathrop Gilb, *Hidden Hierarchies* (1966); Louis Jaffe, "Law Making by Private Groups," 51 *Harv. L. Rev.* 201 (1938); Arthur E. Sutherland, "Private Government and Public Policy," 41 *Yale Review* 405 (1952); W. Willard Wirtz, "Government by Private Groups," 13 *La. L. Rev.* 440 (1953); Frederick H. Beutel, "Law Making by Professional and Trade Associations," 34 *Nebr. L. Rev.* 431 (1955); "Legal Responsibility for Extra-Legal Censure," 62 *Col. L. Rev.* 475 (1962). There still is no general history of the professions in the United States.

pervades the entire academic community has forced the subject into a sterile rut by virtually prohibiting any but sociologists from treating it.

Occasional exposés of a given profession, such as Jessica Mitford's *The American Way of Death*, cause outbursts of public indignation at the sharp and shady practices revealed. Miss Mitford's book even sparked investigation by the Senate Antitrust and Monopoly Subcommittee.[4] But no one has been disposed to see anything but aberrant behavior in a particular profession. *Time Magazine* charged in a cover article that "medicine is the only big business in which the ultimate consumer has no control over what he buys"[5] at the same time that a popular book, Murray Teigh Bloom's *The Trouble with Lawyers*, imputed an equal power to the legal profession. Both failed to articulate the theory of the professional class; they have failed to see that inherent tendencies in all professions constitute a pervasive social problem.

Professional experts are increasingly able to take hold of our daily existence because they are involved so much with the mundane workaday world that they are largely taken for granted. Professionals are unexciting; fictional heroes to the contrary notwithstanding, their work is dreary and rooted in drudgery; intellectual preparation is the basis for excellence and though such work may sometimes have the ring of drama (the omnicompetent doctor calmly readying the operation room; the nerveless lawyer researching at midnight to defend his innocent client), intellectual preparation means years of routine coping with narrow issues which the public is not expected to understand. Professionals do not normally work before audiences; they shield their jobs from public gaze. Even less often are professionals hauled before Congressional committees to justify their work routines; indeed, their very jobs presume they will be left alone to pursue the work about which we know little but without which we could not long survive.

---

[4] *Antitrust Aspects of the Funeral Industry,* Hearings Before the Senate Antitrust and Monopoly Subcommittee, 89th Cong., 2d. Sess., 1964.
[5] *Time,* February 21, 1969, p. 53.

The point has been made most tellingly by the eminent sociologist Everett C. Hughes, who recalls that "the very same engineer kept the waterworks to Paris going before, during, and after the French Revolution."[6]

A widespread assumption that professionals are just technical specialists doing a job contributes to the invisibility of the take-over. A benchmark of this assumption was President John F. Kennedy's Yale Commencement Address in 1962: "You are a part of the world [he said to the graduates], and you must participate . . . in the solution of the problems that pour upon us, requiring the most sophisticated and technical judgment. . . . The central domestic problems of our time . . . relate not to basic clashes of philosophy or ideology, but to ways and means of reaching common goals — to research for sophisticated solutions to complex and obstinate issues. . . . What is at stake in our economic decisions today is not some grand warfare of rival ideologies which will sweep the country with passion but the practical management of a modern economy."[7] The President did not say it, but the implication was clear: give experts governmental authority over their separate spheres of knowledge. Private associations of specialists, like lawyers, doctors, and funeral directors, wield vast power already.

The professional person says his only function is to perform a service. In the underlying theory of the professional class, however, service is incidental to the principal function of the profession. Maintenance of the legal system as construed by lawyers is the principal function of the lawyer, as the public health is upheld in turn by doctors who define it, and as architects do the same for the national esthetic. What degrades the profession degrades the legal system, the public health, the national esthetic. What is not good for lawyers is bad for law. In short, lawyers *are* the legal system, and doctors the public health. Professionals might deny this, but they take actions based on it, and the contradiction is serious.

<hr />

6 Everett C. Hughes, *Men and Their Work* (1958), p. 145.
7 *The New York Times,* June 12, 1962, p. 1.

2

Contradiction and paradox are consistent partners in American history. There are those who rail against federal bureaucracy only to require an equally or more galling state officialdom. Many who despise government "inefficiency" ignore the bungling of the business concerns they esteem. To some, "states' rights" means the power of the state to be brutal and capricious; they who say otherwise by speaking out for "local rule" recoil in horror at the suggestion that the city have more power to govern itself than the state legislature. Likewise, the champions of "oppressed minorities" often have contempt for any but their own voices; yet those who piously prefer majority rule to the pretentious demands of "minority groups" concoct procedures in Congress and state houses which are quite useful in thwarting votes of the majority.

Contradictions arise because beliefs which were once rooted in circumstance tend to become mere rationalizations when conditions change. Perhaps none is stronger than the belief in the supremacy of the American consumer. "The Consumer is King"; his decisions, so runs the economic litany, not only shape but decisively determine the state of the economy and (hence) his life. This myth has been debunked for some time now, even though a substantial number of people continue to believe it, and a significant number who know better cherish it nonetheless.

In fact, the producer is far more important than the consumer, at least in this regard: the producer decides what the public will consume. There is no longer, if there ever was, a market mechanism through which the consumer can order the production of different commodities. Paradoxically at a time when public appreciation of consumer problems would seem to be growing, the average citizen is becoming producer-oriented; he sees himself primarily as a producer of things and services. If he stops to consider his plight as a consumer, it is only to note with some exasperation that other industries seem lax and incompetent. It does not occur to him that a more underlying cause is at work; that *his* occupation probably strikes others as also being less than conscientious in maintaining values which a consumer in an all-too-rare reflective moment might demand; that there is any tension between his own work time hours as a producer and his off-duty hours as a consumer of products, professional services, and leisure.

The professional, too, is a producer, and he sees gains to be made at consumer expense. Far from respecting the received tradition of "free enterprise," most professionals repudiate it and wish nothing more than to alter it beyond recognition. But, they humbly explain, they seek this variance only because theirs is that rare occupation which for reasons peculiar to itself must necessarily stand outside the marvelous Western economic tradition. The expression of their disbelief in the economics they praise outside the office is to be found in the literally tens of thousands of state and local laws, regulations, and ordinances which license the practice of the professions, fix prices, and define what services and products may be offered for sale and in what manner.

The professional tradition began with doctors and lawyers, and in medicine and law has found its highest successes. But the movement merely began there; it is no exaggeration to say that it has extended itself to more than three hundred occupations since professionalism first took on consciousness after the Civil War.

The rise of the professional spells trouble not only in the economic realm: it threatens the validity of the concept of citizenship. Professionalism strikes at the very core of hitherto accepted notions about the place of the individual in the fabric of a liberal, democratic society. Corporations may control economic life and strongly influence social life, yet they do not, for all their power, determine the general shape of our political institutions. But professionalism does carry this threat; inherent in the meaning of professionalism and the motives of its adherents is the negation of democracy itself, stemming from the incipient belief that the citizen, like the consumer, is incompetent to make important decisions affecting his life.

In the political realm, the professionals are developing an

imperial point of view that corresponds to their producer orientation. Decisions should be made, professionals contend, from the perspective of the professions; men should serve the disembodied will of the discipline — law, medicine, even laundering.[8] This is native imperialism—"native" because it does not extend outward to capture other nations. It looks inward and is at its worst in democracy because it is there that the possibility exists for private control of government. The capture of any part of government by a private group is cause for concern because actions affecting the public are taken without public debate and without the possibility of compromise or change.

The management of public affairs by groups not representative of the public is not an ideal ardently sought by democratic or open-society political theorists or by common men, but it is a reality being achieved by professionals. Professional associations have captured enough of the machinery of government to enforce private policy with public power. By exercising control over the staffing and policy-making of licensing bodies throughout the United States, professional organizations impose their idiosyncrasies on almost the entire populace.

3

Men no longer believe in the power of the individual but in the group, the committee, and the organization. Some of these organizations have combined into super groups, to give us the "military-industrial complex." The society "co-exists" with it and does not erupt into "class war" because there has been a "managerial revolution" which has accommodated itself to the needs of an "affluent society." So, at least, have all these trends and moods been interpreted in a stream of books and articles.

Yet we find ourselves in malaise. We are afflicted with strains and revolutions — of race, creed, and youth. It should not be sur-

---

[8] *Cf.* Edmond Cahn, *The Predicament of Democratic Man* (1961).

prising. A principal feature of our managerial, affluent, post-industrial, frenetic, and compulsive life is a willingness to delegate most facets of it to others. We are trained, but unschooled; lettered but unlearned, intelligent but undisciplined. We have turned over to others the power to make legal, medical, aesthetic, social, and even religious decisions for us. We have put the experts in charge — or at least abdicated our responsibility to them. For some, only the moral decision seems to remain, and at its starkest it says to them: "Your only choice is 'submit or defy.' " It says this to youths because they have no control over most of the institutions which intimately affect their lives. So they believe they have lost the power of rational action, with avenues of change blocked. But the need for change is undeniable — hence "revolution." People revolt because they sense and see the world being subdivided and appropriated by experts who know no more, and often see less acutely, than they. We must recognize the need to accept responsibility for ourselves; to do this we must first learn that, despite the myth, we do not have (or even seem to want) this responsibility.

We have become so inured to our own feebleness in the face of expert knowledge that it will doubtless seem difficult to believe that, for instance, the meaning of "due process" was popularly and vigorously debated during the middle years of the 1800's — not alone by lawyers, but by rude and common men who had no greater stake in its meaning than we today.[9] But we have lost our nerve: debate on due process is lawyer talk when it ought to be part of our daily existence. Similarly, we may be led to think that in national debates over great issues we can participate only if we have direct personal or professional stake. Thus education bills should be left not even to teachers but to "educators," medical laws to doctors. It has not quite gone so far yet, but this is the heresy which professionals would make orthodox.

When we ponder leaving decisions in the hands of experts we

---

[9] See Graham, "Procedure to Substance — Extra Judicial Rise of Due Process, 1830–1860," 40 *Calif. L. Rev.* 483 (1952).

should recall the extraordinary fact that the leaders in the fight to establish inoculation as a cure for smallpox in colonial America were Cotton Mather and his brother clergy. Professor Daniel J. Boorstin reminds us that the leading opponents of inoculation in the 1720's were doctors.[10]

4

There will be those who will attack what follows because, they will say, the Western world is evolving into a system of interlocking specialist control, and this quiet and relatively orderly evolution is the only way to save the world from anarchy or despotism and to deliver to it a greatly enhanced quality of life. Perhaps. But it seems prudent to doubt it, at least for a moment in time, so that we can examine its reach and its defects, as well as its promises.

Attack, in any case, will be good. The theory of the professional class will take time to penetrate the American psyche. When students only discovered the United States Army, chemical manufacturers, and universities in the late 1960's, we need not be apprehensive they will march on the American Medical Association[11] much less the Rhode Island barbers' association. Most students do not consider these organizations relevant problems. But then, professional students, no less than others, are not widely acclaimed for the keenness of their perceptions in that regard.

There is one final reason to suppose a study of the professions will be useful. With the ending of the classical market system went the old reliance on profit-maximization as the rule of the individual firm.[12] That goal has been replaced with others: growth may be primary but solemn pronouncements that social utility is the guiding beacon are as insistent. The professions have long claimed benefit to mankind as their goal and profits limited by ethics as a rule. Theirs should be an instructive example.

[10] Daniel J. Boorstin, *The Americans: The Colonial Experience* (1958), pp. 224–5.
[11] But see p. 288.
[12] See John Kenneth Galbraith, *The New Industrial State* (1967), Chapter 10.

2
Licensing and Self-Regulation

I have settled more strikes for my organization by being a member
of the board of state barber examiners than a dozen local unions
could have done in my home town, and I am secretary of my local.
We have settled hotel strikes where they get scab men in there
without licenses from out of town. I have gone to the police station
and sworn out warrants and taken them out of the barber shops,
and two hours afterward had the boss sign up. Now, these are
some of the things you can accomplish by that law. . . . It keeps
the bums out, and it keeps wages up, and the good barber gets
a chance to earn a lot of money.
> — Barber, quoted by SUMNER A. SLICHTER,
> *Union Policies and Industrial Management*

1

Consider the North Carolina Tile Layer: Here is a craftsman who
lays, sets, and installs ceramic tile, marble, and terrazzo floors and
walls in public and private buildings. In 1937, the North Carolina
Legislature enacted into law a tile layers code which had the
effect of making the tile layer a professional.

The law established the North Carolina Licensing Board for Tile
Contractors. It consisted of five tilers, each of whom had to have
had at least five years' experience as a tile contractor. The Board
was empowered to make rules to govern its own proceedings and to
give examinations throughout the state for those who wished to
practice tile laying. The state made criminal the act of contracting
with or receiving bids from an unlicensed tile layer. To procure a
license, the young professional hopeful must have had two years'

experience as a student in tile laying (except that those who were practicing tile laying on the enactment date were exempted from the experience requirement). It cost $25 to take the examination; thereafter the tile layer was required to spend $50 yearly to renew his license (though he need not be reexamined). The Licensing Board, moreover, was given the power to suspend or revoke licenses for manifest "incompetence" or even "inefficiency." The only exemptions to the statutory scheme were these: contracts in which the total cost of materials and labor was less than $150, and all contracts for hospitals, state colleges, and other public buildings.

The theory behind the passage of this modest professional licensing law was the state "police power" to protect the public health. North Carolina, more scientifically prescient than any other state (for no other legislature had passed such a law), comprehended the danger that improperly laid tile could spread disease throughout the state and adjudged that unless only highly skilled people were allowed to lay it, tile would inevitably be poorly placed.

Twenty years later the tile laying profession had grown splendidly in the state. Only 107 individuals and companies were licensed in 1957, the year trouble started; a steady upsurge in demand for the tilers' skills served to employ the North Carolina brethren comfortably. Then the tile laying establishment was fatally hit by a semiliterate, unlicensed youth.

A young tile layer had failed to pass the licensing examination, and though he attempted to carry on, most architects and contractors refused to accept bids from him, since to do so would have been a misdemeanor. One contractor was satisfied with his skill, however, and would have retained him but for the law. So this outcast brought a lawsuit to restrain the Licensing Board and the courts from enforcing it. The law, he asserted, was unconstitutional—strong language for a modest enactment which merely sought to ensure the best performance and prevent disease. The Licensing Board, in its brief before the state supreme court, insisted that the state had the power to license for the protection of public health and to ensure that the complex jobs for which tile layers were hired would be adequately carried out.

The court rejected the health claim rather perfunctorily. If health were in fact the statutory desideratum, how explain the inconsistent exemptions for people who worked on public projects and hospitals? Moreover, sanitation inspectors had never been given a place in the Tile Board.

At greater length, the court found it possible to see through the state's second contention. Despite the evidence tending to suggest complexity, the court noted that the Licensing Board in its affidavit discussed the publications of the Tile Council of America, included among which were "books of instruction to assure proper installations of their products." These books were designed to teach amateurs to work with their materials. "Nothing in the record," said the court, "shows that a man of average intelligence and some aptitude for such work cannot learn quickly enough to do average work. Successful tile contracting consists in doing the work rather than describing it in a written examination paper. In all probability the average worker could learn to do acceptable tile work as quickly as he can learn to describe it on paper."[1] The court concluded that the tiling apprentice had failed the examination largely because his spelling was poor and his syntax was worse, skills which had only a remote bearing on the ability to lay tile. Declaring the licensing law unconstitutional, the North Carolina Supreme Court stated: "If only those of the highest skills are permitted to do the work, those who are unable to pay the higher prices for tile must use wood, brick, concrete, linoleum, or some other material which the ordinary workman is permitted to install. An average man with an average purse has a right to employ a workman of ordinary skill to perform an ordinary task.[2] The North Carolina professional thus rejoined the Union.[3]

---

[1] Roller v. Alden, 245 N.C. 416, 96 S.E. 2d 851 (1957).
[2] Roller v. Alden, 856.
[3] In both senses: other states did not enact tile laws because the tile unions were powerful enough to achieve their purposes without them.

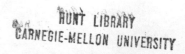

The North Carolina experience is not just a sport among public laws regulating work, nor is the enactment date, 1937, a depression year, without significance. The power of a board to revoke or suspend the license to work because of incompetence and inefficiency, coupled with a power to regulate the supply of workers, are signs that an occupation has entered the preserves of the professional estate, that class of people who perform the vital function in society of transferring "pure" learning to practical ends.[4] It will become clear that the estate is now a large one; if doctors and lawyers occupy its most comfortable rooms, plenty of others have succeeded in settling permanently somewhere inside the gates. Unlike the hapless tile layers, very few are ever directed to leave.

2

Licensing is the imprimatur of status; it serves to label specialists. A complex, interdependent society requires that the method of determining how good or skilled a specialist is be quick, easy, available, and reliable. When it is impossible for the nonspecialist to evaluate the particular expert, he must depend on ratings by other specialists in the same field; the specialist must obtain professional recognition. The evaluation undertaken, the specialist approved, his skill is set forth for all to see in the status which he occupies.[5]

To forestall governmental regulation of their affairs, a few pro-

---

[4] Don K. Price, *The Scientific Estate* (1965), pp. 132 ff. Price sees the professional estate as one of four in a hierarchy which also includes the scientific and scholarly community, devoted to creating theory; administrators, who must coördinate the work of different professionals; and politicians, who must make the "ultimate" policy decisions which shape the direction of the administrators' efforts.

[5] "Licensing can be expected when the variance in the quality of the service furnished by the practitioner is high, when the importance of that variance is great, when the amount of training necessary to evalute the service is large, and when the degree of exposure of the consumer to the practitioner is small." Moore, "The Purpose of Licensing," 4 *J. of L. and Econ.* 93 (1961).

fessions introduced *self-regulation* in the last third of the nineteenth century. Even when state legislatures began to enact licensing legislation at the turn of the century, the impetus came from professionals, not the public. The bulk of existing professional licensing laws was passed at the behest of the professional groups; almost invariably these groups have been given a share of the regulatory power.

At a session of the Wisconsin legislature some two decades ago, caterers, canopy and awning installers, cider makers, coal dealers, dancing school instructors, egg breakers, frog dealers, labor organizers, meat cutters, music teachers, and beer coil cleaners tried unsuccessfully to get themselves regulated. This same state in 1939 did enact legislation requiring examination for house painters; on the strength of this law, friendly citizens who helped relatives and neighbors paint their houses were arrested and fined for failure to possess the requisite license. Unfortunately for the professional painters, the Wisconsin Supreme Court was moved to find a touch of unconstitutionality in the scheme in 1941.[6]

Occupations which currently require licensing are so numerous as to defy classification. Even their listing is tedious in the extreme. A sampling of forty-five occupations controlled by state licensing boards in one state alone gives a fair idea of the magnitude of the licensed estate. By 1938 in North Carolina, these "professionals," among others, were licensed: lawyers, physicians, dentists, dental hygienists, pharmacists, optometrists, osteopaths, chiropractors, nurses, midwives, veterinarians, chiropodists, embalmers, pilots, pawnbrokers, photographers, public accountants, real estate brokers and salesmen, contractors, electrical contractors, mattress manufacturers, dry cleaners, burial association managers, dealers in scrap tobacco, correspondence and commercial school

---

[6] State v. Peck, 237 Wisc. 596, 297 N.W. 572 (1941) (per curiam) (the defendant was convicted prior to the repeal of the statute (§ 101.40 (1939), but the appeal was taken subsequent to the repeal; the court did not find it necessary to elaborate on its short decision); see Ruth Doyle, "The Fence-Me-In Laws," 205 *Harpers* 89 (1952).

operators and their solicitors, liquor wholesalers, slaughterers, architects, auctioneers, barbers, threshers, collectors, plumbing and heating contractors, cosmetologists, engineers and land surveyors, insurance agents and adjusters, fidelity and fiduciary companies, dealers and companies in insurance bonding, investment, dividend, guarantee, registry, title guarantee, debentures and the like; and, of course, tile layers (and others).[7]

By 1952, in addition to the obvious professions, at least one state and usually many more could claim the licensing of the following professions: abstracters, boiler inspectors, private detectives, egg graders, electricians, electrologists, elevator inspectors, guide-dog trainers, hoisting engineers, homeopaths, horseshoers, librarians, manicurists, masseurs, mechano-therapists, milk certifiers, mine inspectors, motor vehicle dealers and salesmen, motion picture operators, naturopaths, oculists, pest controllers, physical therapists, drugless physicians, plumbers, psychologists, certified shorthand reporters, sanitarians, social workers, watchmakers, well drillers, and yacht and ship brokers and salesmen.[8]

Although state laws constitute the largest part of the American licensing structure, the federal government plays its limited role in precisely the same manner: at last count, the Coast Guard administered ninety-eight different licensing examinations for merchant marine masters, mates, pilots, and engineers.[9]

There is probably no organized occupational group in the United States which has not tried at one time or another to break into the ranks of licensed professionals.[10] In 1955 a bill was intro-

---

[7] See Hanft and Hamrick, "Haphazard Regimentation Under Licensing Statutes," 17 *Univ. N.C. L. Rev.* 1 (1938).

[8] See Council of State Governments, *Occupational Licensing in the States* (1952), pp. 7–8.

[9] *Navy Times*, June 25, 1969, p. 7.

[10] A collection of additional professions, businesses, trades, and other occupations in which licensing has been upheld by the courts includes: automobile dealers, bail bondsmen, bottle club operators, brick masons, chattel mortgage and salary loan brokers, cigar and cigarette dealers, coal dealers, commission merchants, creamery station owners or operators, dealers in citrus

duced in the California Assembly requiring the licensing of grass cutters as "maintenance gardeners." Mowing a lawn for pay without a license could cause the criminal to pay a fine of $500 and to stay in the local jailhouse for up to six months. A state board would administer the profession in order to prevent "gross incompetence," negligence, and "misrepresentation." The bill did not pass.[11] A cousin of the maintenance gardener is the "tree expert," who is licensed in several states. In testimony before the Illinois State Legislature in 1959, the chairman of the Illinois State Tree Expert Examining Board calmly noted that "the intent of tree expert law was primarily to protect the public against tree quacks, shysters, and inexperienced persons."[12]

3

As long ago as 1938, a political scientist and sometime member of the New Jersey Legislature pinpointed the source of licensing pressures and their rationale: "Businessmen say that they want less government in business, but that is what they say and not what they want. They are always coming to a legislature seeking regulation. They wish to have the state use its licensing power to give them a competitive advantage over other businessmen, especially over those outside the state. In the session of 1935, bills

fruits, dealers in skins and hides of wild fur-bearing animals or alligators, garage operators, itinerant venders, junk dealers, labor union organizers, transportation agents, nonresident fishermen, parking lot attendants, public dance hall operators, stationary engineers, sugar refiners, travel bureau agents, linen and towel rental service operators or solicitors, theater ticket hawkers, stevedores, and automobile towers. The cases are collected in 16A *Corpus Juris Secundum*, "Constitutional Law," Sec. 659, pp. 1013–15. For some of these occupations, the issuance of a license is admittedly far more routine than for others.

[11] Calif. Assem. Bill. No. 1671 (Regular Sess. 1955). See Hetherington, "State Economic Regulation and Substantive Due Process of Law II," 53 *Nw. U. L. Rev.* 226, 249 (1958).

[12] Quoted in Moore, *supra* note 5 at 93; from the *Chicago Daily Tribune*, May 26, 1959.

were introduced to license bait fishing boats, beauty shops, chain stores, florists, insurance adjustors, photographers, and master painters. . . . Usually the bill authorizes the granting of licenses without examination to persons engaged in the business at the date of the passage of the bill; this provision tends to restrain competition from out-of-state businesses and from new enterprises, and it still does not impose any burden heavier than the cost of the license upon those persons who got into the business early. Arguments are made for these bills, of course, based upon the protection of public health, safety, or security from fraud; but the acts are popular with businessmen for competitive, not for public reasons. There is usually no organized opposition to these measures, and some go through every year. In the session of 1935, a bill was passed setting up a state board for the cleaning and dyeing industry. Two of the three members of the board were to be 'experts in the field of economics' to be appointed by the governor, but Governor Hoffman appointed two of his political adherents, one a Trenton garageman. The law required that the 'third member shall be the executive secretary of the New Jersey Dyers and Cleaners Association.' "[13]

Because there is no organized opposition from either the public or other professional groups,[14] occupational groups find it relatively easy to push their licensing desires into law. The Kentucky Dental Practice Act of 1964, a complete revision of the earlier law, was drafted by a six-man dental committee appointed by the Kentucky Dental Association.[15] Equally adept, through long years of experience, are the cosmetologists, curators of the coiffure. State licensing of beauticians began in Louisiana in 1924. Techniques of the state and national societies were not unlike those offered by many others. In New Mexico, for instance, "when the bill reg-

---

[13] Dayton David McKean, *Pressures on the Legislature of New Jersey* (1938), pp. 56–7.

[14] See Chapters 9 and 10.

[15] See Akers, "The Professional Association and the Legal Regulation of Practice," 2 *L. and Society Rev.* 463 (1968).

ulating the beauty parlor operators was introduced, great hilarity ensued, and the bill and all its works were greatly kidded. All that was needed for a laugh the first three weeks of the session was a casual reference to the beauty parlor bill. The earnest and good-natured young ladies who lobbied the bill to a triumphant finish dimpled merrily at all the jokes, issued frequent invitations to luncheons and dinners, talked quietly. When the bill came up for passage it was regarded as seriously as any other measure in the House." And in Oregon: "When the newspapers began to ridicule our movement, many of us who carried the most advertising stopped it immediately, and made a personal appeal to the editors. They reconsidered and gave us a splendid write-up."[16]

Often the profession is not powerful enough at the outset to gain a full set of professional controls. So it begins circumspectly, achieving a modest measure of public recognition. From the weak grant of public power it initially obtains, the professional group draws enough nourishment to come back to the state house a few years later with thicker muscle and consequently stronger appeal. "When, for example, Louisiana paid heed to its 'beauty shoppe' operators who wished to 'protect' lady customers by reducing the competition for their patronage, the state legislature adopted a relatively mild law to regulate and define the practice of 'cosmetic therapy.' The 'Board of Control of Cosmetic Therapy' consisted of the President of the State Board of Health, a second member drawn from that same body, and only one appointee from among the licensed cosmeticians. Within a few years the beauticians were strong enough to ask for (and to obtain) new powers of control, and to erect much sturdier defenses against competition. The governing board was expanded to six members. The President of the State Bord of Health retained his seat, but the licensees captured the remaining five places for their own. In order, as the state legislature solemnly found, to assure that cosmeticians

---

[16] Both quotations from a member of the National School of Cosmeticians, quoted by Morris Fishbein, *The New Medical Follies* (1927), p. 74.

would be 'well-nourished, strong, and healthy,' the authority to fix prices and prevent 'unfair competition' was lodged in the newly constituted board. Then came closer supervision of the 'beauty schools' which aspiring artistes of the profession were required to attend. A major reform was fixing a minimum tuition fee lest competition among the schools drive down their income. Extensive powers to inspect, to supervise, to direct, and to discipline were of course needed if economic as well as qualitative control were to be effective. So the powers were given."[17]

Since the original cosmetology acts were passed, conditions have become generally more restrictive. Arkansas and New Mexico require attendance at beauty schools; Connecticut requires examinations at each step of the path to becoming a cosmetician — apprentice, operator, assistant, and registered hairdresser. California requires a four-year apprenticeship.

It is not fair to imply that the beauticians were entirely without antagonists. Barbers were not idle; they saw to it cosmeticians could have everything they desired so long as they did not invade the barber's domain. One early beauty culture licensing act, that of Illinois in 1927, defined cosmetology as "the application of cosmetic preparations to the human body by massaging, stroking, kneading, slapping, tapping, stimulating, manipulating, exercising, cleansing, beautifying, or by means of devices, apparatus or appliances, arranging, dressing, marcelling, curling, waving, cleansing, singeing, bleaching, coloring, dyeing, tinting, or otherwise treating by any means the hair of any person." Fair enough, thought the barbers; but this much farther, they persuaded the state legislature to tell the women, you shall not go: "Provisions of this act shall not authorize any registered beauty culturist to cut or clip the hair of any person unless he has first obtained a certificate of registration as a barber."[18] The Illinois law thus distinguished between beauty culturists and barbers by the "cutting" act. Oregon, on the other

---

[17] Walter Gellhorn, *Individual Freedom and Governmental Restraints* (1956), pp. 115–16.
[18] Both quotations from Fishbein, *supra* note 16, p. 70.

hand, distinguished less elegantly (but more practically) on the basis of sex: cosmetic therapy includes manicuring the nails of any person, male or female, and among other things, the removal of "superfluous hair" (a profession which is separately licensed in Connecticut by the State Board of Examiners of Hypertrichologists and is known in still other states as electrology).[19] Removal is apparently not equivalent to cutting since curling and cutting of and numerous other operations on the hair are limited to females only. Who wants to cut a man's hair must be a barber.

Like beauticians, barbers have learned the technique of control well: In Rhode Island, for example, it takes some 1500 hours in a barber school to qualify a man for the job and during this time, student barbers cannot charge for their services. Rhode Island beauticians responded by making mandatory an equivalent amount of training in a hairdressing school. The fine for confusing a man with a woman is $200, three months' imprisonment, or both.[20]

4

As state after state enacted licensing legislation, similarities among professional aims became apparent. Professional organizations, speaking out for the public health and safety, required regulation to ensure competence and they preferred to do the regulating themselves.

One clue to the power of professional organizations is their ability to keep their occupations free from legal requirements imposed on "mere" trades — unless such requirements as American citizenship prove useful in keeping out unwanted competitors. Common trades often require posting of a surety bond and sometimes the law prohibits convicted felons from engaging in them. A study of Illinois trades and occupations in 1961 showed that of sixty-eight industries regulated by the state, such as "breeding of

---

[19] See Conn. Gen. Stat. Ann. (1960) Title 20, Chap. 388, §§ 267–278; Utah Code Ann. (1953), Title 58, Chap. 11, § 12.
[20] Rhode Island Gen. Laws. Ann. (1956), §§ 5–27–22, 5–27–17,5–27–30.

stallions and jacks, equestrian travel, shanty boats, cooperative butter and cheese factories, and frozen dessert products"[21] nearly one-fifth of these required operators not to have been convicted of a felony and one-quarter of them required the posting of a bond. The regulation of professional occupations, on the other hand, showed a marked contrast. Of seventy-three self-regulating professions (such as law, medicine, accounting, barbering, real estate, funeral directing, cosmetology, and tree surgery), only one, private detective work, required bonding and in none was a felony conviction expressly fatal to practice. Furthermore, seventy-one of the professional occupations required their practitioners to be citizens (requirements imposed in 1939 when professionals were escaping from Europe), whereas only six per cent of the businesses regulated by the state required citizenship.[22]

If felony and bonding are not of overarching importance, the power of state boards and private associations over standards are. Both exercise significant control over the professional (and sometimes personal) lives of their practitioners. Both define and limit the practice of the professions. Both are intimately related.

In some instances, in fact, the private association and the public regulatory body are identical. Alabama's state medical association is the state board of health. The same body of men serves in three capacities — as governing body of the medical society (with power to enact legally enforceable medical ethics), as the board of health, and as the official state agency for licensing prospective doctors.[23] Connecticut's Board of Censors of the state medical society is formally the state Board of Medical Examiners. More typically, however, the state professional associations indirectly control the membership of the state examining and licensing boards by sub-

[21] Moore, *supra* note 5, p. 96.

[22] Statistics from Moore, *supra* note 5, pp. 94–97. Businesses were perhaps more reluctant to seek citizenship requirements because of decisions of the Supreme Court in such cases as Truax v. Raich, 239 U.S. 33 (1915). *Cf.* Clarke v. Deckenbach, 274 U.S. 392 (1927).

[23] Henry S. Kariel, *The Decline of American Pluralism* (1961), p. 104.

mitting lists of association members from which the Governor by law or custom chooses his regulators. Sometimes the association will donate funds to the board for enforcement work (this is a common practice nationally, for instance, for dentists). Or, the board by law or custom may contribute money to the association; and if not directly, then indirectly, by paying a full-time salary to a part-time employee who can then donate his services to the association and by picking up the rent bill on association office space.[24]

Yet despite the number of licensing statutes, and the similarity of purpose, there are wide disparities among the state boards; these differences, more than anything else, indicate the degree to which the legislatures have abdicated their responsibility in the drafting and policing of regulatory laws. Throughout the various states and in each state there are vastly different provisions governing the composition of licensing boards and the tenure of their members; fees and administrative procedures vary widely; staffs and records are woefully inadequate; the different professions are unequally treated by the various boards.[25]

A selection of boards in one state, New Jersey, highlights the disparities as well as the relationships between board and private association:

(1) State Board of Public Accountants: 3 members, each of whom must be a certified public accountant (original enactment, 1904);

(2) State Board of Architects: 5 members, four of whom must be architects (1902);

(3) Board of Barber Examiners: 3 members, one each of whom must have been recommended by the State Association of Journeymen Barbers and by the State Master Barbers' Association (1933);

(4) Board of Beauty Culture Control: 5 members, at least three

[24] Akers, *supra* note 15, p. 471.
[25] See "Occupational Licensing Legislation in the States," 25 *State Government* 275, 277 (1952), for a list of criticisms then current.

of whom must be beauticians, one of whom must not be in the business, and two of whom must be women (1935);

(5) State Board of Registration and Examination in Dentistry: 8 members, each of whom must be a dentist with 10 years' practice in New Jersey (1915);

(6) State Board of Mortuary Science: 5 members, each of whom must have had five years' experience in the state (1927);

(7) State Board of Professional Engineers and Land Surveyors: 5 members, each of whom must have had five years' practice in the state (1921);

(8) State Board of Medical Examiners: 11 members, five of whom must be "old-school physicians," three of whom homeopaths, one an eclectic, one an osteopath, and one a chiropractor (1894);

(9) New Jersey Board of Nursing: 5 members, each a graduate of a school of nursing with five years' experience (1912);

(10) State Board of Optometrists: 5 members, each with five years' experience (1914);

(11) State Board of Pharmacy: 5 members, each a registered pharmacist (1901);

(12) New Jersey Real Estate Commission: 5 members, each of whom must have been a broker in New Jersey with ten years' experience (1921); and

(13) Board of Veterinary Medical Examiners: 5 members, each of whom must have had five years' experience (1902).[26]

These licensing and examining boards not only prepare, administer, and grade examinations but also sit as plenary bodies to determine the moral fitness of the candidate. Although the moral requirement is usually perfunctory, there have been times when the boards have used their statutory authority to screen out "bad character" with such vengeance that to outward appearances they became inquisitions. Their power is broad because the standards under which they operate are vague. The New Jersey State

[26] The list from McKean, *supra* note 13, pp. 148–9.

Board of Architects, for example, may not only judge a candidate's "ethical standards and his legal fitness for the practice of architecture" at the mandatory "personal audience examination"; the Board may also look to his or her "natural endowments."[27]   Boards of Bar Examiners occasionally judge candidates by political opinions with the result that most applicants for admissions to the bar profess the same bland belief in the "American form of government" whether or not they actually hold it.   And it can backfire: one candidate, whose story appears later,[28] was refused admission in part because he stated a belief in the principles of the Declaration of Independence.

Means other than control by licensing are at the disposal of professional groups to direct and channel the activities of practitioners.   Memberships in state medical bodies and the American Medical Association are not required by law for the practice of medicine, but the practicing physician who chooses not to be affiliated brooks trouble: "In general a physician's ability to continue his professional development is restricted by the loss of participation in scientific programs and professional relationships. And a rejected doctor is denied the use of the medical societies as a form for bringing his own discoveries before the profession. The non-society member is 'quite generally regarded as an outcast.'   As a non-member he is ineligible for specialty board examinations and ratings.   Referrals and consultation, so essential to the growth of a new practice, are denied him.   Expulsion or denial carries stigma of unethical practice so that members who have professional relations with a rejected practitioner may themselves be considered unethical.   Thus, as part of its enforcement program, one medical society circulated a 'white list' of approved doctors to its members.   The disapproved physician will also be handicapped in caring for his patients.   Unless he relinquishes control over the patient, he may be unable to secure assistance in

[27] New Jersey Dept. of Labor and Industry, *Occupations and Professions Handbook* (1964), p. 10.
[28] Chapter 7, p. 97ff.

time of emergency. Perhaps most important, he will be denied the use of most hospital facilities."[29]

The American Medical Association (AMA) has been able to keep practicing physicians in line for years on such issues as group health practice, insurance, Medicare, and Medicaid by threatening reprisals through the state associations.[30] Reprisals can be exceedingly subtle. One approach is the "not us" ploy. The American Board of Anesthesiology (say) gives examinations for would-be "Board-certified anesthesiologists." The "Board reserves the right to reject any applicant for any reason deemed advisable and without stating the same" and "the right to limit the number of candidates to be admitted to any examination."[31]   But the Board's certification is not legally binding, since a hospital could hire a non-certified anesthesiologist. The hospital would not be likely to hire a non-certified doctor, however, since the AMA's Council on Medical Education and Hospitals stands ready to cut the accreditation of hospitals falling below "minimum standards." Should the specialist without Board certification present himself to the hospital for staff privileges and be rejected, his complaint will fall on unheeding ears: "We only accept Board-certified specialists," says the hospital, "but we are not in the certifying business ourselves." The Board reminds the unhappy doctors that "we do not and cannot compel the hospital to take you on; the decision is entirely theirs." Who is responsible for the doctor's subsequent

[29] "The American Medical Association: Power, Purpose, and Politics in Organized Medicine," 63 *Yale L.J.* 931, 951–2 (1954). Quotations are from Group Health Coöperative of Puget Sound v. King County Medical Society, 39 Wash. 2d 586, 237 P. 2d 737 (1951).

[30] See Oliver Garceau, *The Political Life of the American Medical Association* (1941); Elton Rayack, *Professional Power and American Medicine: The Economics of the American Medical Association* (1967); "The American Medical Association: Power, Purpose, and Politics in Organized Medicine," 63 *Yale L.J.* 931 (1954); *Meeting Health Needs by Social Action*, 337 *The Annals* of the American Academy of Political and Social Science (Sept. 1961); *Medicine and Society*, 346 *The Annals* (March 1963); Louis Lasagna, *Life, Death, and the Doctor* (1968).

[31] *Directory of Medical Specialists* (1966), pp. 715, 727; cf. Rayack, pp. 221ff.

inability to work as an anesthesiologist? "Not us," says the Board. "Not us," says the hospital. And this will still be true though the doctor's failure is unrelated to medical incompetence.[32]

This same type of divided responsibility significantly affects most matters of high medical policy. The supply of doctors can be controlled nationally by the machinations of the AMA's academic accreditation arm, the same Council on Medical Education and Hospitals. By denying accreditation to schools that fall below minimum standards, as defined by the Association, the output of doctors can be reduced below necessary levels. This precisely the AMA did during the Depression when doctors' incomes fell to unacceptable levels.[33] Denied accreditation, schools cannot continue to function, because graduating physicians will be unable to practice for failure to meet the licensing requirement that they attend an "accredited institution."

Racial discrimination is another obvious example of the medical societies' power to control the field of medical practice. Not until December, 1968, did the American Medical Association formally condemn the widespread southern practice of denying the black doctors membership in local medical societies and of thus snuffing out their ability to affiliate with hospitals.[34] Until recently, suits to enjoin a medical society from refusing to admit Negro physicians were unsuccessful because it would always be argued that the medical society is, after all, only a private fraternal organization which need not give equal protection to black and white alike. Recent litigation[35] suggests that the blatantly discriminatory days are waning, but the AMA's resolution was a response, not a catalyst, to other agents of social change.

---

[32] Economists and antitrust lawyers may prefer to think of this kind of covertly consensual agreement in the framework of Interstate Circuit, Inc. v. United States, 306 U.S. 208 (1939) or compare it to the follow-the-leader pricing "agreements" that pervade the oligopolistic sector of the American economy.

[33] See Rayack, *supra* note 30.

[34] *The New York Times,* December 4, 1968, p. 1.

[35] Hawkins v. North Carolina Dental Society, 230 F. Supp. 805 (W.D.N.C. 1964), reversed, 355 F. 2d 718 (4th Cir. 1966).

5

Entrance to the professional estate for the individual is neither easy nor quick. Not only must the prospective professional take a licensing examination before he can work, he must often show that he is qualified to take the examination. In short, he must be an apprentice.[36] In some professions, the apprenticeship requirement is dying out as the years of schooling increase. But even in law and medicine, apprenticeship survives in the form of mandatory clerkships in some states and years of internship and residency which in past years did not, and for the most part still do not, return a livable wage. Architects in many states must serve three years under licensed professionals before they are granted permission to strike out on their own.

Other occupations, in a ratio that seems almost inversely proportional to the amount of knowledge required, demand more rigorous apprenticeships. Laws regulating barbers and beauticians, the building trades, watchmaking, plumbing, and scores of other crafts defer the commencement of professional life to the end of a more or less protracted period of indenture to a master craftsman. The Oklahoma Watchmaking Act of 1945, subsequently invalidated,[37] required the watchmaker to serve a four-year apprenticeship under a licensed watchmaker, none of whom were required in turn to accept any students. The New Jersey barbering hopeful must

---

[36] Apprenticeships are commonplace, but some people cling to the myth that America has rejected all forms of involuntary servitude. When a learned law encyclopedia, purporting to deal with the entire body of American law, repeats the myth, the error is egregious: "Obligatory apprenticeship as an essential to qualification for trades involving skill and practice has apparently never been required by statute in the United States, but all men have been left free to exercise whatever lawful trade they may select, and it has been left to the community in which they reside to determine the extent of their knowledge and skill and to extend patronage to them according to the judgment and individual wants of their patrons." 6 *Corpus Juris Secundum*, "Apprentices," Sec. 1, p. 96.

[37] State ex rel. Whetsel v. Wood, 207 Okla. 193, 248 P. 2d 612 (1952).

apprentice for 18 months under a master barber who is forbidden by law from supervising more than one student at a time.[38]

The most truly heroic legislative establishment of a guild system was the Illinois Plumbing License Law. Under the Illinois Act, a three-man board of examiners was composed of at least one master plumber and one journeyman plumber, each with two years' experience or more. The appointing official, the Director of the State Department of Registration and Education, was bound by law to "give due consideration to the recommendation of the Illinois Association of Journeyman Plumbers and Steamfitters." To procure a master plumber license, the candidates would have to be a licensed journeyman employed by a master plumber for five years or be a graduate of an approved three-year college course and work three additional years for a licensed master plumber. To procure a journeyman's license, the prospective plumber had to be apprenticed to a master for five years or fulfill the schooling requirements and serve two years as a registered plumber. The state guaranteed the student no right to be hired. The master (who would ultimately have to compete with the apprentice) could refuse any candidate for any reason. He could even discharge the student without cause after the apprenticeship had begun, a villainy of such ancient lineage that Parliament made it illegal in 1562.[39] "No matter how well qualified a person may be by instruction and training," said the Illinois Supreme Court when it voided the scheme, "he can never of his own free will and choice become a certified registered plumber's apprentice, a journeyman plumber or master plumber, unless a licensed master plumber so wills."[40] The court declared the system unconstitutional; the state could not sanction and officially protect a system which resulted in the "arbitrary denial" of the "inherent and inalienable right" to engage in an occupation of a person's choice.

---

[38] *Handbook, supra* note 27, p. 19.

[39] Statute of Apprentices, 5 Eliz. I. (1562); see Grant, "The Gild Returns to America," 4 *J. of Politics* 303, 306 (1942).

[40] People v. Brown, 407 Ill. 565, 573, 95 N.E. 2d 888 (1951).

The plumbers did not go the way of the North Carolina tile layers, however.[41] The current plumbing license law, milder but still on the books, requires apprenticeship for five years under a licensed plumber or completion of an approved course in plumbing. Yet the justification for such requirements is still doubtful in light of the statutory provision exempting lessees or owners who wish to install plumbing facilities in their own single-family residences from the necessity of obtaining a license. Plumbing facilities are not self-contained; non-licensed plumbers will necessarily link their pipes to pipes they do not own. Some day they may even sell their homes or not renew their leases. Property rights are not respected by disease-carrying germs.

The apprenticeship system, in a less obnoxious form, endures in Illinois, as it does in many other states for many other professions. Though the logic of the state supreme court case reaches these others, Professor Walter Gellhorn suggests that "the escape route is fairly plain. The state laws will probably be interpreted as conferring on the licensing body the authority to discipline a licensee who abuses his power with respect to their apprenticeships. Thus the apparent possibility of discriminatory or exclusionary policies will be said to have disappeared. The reality of their existence will remain. Youngsters who fail to become apprentices are not likely to press charges before an official body. And if they do, the official body, which is usually representative of those against whom the charges might be brought, may not proceed with crusading zeal."[42]

6

Inherent in licensing and self-regulation is a territorial (or jurisdictional) limitation. A demarcation must obviously be fixed:

---

[41] The annotators of North Carolina law apparently do not believe in the authority of state supreme courts to void statutes. The tile contractors' law is still carried in the code book without any annotation as to its invalidity. This curious practice is not confined to North Carolina; an invalid photography licensing law is still carried in the Georgia Code Annotated.

[42] Gellhorn, *supra* note 17, pp. 124–5.

There must be an area of expertise carved out to correspond to the competence without which professionals could not be licensed. Statutes sometimes define the areas of "authorized practice." More often the line between authorized and unauthorized practice is drawn by the professionals, through their associations. Although the lines may be sensibly mapped on the outer boundaries, the interior county lines are often far fuzzier.

The jurisdictional boundary is two-fold: It fixes and regulates the right of a particular person to engage in an act; it stakes off the area or kind of action involved. The first step, usually legislative, is to prohibit all but lawyers (say) from practicing law. The next step is more difficult because it involves a definitional jump: The qualifications for becoming a lawyer are tolerably clear, but what is "the practice of law"?

To illustrate: It was long a common practice in Arizona, as it is in most states, for real estate and land title companies to draft and use documents of many types. A contract to purchase property and rental agreements are two of these. Salesmen and other employees usually fill in the blanks of already printed forms to make a deal. The State Bar of Arizona found the practice a threat to consumers and sued to enjoin a number of companies from so conducting their business. The Arizona Supreme Court, declaring that inherent in the "judicial power" is the power to decide who may lawfully practice law, defined law practice in 1961 so as to exclude real estate brokers and land title company officers from preparing "by drafting or filling in the blanks, deeds or conveyances of any kind, forms of notes, mortgages, contracts for sale of real estate," and some dozens of other documents.[43] The decision was not reversible by the legislature since in context it was a construction of the state constitution; a bitter political fight shortly thereafter led to a constitutional amendment permitting some non-lawyers to fill in the blanks.

[43] State Bar of Arizona v. Arizona Title & Trust Co., 90 Ariz. 76, 366 P. 2d 1 (1961).

Even lawyers are not entirely safe from the possibility of stray-- ing over the authorized line. In Connecticut, the Supreme Court of Errors has held that attorneys employed by banks cannot draw up legal papers for estates and other fiduciary matters and appear with them in court because, since a corporation cannot "practice law," neither can its agents, even when they are licensed lawyers.[44] Quoting an earlier Massachusetts Supreme Court decision, the Connecticut opinion proclaimed: "No statute can control the judi- cial department in the performance of its duty to decide who shall enjoy the privilege of practicing law."[45]

These are not isolated cases. The enunciated doctrine cuts deep. In Illinois a group called the Association of Real Estate Tax-Payers was formed during the early years of the Depression to provide a large enough coffer so that individual taxpayers could afford as a group to question the legality of certain tax assessments. By 1932, some 23,000 Cook County taxpayers had sent $350,000 in membership fees to the Association. With the rhythm of mort- gage foreclosures and tax sales on the upbeat, association attorneys filed nine suits on behalf of 76,343 separate parcels of real estate; at least one of these suits would have cost more than $200,000 had a private attorney been retained. Association counsel performed other duties: It was charged, for instance, that $16 billion of assessable land was left off the tax rolls, and the Association's attorneys sued to have the property placed on the tax books. Many of these cases were pending before state appellate courts (including the state supreme court) when the Cook County pros- ecutor brought suit to hold the Association in contempt of court

---

[44] State Bar Association of Connecticut v. Connecticut Bank and Trust Co., 145 Conn. 222, 140 A. 2d 863 (1958). Although the belief that a corporation cannot "practice law" persists, the fact of the matter is that lawyers, doctors, and other professionals are now permitted to incorporate themselves in at least 43 states. Opposition does not seem to be springing from the courts; the only concerned institution, in fact, is the Internal Revenue Service, which perceives a tax dodge in the movement. See Business Week, July 12, 1969, p. 80.

[45] Opinion of the Justices, 277 Mass. 607, 611, 180 N.E. 725, 727 (1932).

for practicing law unlawfully. The Illinois court obliged: "That relation of trust and confidence essential to the relation of attorney and client did not exist between the members of the respondent association and its attorneys," declared the court; the association "has beyond question, deliberately engaged in unauthorized practice of law. . . . That it used for that purpose the services of licensed attorneys in its employ does not alter the fact that it was thus practicing law."[46]

If it is sometimes difficult for lawyers to practice law in their own states, it often becomes impossible when they go across the border. In southern states, for example, civil rights defendants can practically never find local attorneys to defend them. When the Lawyers Constitutional Defense Committee and the Lawyers Committee for Civil Rights Under Law were formed in the mid-60's to export counsel to southern strongholds, they were shortly met with cries of "unauthorized practice." Though licensed elsewhere, outside counsel may handle individual cases in most states if affiliated with local lawyers. For a brief time, the two committees used this device to send in droves of lawyers to sleepy towns that never saw black men defended before. But "the volunteer lawyers were too diligent. They appeared in every court in the three states [Alabama, Louisiana, Mississippi], defending several thousands clients — mainly local Negroes since the number of out-of-state civil rights workers never numbered more than a few hundred even at the peak — on charges of everything from minor traffic violations to felonies. And they constantly thwarted local authorities by removing cases from local and state jurisdiction to Federal courts under Reconstruction statutes that authorize such action when civil rights are involved and a local fair trial is unlikely."[47] When the carpetbaggers began to go beyond defense — seeking by lawsuit to bring federal law into southern principalities — local lawyers simply refused to coöperate

[46] People ex rel. Courtney v. Association of Real Estate Taxpayers, 345 Ill. 102, 187 N.E. 823, 826 (1933).
[47] *The New York Times,* March 12, 1967, p. 8E.

with the northern attorneys, and they began to be prosecuted themselves for illegal practice. That is a handicap few lawyers can labor under, and many left.[48]

Restrictions on interstate practice are not motivated solely by political passion and they are not confined to the south. A California lawyer who came to New York to give advice and to consult with local counsel of a client suing for divorce in Connecticut found that he could not collect his fee through the courts when the lady refused to pay. New York's highest judicial tribunal, the Court of Appeals, held that the West Coast attorney, not being licensed in New York, had unlawfully practiced law and under a state statute could not therefore collect a fee.[49]

Lawyers use the courts to enforce their boundary decisions; other professions, while they do not have such organic ties with the ultimate law interpreter of the states, can nevertheless divide their practices sufficiently to suit themselves. Medical specialties, for instance, are decided upon by medical societies and enforced by arms of state medical examining boards, local societies, and the AMA. For formal requirements to be "Board certified," the medical agencies can usually agree on policy. Occasionally there are disputes; in hospitals different specialties may claim access

---

[48] See, for an example of the federal response to local restrictions on lawyers in civil rights cases, Sanders v. Russell, 401 F. 2d 241 (5th Cir. 1968). The District Court for the Southern District of Mississippi enforced its rule permitting an appearance of out-of-state counsel in non-fee-generating civil rights cases only when attorney is non-resident, when appearance is limited to one case every twelve months, and when admitted to Mississippi bar for at least five years, except in the event that the federal district court of home state admits Mississippi lawyers to practice under less stringent rule. The rule operated to preclude competent and experienced civil rights attorneys from litigating federal law by preventing out-of-state attorneys from residing temporarily within Mississippi in order to follow the course of litigation, by requiring an inordinately larger number of attorneys than necessary to handle related cases, and by imposing such licensing criteria on lawyers generally as to preclude all but a handful. The Court of Appeals reversed, holding the rule violative of the Civil Rights Act of 1964.

[49] Spivak v. Sachs, 16 N.Y. 2d 163, 263 N.Y.S. 2d 953 (1965). See Nahstoll, "Freedom to Practice Law in Another State," 55 ABAJ 57 (1969).

to the same diseases and malfunctions, since the body does not entirely respect the convenience of medical allocation.[50] A medical arbitrator with wide experience in resolving disputes recalls "one case where we decided to give all the fractures to the orthopods [orthopedic surgeons]. No go. The general surgeons decided they just weren't going to hand over all those cases. Eventually there may be enough orthopods to change the ground rules and make them stick. Meanwhile, both factions have access to the disputed area of fractures."[51] Disputes between a more distinct set of professionals are still at a primitive stage; clinical psychologists and psychiatrists have been squaring off for years without satisfactory resolution of the conflict. "The lay psychotherapist [meaning, clinical psychologist] is . . . a quack," says the psychiatrist.[52] The psychologist replies: "The psychiatrist is a person who practices psychotherapy without even a Ph.D."[53]

Jurisdictional fights may seem nothing more than pedantic or economic squabbles, but they are crucial to the identity of many professions. Defining unauthorized practice is a necessary con-

---

[50] The body's recalcitrance creates a serious problem for a subdivided profession. An ulcer, for example, can be treated by surgery, analysis, or medicine – depending on the ulcer. Which method of treatment is used may be determined fortuitously, rather than medically: Which specialist the patient first sees may discover only his own special causes at work in the stomach – an excisable growth, a nervous worry, a hyperacidity. See Rayack, *supra* note 30, p. 238.

[51] Quoted in Rayack, pp. 224–5; from *Medical Economics*, April 5, 1965, p. 90. Once set, functions are not necessarily permanently fixed: "The preparation of drugs, the taking of blood pressures, the giving of anesthetics, the keeping of medical records, the collection of bills, the cleaning up of operating rooms, the administration of hospitals – these are but a few of the tasks which have been allocated and reallocated within the medical division of labor in fairly recent years." Everett C. Hughes, *Men and their Work* (1958), p. 122.

[52] Quoted in Goode, "Encroachment, Charlatanism, and the Emerging Profession: Psychology, Sociology, and Medicine," 25 *Am. Soc. Rev.* 902, 908 (1960); from Galdston, "The Medical View," 4 *Am. J. of Psychotherapy* 422 (1950).

[53] Goode, p. 908.

comitant of licensing; it is extended and refined by the power of self-regulation. Together, licensing, self-regulation, and the line of authorized practice constitute the territorial components of the professional class.

Because it has taken relatively recent legislation to shape the professional estate and to help it expand, it should not be concluded that self-regulation is a new phenomenon, whose dimensions and possible dangers are unknown. Indeed, as we shall next see, it is a phenomenon that in the pre-industrial age was very widespread.

3

Status and Contract

Science has brought us back to a set of political problems that we thought we had disposed of forever by simple Constitutional principles. These are the problems of dealing not only with territorial subdivisions of government, and not only with economic interests and classes, but also with various groups of citizens which are separated from each other by very different types of education and ways of thinking and sets of ideals. This was the problem of the medieval estates.

— DON K. PRICE, *The Scientific Estate*

1

The claim of specialists to a competence — or at least a right — to regulate is an old one. By the fourteenth century, when cities began to dot the medieval landscape, artisans and craftsmen escaped their vassalages and flocked together to form guilds to protect their special interests.[1] (In London, guildsmen had organized tight companies at least as early as the twelfth century.) The medieval artisan realized that good will accorded him was dependent upon the status and reputation of his calling. The waxchandlers protested to King Edward III in 1371 that "there

[1] See Grant, "The Gild Returns to America," 4 *J. of Politics* 303 (1942), and "The Gild Returns to America II," 4 *J. of Politics* 458 (1942).

still is great scandal . . . because they have not Masters chosen of the said trade, and sworn before you, as other trades have, to oversee the defaults that are committed in their said trade, and to present them to the mayor and aldermen."[2]

Edward had earlier granted a charter to the Pellipers, or skinners, of London, reading in part: "Our well-beloved men of our city of London, called the 'Pellipers' [or Pelterers], have entreated us by their petition, before us and our Council set forth, that whereas by the advice and assent of all men of the aforesaid in the said City dwelling, for the common advantage of the community of our realm, to the same city resorting, it was of late ordained that [here follow regulations concerning prices and practices]." The King, "assenting to their entreatry in this behalf, and seeing that the premises are for the advantage of the people of our realm . . ."[3] granted control to the Pellipers over the activities of their members.

The Armourers of London petitioned Edward II in 1322 to grant them autonomy and monopoly of their trade, with the result that it "was ordained for the common profit, and assented to, that from thenceforth arms made in the City for sale should be good and befitting, according to the form which follows"; four Armourers were appointed "to observe and supervise."[4] Thus was established the Gothic blue eagle.

Guild masters demanded compulsory membership: unless they could be responsible for all the members of the trade they could not hope to end abuses. It is probable that the early British guilds

[2] Henry T. Riley, ed., *Memorials of London and London Life* (1868), p. 358.
[3] 1 Ed. III (1327), from Riley, pp. 153–4.
[4] 15 Ed II (1322); Riley, p. 145. Among other occupational groups granted such protection were the Turners (makers of measuring cups for wine), the Heaumers (helmeters), Hatters, Pewterers, Glovers, Shearmen, Furbishers, Braelers, Masons, Farriers, Dyers, Plumbers, Tawyers, Master surgeons, Fullers, Taverners, Haberdasherers, Bowyers, Fletchers, Pouchmakers, Blacksmiths, Leathersellers, Scriveners, Poulterers, Barbers, Hurers, and Cheesemongers. All these grants were by Edward II; the list continued to expand under Richard II and Henry V.

established relatively lax admissions policies, but by the middle of the fourteenth century the guilds deliberately began to curb membership, as it became apparent that unrestricted entry brought prices down to subsistence levels. As early as 1321 the London weavers were accused of limiting the number of workmen by charging high entrance fees. Parliament after a while prescribed maximum entry fees for all guilds, but the associations struck agreements with apprentices in which the novice agreed not to "set up nor keep any shop . . . without license." Parliament was forced to outlaw these agreements also.[5]

One of the most successful tactics for limiting the number of tradesmen was the establishment of long apprenticeship periods, the most common of which was the seven year custom of London crafts. In many cases the guilds had to appeal to the government for legislation ratifying the convention. The Ordinances of the trade called "Whittawyers" (dressers of leather with white alum or salt), for example, provided in 1346 "that no strangers shall work in the said trade, or keep house (for the same) in the City if he be not an apprentice, or a man admitted to the franchise of the said City. And that no one shall take the serving-man of another to work with him, during his term, unless it be with the permission of his master."[6] The Bristol barbers' guild sought aid in 1420; for the next 140 years Parliament acted in special cases until finally the Statute of Apprentices of 1562 prescribed the seven-year system for all "sciences, crafts, mysteries or arts."[7] The apprenticeship custom endured for a long time. Indeed, in 1732 the British government exported it to America to protect the homeland's hat trade; American hatmakers were accepting apprentices for very short terms, had taken over the American market, and were moving into British markets as well.

Long apprenticeship was not the sole means of limiting compe-

[5] 23 Henry VIII, c. 5. See Grant, *supra* note 1, p. 306.
[6] 20 Ed. III (1346); Riley, *supra* note 2, p. 232.
[7] 5 Eliz. (1562); Grant, *supra* note 1, p. 306. See Stella Grammer, *English Craft Gilds and the Government* (1905).

tition. Many unscrupulous guildsmen took on apprentices only to dismiss them shortly before the end of their training period. This widespread practice was finally condemned by Queen Elizabeth in 1562; the Statute of Apprentices provided that the master be fined unless a justice of the peace gave prior consent to the dismissal, which had to be "for some reasonable and sufficient cause."

Severe limitations on the number of apprentices who might legally be associated with a given trade was the next resort to curb entry. Among the hatters the masters could have only two apprentices at once. The master slaters of Newcastle could have a second apprentice during the last year of the term of the first apprentice only so that for six of every seven years there could be but one.

Fundamentally the guilds sought to raise wages by curbing admission. Secondarily they were active in establishing and maintaining standards and methods of fair competition. They enacted codes of ethics which in many cases enabled them to set minimum prices through means strikingly similar to those employed by modern associations.

In some ways the medieval guilds particularly resembled the modern professional partnership. Masters bought and owned the raw materials with which all worked, regulated working conditions and hours, trained apprentices. They were a collection of individual practitioners of the art in a loose sense at best; far more than today, however, they had direct and immediate bearing on the daily lives of their members.[8]   In time they became so ingrown that the ranks of masters were restricted to family members only. This is not generally true of professions, since training for the most part goes on outside the association. But for years many unions have restricted membership by refusing admission to minority races and in at least one notable instance (the pilots

[8] See Henri Pirenne, "Guilds," *Encyclopedia of Social Sciences* (1932), pp. 209–14.

of Louisiana) to any but members of the family.[9] That the old guilds were far more restrictive than today's professional associations is evident from the fact that the position of journeymen became so debased during 1300 to 1600 that in some cities they organized private treasuries to enable them to strike against the masters.

In the later middle ages increasing tides of nationalism washed away from the legitimate order much of the self-regulating guild system. Sixteenth and seventeenth century kings — in their continuing bid for authority and revenue — demanded an allegiance directly to themselves rather than to private social groups. Theorists such as Hobbes "proved" that the state must be sovereign against the people, and Rousseau saw faction as a threat to the effective operation of the "general will." The "social contract" was thought to establish a covenant directly between the state and the people; intermediary groups were believed unnecessary and dangerous. (Compare with today when the state literally gives power to like groups.) At no time were the guilds ever completely moribund, but by the eighteenth century, centralized authority greatly curtailed their activities.

The guilds were weakened by the Industrial Revolution as well. Efficiency and profits demanded in the capitalist system a basis for organization which recognized technical skill. Land, labor, and capital became commodities and their relationships had to

[9] Kotch v. Board of River Port Pilot Commissioners for the Port of New Orleans, 330 U.S. 552 (1947). Under Louisiana law, ocean-going vessels in the waters of the port of New Orleans must be piloted by pilots appointed by the Governor; no one is eligible for such appointment unless he has served a six-month apprenticeship under qualified pilots and has been certified by a state board of pilots. Upon appointment, a pilot has the status of state officer. A group of experienced pilots who had been sailing in ships on the federal waterways sought the apprenticeship but were refused, they alleged, because only relatives and friends of the incumbent state pilots were chosen by being first elected into a "private" association of pilots formed under state law. The Supreme Court denied the requested relief, holding that the Constitution does not require a state governor to select state officers by competitive test or any other means.

bc stabilized by the courts. The feudal hierarchy had fixed all people in definite relationships. Serfs responded not to the inducements of a monetary system but to the compulsion of the status enjoyed by the feudal nobility. A private individual could not contract with a merchant or craftsman unless he belonged to the guild controlling the quality and attitudes in the given occupation. Thus, social position and the guild system both interfered with the operation of a market economy regulated by a monetary mechanism. They were gradually overturned, and contract became all-important.

Inherent in the demand for knowledge and new skills was a different kind of professionalism. As the need for capital grew, the locus of power naturally shifted from land to capital.[10] Land comes in few forms. Capital, on the other hand, manifests itself in an infinite variety of forms: money, machinery, and mental capacity. If a person owned no land, no matter; wealth was more likely found in cultivating capital than crops. One might cultivate it by inheritance or by invention, by theft or by the hard work necessary to convert a one-man shop into a bustling factory. One might also cultivate it by education: transforming the fruits of specialized labor into an indispensable adjunct of the mainline capitalist. As business affairs began to spread geographically, mechanically, and temporally, staff men became invaluable intermediaries. The management of capital required new skills; the businessman saw the need for accountants, engineers, and lawyers alongside him. If some men became fabulously wealthy by crassly combining an instinct for plundering along with a genius for growth, management, and manipulation, far more men became well-to-do by dint of their claim to possess a needed expertise.

The process was a long one; for whole centuries many functions which would later become specialized were carried on by solitary professionals: "Inside the eighteenth-century solicitor half a dozen later professional men — the accountant, the land agent,

[10] Cf. John Kenneth Galbraith, The New Industrial State (1966), Chapter 10.

the company secretary, and others — were struggling to get out."[11]
For several centuries perhaps only a "half-dozen professions provided all those skilled intellectual services upon which the day-to-
day functioning of society depended."[12]

As early as the sixteenth century, professionals in the modern
sense began to develop a group consciousness and to seek royal
protection. In 1518 Henry VIII's charter to the Royal College of
Physicians of London proclaimed that its grant of power was "to
curb the audacity of those wicked men who shall profess medicine
more for the sake of their avarice than from the assurance of any
good conscience."[13]   In 1617, the apothecaries[14] — the lowest rung
of the medical profession — split off from the grocers with whom
they had been identified.   Surgeons shrugged off their association
with barbers in 1745.[15] Sometimes the functions of one group of
professionals would be recognized as relevant to the performance
of another and would be absorbed. Thus the scriveners, who long
monopolized the preparation of formal documents, jousted with
the emerging legal profession, and were unhorsed. The "Society
of Gentlemen Practisers in the Courts of Law and Equity" (the
first voluntary professional association, founded in 1740) succeeded in wresting the monopoly from the scriveners in 1760.[16]

It would be erroneous to imagine the professional from 1600
to 1900 was like his contemporary descendants. With the dubious
exception of law, which had developed extremely intricate methods of pleading and tactics of delay, the professions lacked rigor
and precision. Most fields of knowledge were open to minds which
could roam across them; until the nineteenth century, specialization had not yet taken hold. The eminent philosopher Bishop
George Berkeley, for example, developed in addition to his episte-

---

[11] W. J. Reader, *Professional Men: The Rise of the Professional Classes in
Nineteenth Century England* (1966), p. 27.
[12] A. M. Carr-Saunders and P. A. Wilson, *The Professions* (1933), p. 295.
[13] Quoted in Carr-Saunders, p. 298.
[14] Roughly equivalent to our G.P.
[15] Reader, *supra note* 11, p. 32.
[16] Reader, p. 30.

mology of idealism a practical medical discovery — Tar Water. To a gallon of water he added one quart of tar, fermented the solution for forty-eight hours, then drained the water for medicinal uses. It was particularly good for smallpox, he said; in his 1744 work *Siris, a Chain of Philosophical Reflections and Enquiries on the Virtues of Tar Water*, he wrote that "all those within my knowledge who took the Tar Water, either escaped the distemper or had it very favourably." It was also a cure-all for "scurvy, hysteria, hypochondriacal disorders, plague, erysilepelas, all disorders of the urinary passages, gout, gangrene, and the bloody flux."[17]

In those days, even the most intelligent men dabbled in fields we would today believe utterly beyond their ken. The common folk were entirely taken in: The most magical remedies, nostrums, and cures for diseases were trafficked by apothecaries and others. It is only fair to add in the Bishop's behalf that medicine was probably no more beyond his reach than that of most doctors; very little which has lasted was then known. So it was easy for even reputable doctors to prescribe absurd treatments for all manners of diseases.

Reputable doctors were scarce. Only a small part of the populace was educated and an even smaller part attended the universities. Oxford and Cambridge graduates alone were admitted to the Royal College of Physicians of London, which under its charter had the sole authority to control medical practice in London and the surrounding countryside to a radius of seven miles. Few graduates of Oxford or Cambridge ever learned anything about medicine — the classics, theology, and philosophy being considered the chief virtues of university training.[18]   Only 168

---

[17] Quoted in Eric Jameson, *The Natural History of Quackery* (1961), p. 32.
[18] Indeed, as late as 1875, Sir Arthur Helps, "Clerk of the Privy Council and ghost writer to Queen Victoria," complained that the competitive examinations for entry into public service in England were woefully irrelevant: "I believe [he said] that the present system of competitive examination is a dream of pedantry — dreamed by some Chinese philosopher — and that more witches and wizards were discovered by the notable system of pricking with pins, than judicious and capable men are likely to be discovered by

Fellows were admitted to the College between 1771 and 1833; the College deigned to designate an equal number of associate members, dubbed "Licentiates," who could practice but had no say in the affairs of the College.

These 350 men were physicians. There were others outside the London area and in Ireland and Scotland. There were many more surgeons, but they were distinctly lower class, not part of the "learned profession" of medicine; for years they were regarded suspiciously because of their often deserved reputation as "body snatchers."[19]   Apothecaries, the third branch of medical practitioners, were pharmacists who examined patients and prescribed and sold drugs, often receiving advice from lordly physicians who sat at coffeehouses and charged half a guinea per consultation without seeing any patients at all. Although medical distinctions among physicians, surgeons, and apothecaries were shallow, clearcut social differences resulted in a nation of flourishing quackery and little real medicine.

By the opening of the nineteenth century, legitimate medical practice was tightly controlled. "Family connections, together with the influence of the Royal College, and to some extent parliamentary considerations, dominated the coveted appointments to London hospitals which could be the basis of wide and fashionable practice. These appointments were usually in the hands of the governing bodies of the hospitals, and a serious candidate would find he had to canvass the voters exactly as he would if he were standing for Parliament, and there might be 150 or so of them."[20]

The other professions experienced similar restrictions; the higher branches" of each profession attempted to dominate the

the present system of competitive examination." Quoted by Reader, *supra* note 11, p. 87.

[19] Until 1828, there was no legal way to obtain cadavers; for the next five years, only the bodies of executed criminals could be used for autopsy and dissection.

[20] Reader, *supra* note 11, p. 20.

policies and practices of the entire profession, regulating not only themselves but the sub-professionals whom they considered beneath them in dignity and a threat to their standing. Throughout the nineteenth century in England, as professional groups came to define and limit their areas of special competence, they struggled to achieve the power of self-regulation, much as the guildsmen had centuries before. "By 1860, or thereabouts, the elements of professional standing were tolerably clear. You needed a professional association to focus opinion, work up a body of knowledge, and insist upon a decent standard of conduct. If possible, and as soon as possible, it should have a Royal Charter as a mark of recognition. The final step, if you could manage it — it was very difficult — was to persuade Parliament to pass an Act conferring something like monopoly powers on duly qualified practitioners, which meant practitioners who had followed a recognized course of training and passed recognized examinations."[21]

2

In colonial and post-revolutionary America, the conditions of the people led to very different attitudes toward the professions.[22] The land was open, the people pioneers, their goal adaptation. To restrict the practice of any art to people specially trained would have been intolerable in a country where every man had to be able to be his own farmer, manufacturer, doctor, lawyer, builder, and banker. Until after the Civil War, the would-be professional was not restricted. His competence was not certified by law; neither was his honesty. Lemuel Shattuck, in his *Report of the Sanitary Commission of Massachusetts* in 1850, summed up the prevalent attitude: "Anyone, male or female, learned or ignorant, an honest man or a knave, can assume the name of

[21] Reader, p. 71.
[22] See Daniel J. Boorstin, *The Americans: The Colonial Experience* (1958), and Richard Hofstadter, *Anti-intellectualism in American Life* (1963).

physician and 'practice' upon any one, to cure or to kill, as either may happen, without accountability. It's a free country!"[23]

At mid-century, the American professionals were locally oriented; they had yet to repudiate the feeling of the time, as described by Roscoe Pound, that "all callings should be on the same footing of a business, a money-making calling."[24] The notion of serving a vague "public interest" was limited; where it existed at all, it was that the practicing doctor and lawyer would aid members of the local populace individually.

But professionals were not entirely without a sense that they had interests in common. Doctors had formed medical societies in the cities at least by the end of the eighteenth century. These were relatively small groups of men who came together to discuss the latest theories. No great attempts were made to embrace all physicians in the area. Far from it: Disputes among doctors were so factious that separate groups coalesced around many theorists while controversy ranged in full public view. In 1798, the New York City yellow fever epidemic spawned contagionists, anti-contagionists, and quasi-anti-contagionists — all of whom attacked each other bitterly. Controversies continued during the epidemics of cholera and other diseases during the 1820's and 1830's. So heated did these arguments become that a leading New York doctor, Samuel Bard, complained: "Here it has become a *personal* question. Will you side with certain men, or will you join their enemies? The violence on this subject, and the aspect which is given to the controversy is, no doubt, intentionally excited by designing men. They have taken this road to *importance,* because they cannot succeed in becoming the leaders of a party by more honorable means."[25]

It was this kind of intensive sniping about which Bard complained that led to pressure to harmonize the profession, though

---

[23] Quoted in James Harvey Young, *The Medical Messiahs* (1967), p. 19.
[24] Roscoe Pound, *The Lawyer from Antiquity to Modern Times* (1953), p. 182.
[25] Quoted in Daniel H. Calhoun, *Professional Lives in America: Structure and Aspiration 1750–1850* (1965), pp. 49–50 (italics in the original).

harmony meant elevating the virtues of the group over those of the individual. "Repeatedly, men seeking the advancement denied them within the communal profession tried to expand their chances by using the whole population of practitioners as a base on which to erect new, more elaborate, more formal, less personalistic institutions. . . . The way out from social disorder led American doctors to a kind of cultural impersonality that minimized the importance of individuality to discovery and insight. To them, ambition was less likely to stimulate research than to corrupt judgment."[26] By 1847, the American Medical Association was formed.

Other professional associations followed more slowly. Formal bar associations began with the founding of the Association of the Bar of the City of New York in 1870; the American Bar Association was born eight years later. By the end of the nineteenth century, as more and more professions emerged, associations of engineers, architects, social workers, and undertakers were established.

Their purpose was not to enforce standards so much as it was to create them. Except for medicine and law (though not in all states), the practice of the professions remained unregulated. Educational requirements were nonexistent. The standards of medical education, for instance, were appalling. Of the 155 schools examined in the famous 1910 Flexner Report, *Medical Education in the United States and Canada*, only 22 required one or more years of college; some 50 required high school diplomas or the "equivalent"; the rest accepted a junior high school education or were unabashed diploma mills. An earlier unpublished report of the AMA's Council on Medical Education (formed in 1904) caused a number of schools to close or consolidate by 1910. By 1915, sixty-seven schools were approved and the total number of schools had fallen to 104. By 1920, the approved numbered seventy and the total, eighty-eight. By 1930, seventy-six were

26 Calhoun, pp. 57–8.

approved, and there were no others. The physician-population ratio declined twenty per cent during those first thirty years of pressure.[27]

If the motives of some professionals were pure, the motives of professional associations were mixed, combining as they did the differing aspirations of many. During the 1890's, when Congress responded to the threat of Big Business by enacting antitrust legislation, state legislatures were being importuned to help cure a few economic defects also. One defect was competition. Horseshoers, barbers, undertakers, dentists, pharmacists, doctors, nurses, veterinarians, optometrists, midwives, osteopaths, and embalmers, among many others, were succeeding in their push for occupational licensing.[28]   Typical of the sentiment then current was that voiced by an Illinois druggist: "Some provision should be made so that upon passing the examination as a registered pharmacist [an assistant] cannot immediately start a drug store. This business of making it easy for young men to pass an examination and immediately start in business is what is hurting us."[29]

During this period, the expert came to be accepted in public government, at least for some purposes by some governments. By 1871 Congress authorized the President to promote efficiency in the Civil Service by prescribing regulations governing federal employment. President Grant established a civil service commission which lapsed two years later, but in 1883, subsequent to the assassination of President Garfield by a disappointed office-seeker, the Civil Service Act was adopted. It was at this time that professional associations were formed in earnest.

One important reason for the expert's ascendancy was the

[27] Elton Rayack, *Professional Power and American Medicine: The Economics of the American Medical Association* (1967), Chapter 3 *passim*.

[28] See, generally, Friedman, "Freedom of Contract and Occupational Licensing, 1890–1910: A Legal and Social Study," 53 *Calif. L. Rev.* 487 (1965).

[29] Quoted in Friedman, p. 501; from the Proceedings of the Twenty-Sixth Annual Meeting of the Illinois Pharmaceutical Association (1905).

"Wisconsin idea." In 1892 the School of Economics, Political Science, and History was founded at the University of Wisconsin. It was to "become a center of training in administration and citizenship, and would evolve into an efficient practical servant of the state."[30] Shortly thereafter the Legislative Reference Service, an independent Wisconsin agency, was inaugurated. The machine had created so many complex problems that legislators could not realistically hope to solve them without a vast accumulation of information. "The only sensible thing to do [remarked the School's founder, Charles McCarthy] is to have experts gather this material."[31]

The presidencies of Theodore Roosevelt and Woodrow Wilson did much to further the place of the expert in government. Roosevelt, in particular, "did more to restore mind and talents to public affairs than any president since Lincoln, probably more indeed than any since Jefferson."[32] Wilson built on the Roosevelt legacy and as new regulatory commissions were established, it was apparent that experts must staff them. Even the dismal record of the '20's did not eradicate the experts' influence in high councils. However misused and wrongly directed they were, experts were decisive for the practical implementation of the immigration exclusion policies debated and developed throughout that period and finally promulgated by President Hoover in 1929.

The Depression brought the expert home to stay. As regulatory commissions proliferated, as Congressional and executive committee investigations increased and broadened their scopes of inquiry, the expert was imported into every level of governmental thinking. It has hardly been possible since then to read the daily newspapers without discovering what some "expert" or other thinks about almost any topic under current debate.

[30] Hofstadter, *supra* note 22, p. 200.
[31] Quoted in Hofstadter, p. 201.
[32] Hofstadter, p. 207.

3

We seem to be coming full circle. The medieval estates fixed
the relationships of all their peoples toward each other. The
medieval man was born into a rigid hierarchy; his only escape
from the secular land-based system — but a partial one, at that —
was to enter the Church (thus to be trapped in its striated web).
Status was the ruling force of the medieval age. The determination of what duties were owed and to whom, as well as the kind
of justice received, depended upon the individual's place in the
feudal scheme.

The thrust of history, as the range of human alternatives began
to broaden, was toward a contractual organization of society.[33]
The thrust was a long one. When illiteracy was almost universal,
life short, plagues, battles, and turmoil the rule, and the only task
to be done that which long-departed forefathers had done in
identical ways, contract was unnecessary. But as trade and
industry developed, as scientific and technological revolutions
made the organization of society complex and dependent upon
specialized tasks, the old estates broke down and the rigidly
organized guilds crumbled away. The right of any man to do
as he could and as he pleased — to contract freely with another
for the mutual advantage of both — became the cherished goal,
if not always the realized practice, finding its highest expression,
as we shall see,[34] in a host of Supreme Court decisions that the
states could not establish hour and wage laws because they interfered with the workingman's inalienable liberty of contract. But
that onesided understanding of a useful principle could not forever withstand the pressure of those who could never benefit by
an unfettered right to contract. Nor could it, having first been
overturned by those with legitimate grievances, come back to

[33] See Sir Henry Maine, *Ancient Law* (1875), pp. 163–165, for the well-known
dictum that "the movement of the progressive societies has hitherto been
a movement from status to contract."
[34] Chapter 11.

confront the pressure of those for whom status was more comfortable than contract.

De Tocqueville's observation that lawyers formed a class of aristocrats[35] became applicable to a number of other occupations. Professionalism was soon identified with status, not of nobility but of merit and achievement, of knowledge and skill. The privilege of status has returned, as R. H. Tawney aptly noted, "the creature no longer of unequal legal rights . . . but of unequal powers springing from the exercise of equal rights in a world where property and inherited wealth and the apparatus of class institutions have made opportunities unequal."[36] If one profession can claim to be part of a class institution for which status is necessary, why then so too can all occupations claim to be part of it: The professional estate is open to anyone with a claim to skill. Thus real-estate agents have become realtors; undertakers, morticians; junk dealers, salvage consultants; laboratory technicians, medical technologists.[37] Thus the ditchdigger and sewer worker have become drainage engineers. Thus the salesman of burial plots is no longer merely a salesman; he is a "professional memorial consultant" and has a diploma issued after a one-week training course to prove it.[38] And thus the "hospital orderly, whose lowly job in the hospital hierarchy includes the removal of the repulsive debris of medical activity, may describe himself as a 'cuspidorologist' and perhaps even get away with it."[39]

The return toward status is patent, and its appearance is not less troublesome because it is incomplete.

---

[35] Alexis de Tocqueville, *Democracy in America* (1966 Mayer and Lerner ed.) pp. 242–8.

[36] R. H. Tawney, *The Acquisitive Society* (1948 ed.), p. 37.

[37] H. M. Vollmer, *Professionalization* (1966), p. 20.

[38] Jessica Mitford, *The American Way of Death* (1963), p. 135.

[39] Peter L. Berger, *The Human Shape of Work* (1964), p. 216. Thus also the American Culinary Association deplores the use of the word "cook" because it is "loathsome." See S. I. Hayakawa, *Language in Thought and Action* (1964), pp. 94–5. Hayakawa also notes that the Artificial Limb Manufacturing Association has become the American Orthotics and Prosthetics Association. See p. 100 for other examples.

4
The Theory
of the Professional Class (I)

The professional man, it has been said, does not work in order
to be paid: he is paid in order that he may work.
> — T. H. MARSHALL, "The Recent History of Professionalism
> in Relation to Social Structure and Social Policy"

1

When a problem arises, when trouble jolts the public from its
easy torpor, when anything at all happens, a phalanx of experts
is summoned. This is an everyday occurrence, and verification
is but a moment's thought. Are there riots in the cities, do the
students seem to want something, should the United States be
"safeguarded"? The solution is inevitably to appoint a commission of experts, or at least to call them to Washington to talk.

Great public issues, unfortunately, have a way of eluding the
precision of physicists, military strategists, city planners, and economists. Their advice is not unhesitatingly accepted. Yet there
is another class of experts employed to combat a lesser brand of
evils, whose advice is usually impossible to avoid. When the baby
is sick, when the motives of an assassin require analysis, when the
tax payment seems too large, when a community must have a
sewage system, when a manufacturing company needs a vice-
president for marketing, even when a Saturday evening dinner

party compels coiffure, it is the natural instinct to reach out for the professional.

A modern nation without professions is impossible to conceive. The important things in life are in the province of the professionals: from agriculture to zoology, that which daily touches human life has been filtered through their hands. And though Americans sing paeans to the enthusiastic hobbyist, they generally go to salaried garage mechanics for automobile repairs. Americans tolerate amateur painters, and even buy their works, but artistic quacks are quickly transformed into professionals if they spend most of their working day at it.

Traditionally the professional was outside the orthodox boundaries of political and economic functions. The professional was assuredly not a mere tradesman or merchant — not a public official, judge, legislator, chief executive; not exactly a capitalist; but something else. In a paradoxical way, however, as the lines separating powers and possibilities blur and merge, the professional is becoming all of these. He legislates and adjudicates, administers and formulates, produces and sells. Yet he remains apart. Quacks may please their clients; good, even brilliant, professionals may not. But the former are condemned and the latter more than tolerated. Despite all criticism and doubt as to his desirability, the professional persists. What is he?

No easy formula will tell. "The concept 'profession' in our society is not so much a descriptive term as one of value and prestige."[1] Occupations are at various stages of development; there is no magic point at which an occupation like accounting or librarianship[2] or tile laying crosses the professional threshold. But there are characteristics which many professions share in common: attitudes, lifestyles, motivations, rationalizations, training, and authority. Many of these aspects are not necessary to make an occupation a profession, but their absence may indicate

[1] Everett C. Hughes, *Men and their Work* (1958), p. 44.
[2] See Goode, "The Librarian: From Occupation to Profession?" 31 *Library Q.* 306 (1961) and related articles in this issue.

that a particular occupational group is not fully developed or is at a dead end.

2

First among equals in the professionals' claim to uniqueness is preoccupation with a specialized skill premised on an underlying theory. The earliest students of the professions classically held the "chief distinguishing characteristic of the professions" to be "the application of an intellectual technique to the ordinary business of life, acquired as the result of prolonged and specialized training."[3] Paradigms are, of course, medicine or law, professions requiring vast amounts of theory, special techniques, and intensive schooling.

The skill which most professionals claim to possess is not simply that kind of manual operation which a housewife may learn at a one week afternoon training course. It is a skill which is measured by the probability that a layman would fail at the assigned task with varying degrees of practice.[4] A layman who, without training, has tried his hand at balancing a set of books, writing a brief, or analyzing a blood sample, will readily concede that a skill is required and will perceive the need for prior education, formal or otherwise.

Another way to consider the nature of the professional skill is to contemplate the danger to be anticipated from an incompetent exercise of it. Brain surgery would be conceded by all without debate; psychiatry by most, after only a short argument. A businessman with no training in accounting would know better than to attempt to straighten out his accelerated depreciation tax reserves. The danger contemplated may be more or less serious, but it is one which touches us in important ways. On the proper

---

[3] A. M. Carr-Saunders and P. A. Wilson, *The Professions* (1933), p. 491. See also Morris L. Cogan, "Toward a Definition of Profession," 23 *Harv. Educ. Rev.* 33 (1953).

[4] Hughes, *supra* note 1, p. 89.

exercise of the skill our life, liberty, property, or sensibilities may turn.

Schooling was not always a prerequisite for the achievement of professional skill. Lawyers used to gain their knowledge of the law by clerking in an office. A century ago, a classical education with a course or two in anatomy was considered sufficient training for a doctor. Today, however, "preparation for a profession . . . involves considerable preoccupation with systematic theory, a feature virtually absent in the training of the nonprofessional. And so treatises are written on legal theory, musical theory, social work theory, the theory of the drama, and so on; but no books appear on the theory of punch-pressing or pipe-fitting or brick-laying."[5] Treatises require schools. Many groups, as they come to claim professional status, appreciate the overwhelming necessity for intellectual preparation. They create courses of instruction in their crafts and write their treatises. Barbers, to choose but one example among numerous others, go to schools in many states and read treatises on barbering[6] in order to satisfy the intellectual requirement of professional status.

Special skill creates special status: professionals are given leave to do dangerous things, to talk about things in a shocking way, to do what others would not dare, and "to get – and in some degree, to keep secret – some order of guilty, or at least potentially embarrassing and dangerous knowledge."[7] Psychiatrists hear the inner torments of disturbed men and women. Engineers build bridges which the public will cross, doctors prescribe drugs with possibly devastating side effects, and they, like lawyers, talk about people as though they were just so much mangled tissue of skin and rights. Anyone who has ever heard a doctor talk clinically about his patient or a lawyer about his client knows

[5] Ernest Greenwood, "Attributes of a Profession," in Sigmund Nosow and William H. Form, eds., Man, Work, and Society (1962), p. 208.

[6] E.g., Sidney Coyne Thorpe, Practice and Science of Barbering (1967); L. Sherman Trusty, The Art and Science of Barbering (5th ed., 1963).

[7] Hughes, supra note 1, pp. 81–3.

that very real sorrows are ordinary occurrences to the dispassionate professional.

The matter-of-factness which the professional's approach engenders may seem callous, but it is another important and usually necessary characteristic of the specialist. He seems unfeeling only because he does not react emotionally to crisis. He is trained to remain calm because it is his job to help clients and patients when problems that are beyond their solving arise. A large measure of professionalism has been said to be detachment and equanimity in a time of crisis. The trouble may seem less so because the professional has seen similar problems before and knows that there are solutions; or a problem may seem more critical to the professional than to his client because the specialist may recognize what the layman does not. But in any event, the professional will bring calm consideration to bear on another's problem. (That is an important reason why a doctor will usually not treat himself and a lawyer who acts as his own counsel is said to have a "fool for a client." Detachment toward others is a professional virtue that is far more difficult to display towards oneself.)

Along with equanimity must go neutrality. The engineer whose loyalty was to faction rather than to the waterworks could have seriously affected the distribution of water in Paris during the 1790's. All partisans agree that some things are better left free of political and social bias.

The professional maintains his neutrality against encroachment by insisting as a fundamental proposition that his motivation is altruistic. He professes a desire to serve all and to serve to the maximum of his ability, regardless of the size of his compensation or other material reward. The professional asserts that the skills he has to offer are actually or potentially beneficial to all. Of course the professional can say this without believing it, but it is important that he act on it.[8]

---

[8] "The social invention of the professions institutionalizes altruistic behavior. The profession does not require practitioners to *feel* altruistic (although that might do no harm); it only requires them to *act* altruistically (at least

To achieve a basis for applied altruism, the professional sets
standards for himself, preaches professional ethics, limits the
degree of competition with his fellows to which he is willing to
submit, and disavows advertising. And because his is a specialized task which by definition no one else can fully comprehend,
the professional demands autonomy in order to enforce and preserve his standards.

There is an equally important consideration requiring professional commitment to autonomy. Like the businessman, the professional fears control by a government bureaucracy from which,
presumably, he would be bound to take orders. Much of his
concern is self-serving; every man wants to be free of official
scrutiny and able to bury mistakes. But there is a basic reason
why autonomy is desirable: If in every case the specialist had to
submit his plan for treatment or service to an agency, he would
never have time to do his work, nor in the end, would it be his
work. Part of the specialist's skill is the ability to do unsupervised
work; if others could do it for him, then he would not be much
of a specialist.

The requirements that the professional possess a specialized
skill and that autonomy is necessary for its exercise have an important corollary. The professional assumes the right to define "what a
failure or a mistake is in any line of work."[9] The proper method
of treatment for a particular disease is prescribed by physicians,
not by legislators or judges. Thus doctors and many other professionals rarely criticize their fellow practitioners. Public discussion of professional mistakes results in loss of autonomy because
the layman gets a clue to the mystery and a basis for control.

There is another reason for the reluctance of professionals to
criticize each other: In the highly developed professions, precise
definitions of mistakes do not exist. How best to try a lawsuit or
treat an ailment is a complex question, and the more complex the

to a substantial degree)." Robert K. Merton, *Some Thoughts on the Profes-*
sions in American Society (1960), p. 11.
[9] Hughes, *supra* note 1, p. 93.

individual case, the less agreement will be found on how to proceed. And to admit to these theoretical difficulties is doubly dangerous: Not only might a case be prejudiced by an honest disagreement but also the layman may easily conclude that the professional knows no more than he and so take the matter out of the specialist's hands altogether.

Another consequence follows. If the professional defines mistakes, he must necessarily be immune from client control. John Kenneth Galbraith has said that the "accepted sequence" of economic behavior (from consumer to market to producer) is being reversed: Consumer demand is increasingly less important in stimulating production than producers are in stimulating consumer demand.[10] In the sphere of professional services, an analogous "revised sequence" has long been the case: The agent directs the master. Who is not familiar with "doctor's orders"? If the patient consistently refuses to do what the doctor says, the doctor will resign the patient. It is accepted that he should; the patient, after all, is not the expert. The patient has hired the specialist for his expertise; so with lawyers, architects, and dozens more. It is not an adequate answer that there are physicians who will gladly prescribe whatever medication the patient thinks he needs, or that there are lawyers who will do whatever the client wants so long as the client understands the risks and pays. The fact remains, there are ethical professionals and for them, expertise must be permitted to apply.

From the necessity for autonomy and the exclusive ability to define mistakes, the professsional asserts the power to define the needs of the client. This is no great leap: The client who defines any needs would be in a position to control the professional's actions and ultimately thus to usurp his function. Even the ability to describe the basic problem that brought the client to the professional's office is sometimes denied the layman: A common complaint against social workers is that they will not see their

[10] John Kenneth Galbraith, *The New Industrial State* (1967), p. 211.

indigent client's problem from his point of view but insist that he fit into the mold of the social worker's conception of the productive citizen.[11]

The result of the power to define needs should now be clear. The professional asserts the necessity for defining public policy toward his profession. "Not merely do the practitioners, by virtue of gaining admission to the charmed circle of colleagues, individually exercise the license to do things others do not do," says Professor Hughes, "but collectively they presume to tell society what is good and right for the individual and for society at large in some aspect of life. Indeed, they set the very terms in which people may think about this aspect of life. The medical profession, for instance, is not content merely to define the terms of medical practice. It also tries to define for all of us the very nature of health and disease. When the presumption of a group to a broad mandate of this kind is explicitly or implicitly granted as legitimate, a profession has come into being."[12]

To sustain the professional perquisites, something more than an intellectual creed is required. The professional must be separated from his fellow man and brought into a distinct way of life. "The profession claims and aims to become a moral unit."[13] Com-

---

[11] "Social workers, especially those in family agencies or child guidance agencies and those serving and attached to courts, have an especially fine opportunity to play God. They can tear a family apart by convincing a spouse that divorce is the answer to his or her needs. They can recommend that a child be torn from his parent or parents and be placed in a foster home. They can make recommendations to a court that determines the length of a sentence or whether a sentence is to be suspended or not. They can 'close a case,' which means that a client is denied welfare, and they can recommend that legal or common-law husbands be jailed for failure to provide support to wife and children." Joseph Bensman, Dollars and Sense: Ideology, Ethics, and the Meaning of Work in Profit and Non-Profit Organizations (1967), pp. 97–8.

[12] Hughes, supra note 1, p. 79. For the suggestion that librarianship is not yet and will not become a profession until it asserts itself as a guardian of something more significant than the door to the library, see Goode, supra note 2.

[13] Hughes, p. 33.

mitment to the way of life begins early. A student must decide while still in college the direction of his career. The senior who has a sudden surging interest in medicine cannot go to medical school without extensive prior preparation. The would-be economist will not find it easy to enroll in graduate school in his newly acquired subject if he does not have a thorough grounding from his undergraduate years. To gain a specialty, the student often forfeits the chance to acquire a broad background.

The student who opts for professional life is transformed during his academic sojourn. He is initiated into a great mystery, over whose secrets he will someday preside as trustee. He will learn a ritual and a language; he will learn an art as well as a science. For at bottom, no matter how much a professional may claim to rely on systematic or scientific theory, successful practice depends as much on intuition as on recall. Certainly no one is any longer deceived by the archaic writers who spoke of the "science of law." Even chemistry and biology — "pure" sciences — depend for success on a hit or miss practice that eludes rigor and initial precision and demands a gifted artist.[14]

3

These aspects of professionalism serve the professions but they also handicap them. The professional is often so important to a soul in trouble or so necessary for the job at hand that any remoteness can sour the client. Although clients "could not stand it if the expert to whom they take their troubles were to show any signs of excitement" people often resent the cool attitude of the specialist. "In times of crisis, detachment appears the most perilous deviation of all, the one least to be tolerated. The professional mind, in such a case, appears as a perversion of the common sense of what is urgent and what less urgent. The license to think in longer perspective thus may appear dangerous."[15]

[14] Cf. James D. Watson, The Double Helix (1968).
[15] Hughes, supra note 1, pp. 55, 84.

Not just the ability to stay calm, but also the possibility of failure, create a widespread ambivalence toward the professional in America. Those who think that a problem must necessarily have a solution are quick to blame the professional. It is not a paradox that in spite of the desperate need for specialists, there is in the folklore as well as the personal experience of most an uneasy belief in the stupidity, inefficiency, even cupidity of professionals.

The ambivalence is deep. There are too many experts and there are not enough; the expert is too aggressive and yet he is overly placid; he is self-satisfied but neurotic; revered but despised, praised yet derided. Any number of disadvantaged and ill-used mothers may believe as fervently as they know God is their friend that the lawyer is an unscrupulous rascal bent on gouging the helpless. Yet these same women could find no greater happiness than for their sons to go to school to become — lawyers; nice, respectable people, who will uphold the rights of the poor and defend the sacred institutions of the country against all attack.

This ambivalence is due partly to the not-so-astonishing fact that the ideals of the professions are measurably higher than the perspicacity with which they are sometimes carried out. It is due just as often to the fact that professionals deal frequently with sets of problems which have no solution. A profession is not an exact science and this realization can be a bitter one. Many people express it in resentment toward the professional, failing to recognize instead the bittersweet in life. A lawyer may claim he can help with a complex lawsuit, but the fact is that people often seek lawyers too late, after the damage is done. Doctors are expert in saving lives, but people have been known to die on the operating table. Professions thus often suffer from their own pretensions.[16]

---

[16] Professionals themselves occasionally fall prey to these pretensions. Admiral U. S. Grant Sharp, formerly Commander-in-Chief, U. S. Forces Pacific (CINCPAC), wrote upon retirement that the war in Vietnam could have been ended perhaps by 1967 but for arbitrary actions of the Secretary of

Sometimes, on the other hand, professions suffer from the pretensions of laymen. Many laymen indulge rather too much their belief in their own intelligence and sophistication when they evidence their distrust of professionals. Our early history was founded on a skepticism that the professional knew anything at all; it is not a twentieth century discovery.[17] This indulgence is only conceit and ignorance, of course, for the most sophisticated people are the most trusting of professionals. Not only do the most sophisticated have the wherewithal to retain the blue-stocking specialists, they number among themselves far more who are experts in their own right. To question another expert, to deride him or doubt him, is obviously to risk the seal of your own Pandora's box.

Moreover, the public has been conditioned since the Korean War to believe that all problems can be quickly solved. The impossible may take a little longer, but since nothing is impossible (the moon having been reached), the remaining problems are merely difficult and should, therefore, be solved immediately. That is the prevailing theory of problems and their solutions, and it is drilled into us constantly by entertainment programming on television, which shows that the right thing always happens. It depicts the split-second capturing before (a regrettable) murder can be accomplished and the nearly instantaneous conviction of all criminals by resourceful and ever-polite FBI and police agents; contrariwise, it shows the successful defense of every case that certain lawyers try. Television is filled with nightly exhibits of such horrors as nuclear fail-safe systems sabotaged by madmen, but it always intones that the worst will never be permitted to

Defense. "We Could Have Won in Vietnam Long Ago," *Readers Digest* (May, 1969), p. 118. As one newspaper editorially commented: "It panders to an ancient American belief, that things go badly not because they are inherently difficult (or intractable) but because someone was stupid, or cowardly, or false." *The Washington Post*, May 1, 1969, p. A18.

[17] See Daniel J. Boorstin, *The Americans: The Colonial Experience* (1958), Part 7: "The Learned Lose their Monopolies," and Part 8: "New World Medicine."

occur: shortly after the penultimate commercial the insouciant hero singlehandedly saves the world from utter holocaust in the last possible five seconds before communications are cut off from nuclear-armed Air Force bombers deep into Russian territory. That the right person correctly solves the problem and ends the danger nightly is scant comfort to us during the day, however, when the real world consistently fails to measure up to the fantasy world we passively watch. Even worse, on television the danger is perceived at the outset and the viewer explicitly told what it is and how it affects him. Unfortunately, the Author of our daily lives does not usually provide such sure guides even to recognizing dangerous situations outside the television set.

Both laymen and professionals are to blame for the corrosive ambivalence. Did the professional not reach for so much he would not fall in estimation so far. Were the layman to accept some responsibility instead of leaving all to the expert, he would have less to resent. The professional deals with the mysterious problems of the world, but he is no magician.

4

Two important qualifications must be added to what has just been said of the characteristics of professionals. No matter how much skill, training, coolness, neutrality, or autonomy the expert possesses, he cannot operate a professional in fields considered morally depraved or utterly foolish. Social acceptance is imperative. Otherwise, two eminently respected types of workers would be graciously admitted to the professional estate: prostitutes and astrologers.

The prostitute has a strong claim to such status; she belongs, after all, to the "oldest profession." There is unquestionably a body of knowledge involved. Many cultures have had distinct classes of women to serve as public mistresses higher in esteem than common prostitutes. The skill and training of some of these are legion. The *hetairae* of ancient Greece, for instance, were highly accomplished mistresses, learned in the arts, devoted to social intercourse as well, and available only to the eminent men of their time. One of these was concubine to Pericles: "Her house became the center of Athenian literary and philosophical society, frequented by no less a person than Socrates."[18] Many societies have linked prostitution to religion, delivering young girls to the care of those who train them to sing, worship, and submit. Often the prostitutes' position as entertainers made them the only women who could sing, dance, and read; but because they were paid meager salaries as official or religious courtesans, most moonlighted.

Yet the *hetairae* did not rank co-equal with philosophers; they were usually aliens and not respectable for all their influence. And the fact that church ladies could read sometimes acted to keep respectable women from gaining education for fear of a hasty confusion between two talents. To suggest that the failure of prostitutes to achieve professional status is because prostitutes, whether educated or not, do what any woman could do, does not settle the matter; any woman *could* become a lawyer.[19]

The fact that the depravity may be only in the minds of the self-righteous does not avail the woman seeking to increase her prestige. Prostitutes have long been roundly condemned by many who have had recourse to them; this is simply an illustration of the contradiction that arises when men do what they think others might dislike. Like business magnates who deplore welfare "hand-outs" to the poor but accept federal subsidies to support "crucial" enterprises, those who condemn thereby banish their lingering doubts of the propriety of their own behavior at the same time that they shield their own activities from view by throwing off those who might otherwise look.

"The harlot's return," it has been argued, "is not primarily a reward for labor, skill, capital, or land (rent). It is primarily a

18 Kingsley Davis, "Prostitution," in R. K. Merton and R. Nisbett, eds., *Contemporary Social Problems* (1956), pp. 267–8.
19 Though, to be sure, the capital investment is higher.

reward for loss of social standing."[20]   This is implausible.   She rents her body and, like a lawyer, sells time, which she spends in bed.   Some women command enormous fees and do not decline in social prestige at all because the proper clientele is a guarantor of privacy.   But a professional does not hide his status from the public; the best prostitutes must.

It might be otherwise, of course.   Prostitutes are licensed in some countries.   But the suggestion that they be licensed in America has never been seriously considered.

If the prostitute is debarred from professional status because her activities are heinous, the astrologer is limited by the conventional belief in his essential absurdity.[21]   "Good" astrologers can claim much devotion to study, as well as calmness, neutrality, and autonomy: No one tells the astrologer how to act or what to say (except perhaps the stars).   Even the contention that astrology is not based on an underlying testable theory (advanced as a reason to show they are not professional) can be dismissed by astrologers. That astrological veracity is not scientifically verifiable is hardly a problem if the prediction of the future depends upon non-scientific theorems.   Zodiacal charts — horoscopes — are evidence that some theory exists.   Yet if a group of astrologers were to petition a state legislature for the right to license members of their "profession," the bill would be laughed to the incinerator, even though there are many guileless citizens who are undoubtedly harmed by pinning hopes on the conjunction of planets and stars.

Astrology was not always so treated.   The great astrologers in Babylonia, China, India, Egypt, Greece, Rome, and even Europe were intimate advisers of kings and emperors, second only to royalty in their influence at court, and sometimes they were first. A famous scientist, Ptolemy, wrote a treatise 1700 years ago on which modern astrology is based.   There is even reason to believe

20 Davis, *supra* note 18, p. 277.
21 See *Time*, March 21, 1969; and Linda Goodman, *Linda Goodman's Sun Times* (1969); Carroll Righter, *Astrological Guide to Marriage and Family Relations* (1968).

that astrology was the seminal occupation from which professionalism itself sprung. For astrologers did not plow fields or march
in armies; they sat in towers gazing at the stars, advising kings
that on the basis of their observations as interpreted by theory the
time was propitious for this or that. And they may have advised
important nobles on medical and legal matters as well.

The point need not be insisted upon, for it is clear that astrologers
do not enjoy much official influence. Although there are many
who work full time at it[22] and who have earned fortunes by giving
advice to "clients" — thus earning the title "professional" as opposed to "amateur" — they are not professional men. The professional may do many silly things, but he does not spend all his
time in bed or on foolishness.

5

A constituent part of the theory of the professional class is its
theory of motivation. A typical statement of the professional's
motivation is as follows: "Professional work is never viewed solely
as a means to an end; it is the end itself. Curing the ill, educating
the young, advancing science are values in themselves. The professional performs his services primarily for the psychic satisfac-
tions and secondarily for the monetary compensations. . . . The
work life invades the after-work life, and the sharp demarcation
between the work hours and the leisure hours disappears. To the
professional person his work becomes his life."[23]

What the professional advances to explain his behavior does
not necessarily explain his behavior, however. Any discussion of
motivation is haunted with the ghost of hypocrisy. "Why did he
do that?" if answered simply "because this" or "because that" is
likely to elicit an immediate retort: "But that wasn't [or couldn't

---

[22] Professionalism has been defined in part as "doing full time the thing that
needs doing." H. L. Wilensky, "Professionalization of Everyone?" 70 *Am.
J. of Soc.* 137, 142 (1964).

[23] H. M. Vollmer, *Professionalization* (1966), p. 17.

be] his *real* reason." It is well to avoid the ghost and the retort altogether by openly recognizing that very few people are so simple-minded as to act from only one motive at a time. In asserting that the "primary" motivation is one of service, I suggest that the professional errs. At least three separate motivations go into the mix that activates the professional: the service goal, the profit goal, and the desire for autonomy. It is useless to hunt for the "primary" motivation among them. At different times, they are strengthened and weakened and combine and recombine in varying proportions in all professionals. It is a possible hypothesis, however, that among a significant number of professionals the profit and autonomy motives use the service motive as a subterfuge to advance their primacy. The next several chapters explore the possibility of this hypothesis.

5
Ethics and Profits

The new professional man brought one scale of values — the gentleman's — to bear upon the other — the tradesman's — and produced a specialized variety of business morality which came to be known as "professional ethics" or "etiquette." It is based upon the fact that what the professional man sells, generally, is expert advice, often upon confidential matters. Unless the client can rely on his adviser's honesty, exactness, and devotion to his (the client's) interest, the transaction falls to the ground. Therefore any professional man must cultivate it even more zealously than the ordinary businessman, who deals with other businessmen who know what to expect. It is this sense of being obliged to observe exceptionally high standards which, more than anything else, gives some sense of unity to the professional classes as a whole, diverse though the occupations of their members may be.
    — W. J. READER, *Professional Men: The Rise of the Professional Classes in Nineteenth Century England*

Generally speaking detailed codes have hindered more than helped. I can remember when it was stated to be unprofessional for a doctor to address a public gathering on a health problem. Within twenty-five years we mechanical engineers were prohibited from discussing any engineering concern with the public in advance of taking it up with our professional brethren. Some of the more rigorous specifications covering conduct have never been included in the written codes, such as that which virtually forbids

a physician to answer a call for service if the person requiring
attention is the patient of some other doctor.
    — MORRIS LLEWELLYN COOKE,
    Professional Ethics and Social Change

1

The professional man must eschew a large income in theory and
realize it in practice. This basic tension between two fundamental
motivations of the professional — the desire to serve and to prosper
while so doing — requires an effective mediator if the work of the
expert is not to be corrupted.

The professional must eschew a large income in theory not
merely because it would be unseemly for a man to profit from
others' misfortunes, but more importantly because the special skill
inherent in the professionals' work puts laymen at their mercy.
The consumer does not meet the professional in the marketplace
as his equal. Since there is no reason for a man in need of expert
assistance to trust the opinions of a man bent solely on profit, the
professional advances as a fundamental aim his desire to serve.
Caveat emptor has no place in the professional's lexicon.[1]

Yet the professional must realize wealth in practice, for in order
to subsist without it he would be reduced to giving hurried, care-

---

[1] "Ethical codes are based on the belief that between professional and client
there is a relationship of trust, and between buyer and seller there is not.
In so far as the professions purvey services and the trades commodities, the
difference is obvious. The commodity can be inspected before it is paid for:
the service cannot." T. H. Marshall, "The Recent History of Professionalism
in Relation to Social Structure and Social Policy," 5 *Canadian J. of Econ.
and Poli. Sci.* 325, 327–8 (1939). But the difference is no longer so obvious:
An automobile is not readily inspected by the non-mechanical purchaser, so
warranties are supplied, and these also imply service and trust, because few
would or could go to court over an interpetation of an ordinary car warranty
when a minor repair is necessary. Even the professional is trapped: Drug
companies sell thousands of drugs and the doctor must depend on the company for a drug's efficacy and safety; he cannot subject each pill or each
type of pill to chemical analysis. Yet few drug manufacturers hold to a
hearty code of ethics.

less service to many whose problems he does not have time to consider fully. Only if he can expect large fees from relatively few clients will the practitioner be able to devote sufficient time to each and feel compelled to do so. This, at any rate, is what most professionals will argue when asked why it is that certain professionals have inordinately-sized incomes.

Because there is a tension between what professionals say and do, a mediator is required. By the turn of the twentieth century, the leaders of many professions themselves recognized the need to impart a sense of responsibility to each of their professions as a whole. The goal was to remove the thought of *caveat emptor* — and the actual practice of it, where possible — from the experience of the public. To instill a sense of public responsibility, the professions drew up codes of ethics.

The ethical precepts of the professions did not, in most cases (at least at the outset), have the force of law. Neither were they always as vague and ambiguous as traditional moral dictates. "Be honest" was not enough; it was precisely because morality had no place in the market that something else was required

Law, morality, and ethics are all essentially systems of belief which perceive various modes and degrees of sanctions to be used against those who fail to believe in or abide by them. As a practical device, conventional religious morality has its limitations because it must sustain a lust for heaven and a fear of hell. The Church was once able to enforce its moral (and ethical) precepts because it had believers; people took it for granted, at least after a fashion, that the Church truly spoke for the will of God, that He condemned immoralists, and that the fate of these sorry people would in truth be hell. That belief is fast waning. With neither divine punishment nor divine reward as part of its motivational structure, religious morality has been heavily discounted.

This is not to say that a moral system has no value in modern life. Quite the contrary: Most people do not commit murder (say), do not even contemplate the possibility, because it is simply "wrong" to do so. This kind of morality does not depend on any

external institutions, other than education and "proper upbring-
ing," to enforce its rules. In essence, what we would put into law
as a rule of behavior if we could devise a program to administer
it — and what we sometimes do regardless — is what we mean by
"morality." For ultimately, morality and law spring from the
perception that some kinds of behavior are good or bad for certain
ends, even if those ends are only our own peace of mind.

If morality would not work, the professionals could have
turned to law. But law is not an entirely satisfactory mechanism
when the question is regulating the moral quality of a man's
conduct, because the variety of misdeeds is so great. Professionals
sensed early, furthermore, that laws that defined standards of
professional conduct would require large administrative agencies
to probe their work. Between the full panoply of institutions
imbedded in the legal system and the relatively flimsy and ephe-
meral devices for maintaining the moral order, lies a middle system
of control: those rules which have increasingly come to be called
"ethical." Canons of ethics are nothing more than sets of rules
(with some institutional means of enforcement) devised by a
private group.

Codes of ethics were developed at the beginning of the century.
Their explicit rationale was the belief that thus an honest body of
practitioners could be fashioned. Specialists will not abuse their
positions of trust and responsibility if they know that punishment
awaits those who do. The only practicable sanction the professional associations could offer when they promulgated their codes
was the suspension or expulsion from the association. This threat
will evoke a fear in direct proportion to the power and importance
of the association. As the organized professions matured, their
power extended to more drastic sanctions. Lawyers can be disbarred from practice if a court should view their "unethical"
behavior in a grave enough light. For lawyers in many states,
codes of ethics have come to have the force of law. Doctors stand
to lose valuable privileges if they should forfeit local medical
society affiliation: Intellectual contact with fellow practitioners

disappears, a stigma of incompetence attaches, and the loss of hospital accreditation and referral services quickly follows. And though it is difficult to conjure the deeds of an unethical maintenance gardener, doubtless sanctions would be devised and applied were the profession organized.

In acting as mediator between two hostile forces, there is danger that the mediator will be bought off by one side or the other. It should not surprise us that when one of the forces has the wherewithal to pay and the other does not the mediator will be put to a terrible temptation. In the case of professional ethics, it is arguable that the mediator has succumbed altogether.

Consider, for example, the difference between the great Samuel Williston's withholding evidence from the other side on behalf of his client in a civil suit and the position of an attorney who works for a salary on behalf of others to save them the cost of large contingent fees. Were the first condemned and the second applauded, any concern we might have over the course of professional ethics would be theoretical. Yet the surprising fact is that when Professor Williston withheld from the other side evidence he knew to be true but damaging to his client he was not condemned; quite the reverse: His conduct was justified as the work of a skilled advocate ably aiding his client by obscuring the issues. The union attorney, on the other hand, was said by the Illinois Supreme Court to have acted so unethically that an injunction barring him from such a role in the future was upheld. Half-truths are ethical but low fees are not.[2] Ethics is not as obvious a science as it might seem.

2

Central to many codes is the prohibition against "group practice," in which professionals team up with a union, hospital, or other group to provide services for the members — on a salaried, rather than fee, basis. Two notorious incidents are illustrative.

[2] See Opinion No. 309, in *Opinions of the Committee on Professional Ethics* (ABA: 1956); United Mine Workers v. Illinois State Bar Association, 35 Ill. 2d, 219 N.E. 2d 503 (1966).

In 1963, the United Mine Workers of America District 12 (Illinois) hired an attorney who received an annual salary of some $12,000. His function was to aid union members, upon request, primarily in the area of workman's compensation law. A letter from the Union to the attorney stated in part: "You will receive no further instructions or directions and have no interference from the District, nor from any officer, and your obligations and relations will be to and with only the several persons you represent." Union members were not obliged to use the attorney, and he frequently advised them of this fact. The particular attorney chosen served also as an Illinois state senator and carried on an additional private practice. His work was largely confined to preparing the proper papers for submission to the Illinois Industrial Commission whenever an injured employee or his next of kin wished to prosecute a claim against the coal company. A large part of the work is apparently perfunctory; the attorney rarely spoke to clients for any length of time and the preparatory work seemed to resemble a game of filling in the blanks. During the first three years after he was hired, he managed to win more than $3 million for his clients; had he been a privately practicing attorney he would have taken some $500,000 in contingent fees; instead, the money went entirely to the clients.

The system suited everyone but the local attorneys. In 1966 the Illinois State Bar Association instituted proceedings to enjoin the Union from conducting its legal assistance program. The stated ground of the legal action was a violation of a canon of ethics which forbade the "unauthorized practice of law by any lay agency." This was merely verbiage: "Lay agencies" do not practice law; only people do, and the Union had a lawyer. What the canon actually condemned was practice of law by a lawyer salaried to a lay corporation or other group. This was Illinois, and the principle of the *Real Estate Taxpayers* case was still very much a part of public policy.[3]

[3] See discussion, p. 32f.

The state bar association did not charge that the lawyer was sloppy or dishonest, that he asked for less than he could have recovered, or that he conspired with corporate employers to keep down the level of recoveries or with the union to appeal a given case to test a novel legal theory. Indeed, the record speaks for itself that he did well by the union members. The bar did not charge any union official with directing the attorney to act in a particular manner or to take any specific actions. Nor did it charge that anyone else was practicing law in an unauthorized fashion. But the Illinois Supreme Court found the element of unauthorized practice too overwhelming an affront to the canons of professional ethics, and the Union was enjoined.[4] Union members could have recourse to private practitioners who, though they might charge more, could fill in the blanks untainted by a union salary.

A remarkable aspect of the suit was the court's solemn declaration that although the canons of ethics "do not have the force and effect of judicial decision or statutory law they nevertheless are of interest to this court, provide guidelines to members of the profession, and are helpful in reaching determinations in particular cases."[5] What is not law will be enforced as such, the court seemed to be saying. In affirming the injunction the court was promulgating economic regulations by itself. To be sure, the court rested on precedent, but that is simply to say that early in the development of ethical codes the court presumed the power — guided by ethics — to determine what was right and what was wrong in the manner of a lawyer's employment. The Supreme

---

[4] *United Mine Workers, supra* note 2.

[5] *United Mine Workers,* at 507. It should be obvious that a rule, no matter how characterized, has become law when a judge grounds his decision on it. The bar association, in other words, had successfully enacted its own law which it then used as a basis for suit. Cases relying on private codes of ethics are innumerable. In United States v. Standard Oil Co., 136 F. Supp. 345 (S.D.N.Y. 1955), a government motion to disqualify an attorney under Canon 36 because he had worked for the government before his employment with the law firm representing the company failed only because on the facts in the case the attorney had not had the requisite contact with the subject matter of the suit while in federal service.

Court of the United States ultimately overruled the decision, but the point is that in this decision — mirrored in numerous other states — ethics gave judgment for profit, not service.[6]

The American Medical Association feels as strongly about "contract practice" as the Illinois State Bar. Contract practice is nothing more than "a formal association of three or more physicians providing services in more than one field or specialty with income from medical practice pooled and redistributed to the members according to some prearranged plan."[7] According to the canons of medical ethics, "contract practice per se is not unethical." But the code spells out amorphous conditions that quickly make it unethical: "when the compensation is inadequate to assure good medical service"; and "when there is interference with reasonable competition in a community."

In 1937, the AMA grew worried about the burgeoning Group Health Association of Washington, D.C. GHA is a non-profit, prepayment corporation organized by government employees; it hires full-time physicians and pays them a fixed salary. An article in the *Journal of the American Medical Association* (*JAMA*) suggested that nearly three-quarters of the District population could be covered by GHA and prophesied that if even one-half the population were taken in, it would "materially disturb medical

[6] It should be noted that the American Bar Association has adopted a new code of ethics (the Code of Professional Responsibility); five years in the making, it was effective January 1, 1970. According to the *ABA Journal*, 55 *ABAJ* 970 (1969), a series of disciplinary rules accompanying the simplified code "are intended to be legally binding upon all members of the legal profession." Exactly how this intention is to be carried out is not clear, though all it would take is the nod from a judge in a given case. But it is remarkable how explicit the bar has become in promulgating "law." As other "private" groups come to find they too can create law, legislatures will become as superfluous as they are now passé. For the new canon relating to group practice, see note 17, p. 226.

[7] Quoted in Elton Rayack, *Professional Power and American Medicine: The Economics of the American Medical Association* (1967), p. 150; from G. H. Hunt and M. S. Goldstein, *Medical Group Practice in the United States*, Public Health Service Publication No. 77 (1951), p. 10.

practice in the District of Columbia and react against public interest."[8] Two months after the article's publication, the District of Columbia Medical Society's Compensation, Contract, and Industrial Medicine Committee began ousting participating physicians. The AMA coöperated in the purge that was to purify the profession.

The plan of operation was elementary. Those physicians employed by GHA would be expelled from the medical association as would any doctors who, though not employed by GHA, consulted professionally with GHA physicians. Many doctors were expelled and some resigned from GHA rather than face expulsion. A letter of resignation from Group Health was sufficient to remove the stain from the repentant doctor and was the basis of an immediate entitlement to rejoin his brethren in the pursuit of the healing arts.[9]

The plan was under way when the Department of Justice brought suit under the Sherman Antitrust Act, charging both the AMA and the District Medical Society with conspiring "to coerce practicing physicians . . . from accepting employment under Group Health, to restrain practicing physicians . . . from consulting with Group Health's doctors who might desire to consult with them, and to restrain hospitals in and about the City of Washington from affording facilities for the care of patients of Group Health's physicians." The AMA responded by attacking the unethical nature of the GHA enterprise. The attack was unavailing; both medical societies were convicted of antitrust violations and the Supreme Court affirmed on appeal.[10] Against the contention that GHA commercialized the practice of medicine (the same charge as was levied against the United Mine Workers' legal aid program), the Court of Appeals for the District of Columbia Circuit responded that "the activities of GHA are commercial, but because the lay executives do not in any way interfere with the professional work

---

[8] Quoted in American Medical Association v. United States, 130 F. 2nd 233, 239 (1942); from *JAMA*, October 2, 1937.

[9] See American Medical Association v. U.S., 130 F. 2d 233, 239, N. 23 (1942).

[10] American Medical Association v. United States, 317 U.S. 591 (1943).

of the medical doctors, their commercial activities do not tend to commercialize the *practice* of medicine. Medical doctors have long conceded the propriety of medical services furnished by large industrial organizations, to their employees, by doctors also in their employ. There is not greater incongruity in the making available of medical services by a coöperative association or a non-profit mutual benefit association, in similar manner; nor any more reason for suggesting that such industrial organizations are not engaged in commercial activities. In each case the service is rendered in accordance with the standards of the profession and to that extent uncontrolled by the corporate employer."[11]

The professional fear that group practice necessarily corrupts standards is unfounded. The claim that group practice is unethical is based on a faulty chain of reasoning that could be dubbed the "ethical syllogism." Mr. Justice Jackson stated the syllogism (without necessarily endorsing it) as follows: "The ethical objection has been that intervention by employer or insurance company makes a tripartite matter of the doctor–patient relation. Since the contract doctor owes his employment and looks for his pay to the employer or the insurance company rather than to the patient,

---

[11] American Medical Association v. United States, 130 F. 2d 233 (1942). In United States v. National Association of Real Estate Boards, 339 U.S. 485 (1950), the Court held that real estate brokers carry on a trade and that the standardization of commission rates within the District of Columbia is illegal under the Sherman Act. The Government won these cases because the defendants were involved in concerted activity within the District of Columbia, in which the Sherman Act applies. Medicine and other professions have not yet been held to involve interstate commerce, the other basis of the antitrust laws, so the result reached in this case is of limited use. See, generally, James E. Coleman, Jr., "Antitrust Exemptions: Learned Professions," 33 *A.B.A. Antitrust L. J.* 48 (1967). In December 1969, in United States v. Prince George's County Board of Realtors, Inc., the Justice Department brought suit against a Maryland organization, charging price-fixing and alleging that "the activities of the Board and its members are . . . within the flow of interstate commerce and have an effect upon that commerce." See *The New York Times,* December 19, 1969, p. 1. Obviously, people looking for homes and money used to finance them not infrequently cross state lines. The implications of this case are potentially far-reaching.

he serves two masters with conflicting interests."[12]   The syllogism could be rephrased:

(1) Professionals can earn money by helping those who pay them.

(2) Professionals who engage in group practice are not paid by their clients.

(3) Therefore, professionals who engage in group practice will subordinate the clients' needs to the employers' demands.

This is a syllogism that at best draws probabilities from possibilities. The conclusion is illegitimate because, among other reasons, if pay is the thing, a professional might be equally likely to give the patient superficial treatment in order the more quickly to get the pay and in order to get more of it in relation to the work performed.   If the conclusion is to stand up, it would have to be made unethical to be paid at all.

The ethical syllogism is widely deployed throughout the professional estate; thus: "An attorney is licensed to represent persons in their legal activities and the person receiving these services is entitled to the attorney's undivided allegiance. . . . Such allegiance is not *possible* if the attorney . . . is employed and paid by an organization separate from his client.[13]   But of course such allegiance is possible; its probability depends on the nature of the organization.   The United Mine Workers is hardly an "organization separate from" the particular clients.   Likewise, the GHA plan presents these benefits to the patient: "the pooling of the skills of a number of specialists to serve the special needs of the patient; salutary effects of the doctor being subject to observation by his peers; easy access to the services of specialists at little or no additional costs; lower costs through pooling of capital investment; stabilized income for the doctor as he shares in the total receipts of the group; fuller use of ancillary personnel and equipment."[14]

---

[12] United States v. Oregon Medical Soc'y, 343 U.S. 326, 329 (1952).
[13] Derby, "Unauthorized Practice of Law," 54 *Calif. L. Rev.* 1331, 1337 (1966).
[14] Rayack, *supra* note 7, p. 150.

What the professional actually fears, of course, is undue competition. A clinic that is able to serve many patients at reduced costs is a serious threat to the solo practitioner. What better way to obviate the danger than to brand it unethical because it is, as the medical canon says, an "interference with reasonable competition in a community"? The professional represses the unstated assumption that interference with competition means nothing more than that an unprofitable business is an unethical one. By that criterion, medical doctors at Walter Reed Army Hospital or Bethesda Naval Hospital must be unethical indeed.

3

Another important prohibition contained in the ethical canons of most professions is that against advertising. The lawyer or doctor or dentist or architect or accountant who puts a notice in his local newspaper to the effect that "I am available to help you with your problem" runs a serious risk of condemnation by his professional society. The ban on advertising is sweeping. The legal canons of ethics prescribe the typeface size a lawyer may use on professional notices and window signs; the lawyer in many states may not mail even to fellow practitioners a tasteful notice that he has opened an office or is available for specialized services. The New York Dental Society code of ethics proclaims as unethical publishing or broadcasting manuscripts or speeches concerning dentistry to the public unless first submitted for approval to the Society. (That particular canon was recently declared unconstitutional by a New York court.[15])

The advertising ban is grounded on the belief that modern advertising quickly transforms itself from the imparting of information to the creation of want, and the creation of want means that the need is not already there.[16] Professionals resist this impli-

---

[15] Firestone v. New York State First District Dental Society, 299 N.Y.S. 2d 551 (Sup. Ct. 1969).

[16] See John Kenneth Galbraith, *The Affluent Society* (1958), Chapter 11.

cation since manufactured wants of professional services would leave the client open to gross manipulation by the unscrupulous practitioner and the client could not evaluate the services and their quality.[17]   Unfortunately, the damper on advertising prevents it from serving a very useful function: letting those who really do need proper professional care know that they need it. To remedy this defect, professionals publish a host of popular articles and books on problems and needs.   The solution is generally "see your doctor."

The lack of advertising keeps the big strong and the small weak. Although some restraints may be salutary, the ethical proscription masks an important effect.   In the funeral industry, for instance, where it is said to be unethical to advertise prices (though not to advertise services), lack of advertising creates higher prices. Jessica Mitford relates the tale of Mr. Nicholas Daphne of San Francisco, who was expelled in 1961 for advertising $150 funerals. The going price was then $500.   The net effect of his expulsion, owing in part to favorable publicity he received, was price-cutting by other morticians.   The harm in it all is difficult to discern, except to the high-priced operators whose business suffered.[18] The California association obviously handled itself badly and got its members hurt; but many professions, including that which applies "mortuary science" to practical ends, are capable of injuring the transgressing professional's practice.

Again, the ban is rooted in the ethical syllogism: "If individual lawyers could advertise and solicit business *without restriction,* professional reputation would depend upon the effectiveness of an advertising campaign rather than the quality of the services per-

---

[17] H. M. Vollmer, *Professionalization* (1966), pp. 12–13, suggests a related reason for the ban: Advertising would allow the client to make judgments about services and the professional cannot tolerate that client ability.

[18] Jessica Mitford, *The American Way of Death* (1963), pp. 54–5. Following a charge by the Justice Department that the National Funeral Directors Association had violated the antitrust laws, Daphne was permitted to rejoin both state and national associations in 1968. *Time*, January 5, 1970, p. 10.

formed."[19]   The fallacy in this statement is apparent: What might happen without any restriction does not justify a total prohibition.

4

The perusal of published opinions on professional ethics[20] will illuminate the highly developed art of rationalizing the need for profit. The National Lawyers Committee of the American Liberty League (an exceedingly anti-New Deal group) was charged by a disgruntled critic with unethical conduct for organizing a service to develop arguments against New Deal legislation.[21] Might not he who would give gratuitous counsel to the politically oppressed also be seeking clients for other matters by broadcasting his good will? The American Bar Association's Committee on Professional Ethics and Grievances held otherwise, even though the offer of free service was broadcast over the radio.[22] But what is the difference between the conduct of the National Lawyer's Committee and the case of the lawyer who was severely castigated by a New York court for advertising the various services he would perform?[23] And why, for that matter, is it patently unethical for an attorney to go into professional partnership with an accountant unless the attorney cease practicing law?[24] Why is it unethical for a licensed physician to give a lecture to a group of optometrists (whom the

[19] Derby, *supra* note 13, p. 1340 (emphasis added).

[20] See, *e.g.*, A.B.A., *Opinions of the Committee on Professional Ethics and Grievances* (1957), as supplemented, and A.M.A., *Opinions and Reports of the Judicial Council* (1964). See also ABA, *Opinions of the Committee on Professional Ethics* (The American Bar Foundation: 1967 ed.); *Opinions of the Committees on Professional Ethics of the Association of the Bar of the City of New York and the New York County Lawyers' Association* (1956); and ABA Committee on Professional Ethics, *Informal Opinions* (1969).

[21] *The New York Times,* November 13, 1935, p. 15.

[22] Opinion 148 (1935) in *Opinions, supra* note 20, pp. 308–12.

[23] *The New York Times,* April 19, 1969, p. 31.

[24] Opinions 239 (1942), 269 (1945), in *Opinions, supra* note 20, pp. 475–6, 559–60.

AMA has labeled "irregular practitioners")?[25] To what use is the official American Bar Association opinion that "habitual charging of fees less than those established by minimum fee schedules may be evidence of unethical conduct" to be put?[26] If conflict of interest is to be avoided, why has the AMA persisted in its refusal to brand as unethical all types of physician interests in pharmacies or pharmaceutical companies?[27] The answers to none of these questions are satisfactory if professional ethics are supposed to serve to keep the professional honest or at least to mediate between profit and service.

The problem is compounded by the manner in which the codes of ethics are construed and changed. Despite the uses to which they are put, ethics retain the notion of an inherent morality. What is unethical is not only wrong for practical reasons, it is wrong for more basic moral ones. At any rate, that is the theory. In practice, morality is more apt to be legislated by majority vote. For example: a war between doctors and osteopaths has raged for decades. Until 1961, the AMA had condemned as unethical any association by M.D.'s with osteopaths. In that year, the AMA declared a truce, suggested an alliance whereby orthodox doctors will absorb the Doctors of Osteopathy, and its House of Delegates approved a radical change in the canons of medical ethics, permitting M.D.'s "to associate voluntarily with those osteopaths practicing scientific medicine." Yet for some twenty years before this change, osteopathic and medical education were almost identical and M.D.'s had long been using osteopathic techniques for therapy.[28]

A glance at any association's compilation of opinions interpret-

[25] See AMA, *Opinions and Reports of the Judicial Council* (1964), Sec. 3, 13–14.
[26] Opinion 302 (1961), in *Opinions* (Supplement), *supra* note 20, pp. 17–18, overruling Opinion 190 (1939), pp. 375–6.
[27] It is not currently considered unethical for a doctor to own or operate a pharmacy "provided it is in the best interests of the patient." See National Association of Retail Druggists (NARD) *Journal*, November 3, 1969, pp. 53–4.
[28] See Rayack, *supra* note 7, pp. 241–53.

ing its code of ethics will indicate the extent of the association's grip over the practitioner. From the form of the letterhead to the people with whom the practitioner may professionally associate, the association is consulted first, rather like the businessman who submits his latest advertising campaign to the Federal Trade Commision for advance approval.

The various canons of professional ethics run into the hundreds; the formal opinions that interpret and extend them are in the thousands. This cannot be the place for their enumeration. It is sufficient to note that the concern of ethics is said to be public protection, but the rules are privately promulgated. We should require of the professionals what they say they require of themselves: Some way must be devised to limit the grasping for profits now all-too-common. The possibility that there will be a conflict of interest when the special interest group promulgates rules for protection of the public should make us at least consider whether specific rules should not be matters of public law rather than of private ethics.

6

Inconspicuous Production

When the predatory habit of life has been settled upon the group by long habituation, it becomes the able-bodied man's accredited office in the social economy to kill, to destroy such competitors in the struggle for existence as attempt to resist or elude him, to overcome and reduce to subservience those alien forces that assert themselves refractorily in the environment. So tenaciously and with such nicety is this theoretical distinction between exploit and drudgery adhered to that in many hunting tribes the man must not bring home the game which he has killed, but must send his woman to perform that baser office.

    — THORSTEIN VEBLEN, *The Theory of the Leisure Class*

The great error of contemporary American medicine has been to let specialists usurp parts of bodies and certain age groups and erect "no trespassing signs" aimed at general practitioners. We do need specialists for special cases but it is a scandalous waste of manpower and foreboding to medical economics for specialists to handle the usual illnesses, most of which, frankly, are self- limited or lend themselves to simple remedies.

    — DR. HERBERT RATNER,
       "Deficiencies in Present Day Medical Education"

1

Thorstein Veblen had it that the leisure class engaged in an enormously wasteful venture called "conspicuous consumption," mani-

fested by varying degrees of ostentation and distinguished only by
the lack of productive effort necessary to maintain it. The leisure
class goes on. Its spirit has even wafted into the working classes
which today dote on mass-produced items which they slavishly
consume by the millions, thinking that the need for whitewall tires
and psychedelic posters is original with them. This is not, of
course, the highest kind of conspicuous consumption Veblen had
in mind, for those who peopled his leisure class did no productive
work at all.

The professional class, however, must work to support itself.
Yet, next to inheritance, the professional routine is the easiest
door to unmerited opulence. Nor is all of the work involved highly
professional. Throughout much of the "real" world, in fact, is
strung a vein of exceedingly routine, unskilled chores which constitute the bulk of many a practitioner's daily performance. This
work I will call "inconspicuous production," some examples of
which are immediately in order.

Baker, a Wisconsin resident, was named executor of his mother's
will. When she died, his sister and two children were also beneficiaries of the will. He sought an attorney to help him prepare a "final
account and petition for allowance," paperwork that must be submitted to the probate court — in Wisconsin, the county court — in
order for the estate funds to be disbursed. The attorney wanted
$4,800 on an estate valued at $172,000. Feeling that to be an excessive percentage, Baker discharged the attorney and decided to put
the papers in order himself, since all other attorneys were likewise
bound by the state bar minimum fee schedule. After working up
an account of the estate and detailing to whom it was to be distributed, Baker presented the papers to each of the beneficiaries,
all of whom then consulted their own attorneys. The distribution
was approved by each attorney. At last Baker submitted the "final
account and petition for allowance" to the county court, which
refused to order the estate's assets distributed. Since he was not
himself a lawyer, Baker had engaged in unauthorized practice of
law; it would be legally necessary for him to hire an attorney to

ratify what he had already done before anyone would collect so much as a penny. Baker appealed to the Wisconsin Supreme Court. No one had questioned his honesty or the propriety of the settlement, and he sought an order requiring the lower court to probate the estate. The Wisconsin Supreme Court turned him down: "The need for protection of beneficiaries in general from practice by unlicensed persons," it said, "justifies the existence of a general rule and its application to this instance. To require the county court to determine, case by case, whether an unrepresented executor had properly protected the rights of all beneficiaries would impose an unmanageable burden."[1] In a remarkable reading of the Wisconsin constitution, which says that anyone has the right to appear in any court "by an attorney or by an agent,"[2] the court held that the word "agent" means "attorney" only. It is not uncommon for courts to get around uncomfortable laws by saying day is night, so no one ought be surprised at how easily the constitution succumbed to the state legal profession. Indeed, the constitutional provision was quite beside the point; many other state courts have similarly decided the issue without the necessity of overcoming a constitutional presumption to the contrary.

What lay at the bottom of the decision was the common understanding that lawyers thrive on estate work. As the court noted, the bar had set minimum fees to which lawyers working up estates for the county courts would have to adhere at the peril of being branded unethical. Of course the court did not say it was for lawyers that the case was decided against Baker; its immediate decision was that lawyers were necessary in all probate cases because *otherwise the judges would have to work.* To ask the county courts to exercise their jurisdiction intelligently — to determine whether the rights of all beneficiaries were protected by the executor — would be impossible: This was the gravamen of the upper court's holding. The reader who reflects that the implication

---

[1] State ex rel Baker v. County Court of Rock County, Branch I, 29 Wisc. 2d 1, 138 N.W. 2d 162, 167 (1965).
[2] Wisconsin Constitution, Art. VII, Sec. 20.

of the case is that county courts do not bother to check the papers at all when an attorney represents the beneficiaries — that is, do nothing — would not be much amiss. For the fact of the matter is that most of the paperwork is routine and could be done by anyone with a modicum of training. To be sure, not all estates could be prepared in satisfactory form by all laymen. Many would be well advised to seek professional help. But it is a fair example of inconspicuous production when a court is held not to have to exercise a power granted it because it might have to exert itself. If the county court can assume the work is properly done when a lawyer is retained, then the county court has no reason to have probate jurisdiction.

The judges' decision that even simple cases of probate require attorneys rests on the inconspicuous production of judges. The court says it would be an unmanageable administrative burden: a familiar argument of regulatory agencies for flat prohibitions where, were there greater amounts of staff and time, lesser restrictions would be imposed. But this administrative burden is precisely the job for which probate jurisdiction was established. The uncluttered point of the decision is simply that the judges do not want to work.

Lawyers do not understand this, however; at least they profess not to. Indeed, why should they profess it? An excellent way to make money is to perform duties that do not require doing in order to be paid consonant with a fee schedule determined in advance by the group that exclusively does the work. Thus the New York County Lawyers' Association unsuccessfully sued to enjoin the publication of non-lawyer Norman Dacey's *How to Avoid Probate* on the ground that it constituted unauthorized practice of law.[3]

Inconspicuous production does not exist merely at the margin of the legal profession. It is pervasive. It was the motivating factor

---

[3] New York County Lawyers' Association v. Dacey, 21 N.Y. 2d 694, 287 N.Y.S. 2d 422 (1967). The Court of Appeals dismissed the Lawyers' Association petition and reversed the order of the Appellate Division, which had enjoined publication, distribution, advertising, solicitation to purchase,

of the United Mine Workers' case in Illinois. It is the motivation of
many lawyers in the Texas civil commitment procedure. Under a
tightly-drawn statute, an allegedly mentally ill person is entitled to
a hearing and to be represented by legal and medical counsel
before he can be adjudged insane and incarcerated in a mental
hospital. One investigator took the trouble to observe one of these
hearings: "Forty-one cases were heard in an hour and five minutes,
an average of 66 seconds per case. . . . The judge read the patient's
name and the date of medical examination, and asked the doctor,
'Is it your opinion . . . that he is a mentally ill person and needs
medical care and treatment for his own welfare and protection or
the protection of others and is mentally incompetent?' The doctor
answered 'Yes,' and the next case was called. Only two of the
forty patients [one of the cases did not involve a hospital patient]
actually appeared at the hearing. The attorney *ad litem* earned
four hundred dollars for sixty minutes of work plus travel time. He
had no contact with his clients and had never seen nor heard from
most of them."[4] This magnificent example of American due process is a taxpayer's boon: Ten dollars a case is obviously cheaper
than the salary of public defenders, even though the attorney here
gets it for doing almost nothing at all. We may take heart from it
only because the Texas law is better than most.

Inconspicuous production in the guise of unauthorized practice
was raised to a constitutional height during the Arizona real estate-
attorney battle when the Arizona Supreme Court declared that it
was the final arbiter of who might lawfully practice law. The
question was whether real estate salesmen and brokers could lawfully fill in preliminary sales agreements and certain other forms;
the court held they could not.[5] Only lawyers were authorized to

and sale of the book. The Court of Appeals held that the publication of a
book stating what the law is does not constitute law practice, regardless
what use the reader makes of the book or forms it contains.

[4] Weihofen, "Mental Health Services for the Poor," 54 *Calif. L. Rev.* 920,
938–9 (1966).

[5] State Bar of Arizona v. Arizona Land Title and Trust Company, 90 Ariz.
76, 366 P. 2d 1 (1961); 91 Ariz. 293, 371 P. 2d 1020 (1962) (supplemental
opinion).

do that: At every stage of the real estate transaction, lawyers would have to be retained. The upshot was a successful realtors' campaign to amend the state constitution, permitting them the right also to fill in a few blanks.[6]

2

Professionals base their definitions of "unauthorized practice" on their claim to expert skills; the public must be protected. Less pretentiously, professionals arrogate to themselves special areas of practice not because of skill but because of routine. The routine performance of narrowly-drawn tasks is a voluminous business in a modern society with a large middle class. The routine is in demand, is easy to perform and will command high prices when controlled by a monopoly. But precisely because it is routine, a skilled monopoly is unnecessary. The routine can be accomplished by anyone with a modicum of training — if routine enough, in fact, it can even be adapted to the machine.[7] The Arizona real estate decision rested rather less on the specialization of the lawyer than the lack of it: Many lawyers are poorly trained, unadaptable people to whom writing in names on boilerplate is a real challenge. These people and others have cast Veblen's distinction[8] between exploit and drudgery in fine modern form: The lawyer brings in the client and the secretary fills in the forms. For all of the inconspicuous producers, the fight for monopoly is the fight for survival.

Inconspicuous production is not confined to the legal profession; it is widespread. At its best it repesents the profession ekeing out a living by making incantations the public is bound by law to respect and to pay for. At worst, it represents precisely that predatory nature of man that Veblen noted the average American so

---

[6] The fight and its background is discussed in Murray Teigh Bloom, *The Trouble With Lawyers* (1968), pp. 109–121.

[7] Thus, though few will admit it, there are lawyers and law firms which charge steep prices for wills drawn up by computers with capacious memory cells.

[8] See p. 85.

easily accepts: Plundering by trickery is better than honest effort, especially when the economic system holds out the opportunity for everyone so to profit.

The constant vigil to restrict professional practice inevitably leads to featherbedding. This is inherent in all systems of specialization. The specialist insists on doing work which lesser trained men could easily do. Thus, there has been for decades a savage battle between ophthalmologists — licensed M.D.'s — and optometrists, who do not have the M.D. but who are licensed to perform refractions — examinations — of the eyes and to prescribe and fit lenses. The optometrist does a simpler job when measured against the learning and licensed skills of the ophthalmologist, who is a specialist in the diseases of the eye and their treatment. Yet the ophthalmologists have waged an intense struggle to keep the refraction business for themselves, though it is a job which can quite competently be performed by the optometrist. The ophthalmologist seeks to monopolize the simpler business because it is so much more routine, and not so incidentally, very lucrative. For some years eye doctors were in the habit of receiving kickbacks from opticians and optometrists on glasses they prescribed. When this was made an unethical practice in the early 1960's, ophthalmologists across the country began to prescribe and sell eyeglasses themselves. This time — and so far — ethics has not intervened. Eye medicine maintains its status as a commercial enterprise.[9]

Some entire industries are erected on the belief that useless work is imperative to survival. The claim is advanced, for instance, that embalming is for sanitation; the industry has among its proponents those who believe they share with medicine the happy (and selfless) power of reducing the death rate.[10] Morticians are not alone in claiming sanitation as a basic rationale for their existence. Health, after all, is an accepted condition for public legislation; the

[9] See Rayack, *Professional Power and American Medicine: The Economics of the American Medical Association* (1967), pp. 258–65, for a discussion of the intra-professional struggle.

[10] Jessica Mitford, *The American Way of Death* (1963), p. 81.

aesthetic far less often is. Hence morticians embalm and barbers learn health secrets — and legislatures leave them alone — to preserve the public welfare. If those who oppose dump yards and billboards and other monstrosities of our environment would learn to oppose with phrases such as "dangerous to the public health," and eschew "beautification" campaigns, the same result would be achieved far more quickly. Hypocrisy must be fought with parody; honesty will never do.

Professionals, who can produce inconspicuously because laymen cannot always penetrate their mysteries, can produce even less conspicuously when the federal government stands ready to fund them. Then, except for false documents, there is not even a pretense of work. Physicians and dentists who fought government-sponsored health programs for years found it advisable to cash in once Medicare became operational. In a physical check of New York City dental patients in 1969, nine per cent of 1300 patients were found to have had no work performed at all; the city was billed nonetheless. An equal percentage of patients were discovered with painfully inadequate treatment.[11] Lucky — and by no means isolated — was the Eastern Kentucky pharmacist who reportedly received $328,000 in Medicaid funds for his work in a town of 750 people. Said the grateful man: "I think Medicaid has been good to me and I think I've been good to it."[12] This enterprising American is no more to be condemned than countless other physicians who find revolving-door diet clinics and their own pharmacies valuable adjuncts to a professional practice.

Something for nothing is an old dream. Manifestations of the dream are prominent in all walks of life. Doormen at luxury apartments get large tips for doing essentially nothing, but it is at least

11 *The New York Times,* June 20, 1969, p. 1.
12 *The Washington Post,* June 15, 1969, p. 1. A Senate Finance Committee report on Medicare and Medicaid released in February 1970 gives numerous other such examples, and it noted the propensity of some doctors to charge higher fees to Medicare than to private insurance programs for the same service. See *The New York Times,* February 15, 1970, p. IV-6.

arguable that because they serve more to adorn than to work their cost is no more inflated than works of low-grade art. Inconspicuous production is far more serious and costly at the level of professional services.

There is a sound reason why inconspicuous production is a function more of service industries than the manufacturing crafts. Those who make things, or push them through assembly lines, can be evaluated; the quality of their work is discernible and assessable. The quality of services is something else again. Although quality is the core of the "commodity" which professional people produce, it is one which cannot be assessed by any but the experts themselves. And since professionals have an immediate stake in maintaining their status, they do not often investigate and root out the unartful practitioners in their midst. Occasional studies, as we shall shortly see, show how seriously deficient in needed skills are those who claim them most.

It is time to realize that many of our most pressing problems are due to the inconspicuous production of people in critical jobs. An incredibly large number of municipal and state justices of the peace and trial judges, prison officials, and keepers of the mental wards suffer from it. Many "middle managers" of the large bureaucracies — in the business as well as the government enterprise — are notorious for their capacity to spend their time in nonproductive work. Anyone who ever served on active military duty can attest to the lazy ways of many career officers whose salaries and retirement benefits are guaranteed.

All these individuals are comfortable in being lazy or foolish or harsh or vindictive, but they are professionals and it is not politic to go on record attacking a pro. Charges of "you can't understand what we're dealing with" fly thickly through the air like intellectual pollution as soon as anyone mentions outrages that occur daily. Most people lean back and nod, agreeing that they are no legal experts; nor penal experts; nor professional soldiers. The problem is inherent in the autonomy of these professions; it will not be solved by proposing to find "better" people to install as municipal judges or wardens or dentists or morticians. Some portion of all strata of society will work hard at avoiding work so long as no one but their brothers are their keepers. As the chapter following illustrates, control of the professional by his fellow practitioner is a sedulously fostered illusion.

7

Reputation and Autonomy

I was dining at the Duke of Richmond's one day last winter and there came in two notes, one from Sir W. Farquhar and the other from Dr. Hunter, in answer to an enquiry whether or no His Grace might venture to eat fruit pies or strawberries. I trembled for the honour of the profession, and could not conceal my apprehensions from the company: Luckily, however, they agreed tolerably well, the only difference of opinion being on the subject of the pie-crust.
— THOMAS YOUNG, quoted in *Professional Men: The Rise of the Professional Classes in Nineteenth Century England*

A music teacher was forced to resign from a junior high school job when identified as a Communist by a witness testifying before the House Un-American Activities Committee. He turned to piano tuning but was denied a Washington, D.C., license on the ground that he was 'under Communist discipline.'
— American Civil Liberties Union Thirty-Fifth Annual Report

One of the arguments for hushing up [the problem of medical mistakes] is that the public might lose confidence in physicians or hospitals. . . . A serious rail, air, or sea accident leads to inquiries, publication of the findings, and compensation for the victims, without destroying public confidence in the safety of trains, planes, and ships. The difference between such accidents and those in the

95

hospital is that public accidents cannot usually be hidden, whereas those in the hospital can be and often are.

— Louis Lasagna, *Life, Death, and the Doctor*

1

Ethics are not necessary solely for the protection of clients; a set of ethical rules is essential also to set the moral tone of the profession and thus to present an unsullied face to the public. A profession must be purified not only of incompetents but also of those who are otherwise unworthy to carry on the high office of the art. Unworthiness comes in several forms, chief among which are unhealthy political views and dark skin.

The professions have two principal methods of preserving the quality of the practitioners within their domain: refusal to admit them to practice or to membership in the society, and suspension or eviction when a character defect becomes apparent. Some prominent cases should make the matter clear.

Clyde W. Summers was refused admission to the Illinois Bar in 1943 solely because he stated that as a conscientious objector to war he would be unwilling to serve in the Illinois militia during wartime. He based his objection to bear arms on his religious convictions, and it was unquestioned that he was sincere: The United States Selective Service had already classified him a conscientious objector. The state supreme court, following the failure of the Committee on Character and Fitness to certify him (all other requirements having been met), refused to admit him to practice. His unwillingness to serve was characterized as a failure to "support the Illinois Constitution," though he was, the court agreed, willing to take an oath to support that constitution. The court refused to consider his willingness a valid demonstration of loyalty, however, deeming his statement that he would not serve if impressed into the state militia an indication that his oath would not be conscientiously sworn. It was uncontroverted that Illinois had not drafted men since 1864 and that its law in 1943 specifically exempted men who were exempt under federal law. In other words, Illinois refused to allow him to practice law because he would not do what under state and federal law he need not do.

His appeal to the Supreme Court was unavailing. The Court found his stated unwillingness to serve sufficient to justify exclusion. In an interesting *non sequitur*, Mr. Justice Reed for the majority compared Summers' stand with the law that an alien who refused to serve in the U. S. armed forces when needed is barred from citizenship. But power in Congress to exclude aliens from national citizenship should hardly be support for state power to deny employment. The difference is marked, even if Summers had been called, like the alien; that he was not called made the analogy all the more unworkable. As Mr. Justice Black said in dissent: "Such a belief [cannot] be penalized through the circuitous method of prescribing an oath and then barring an applicant on the ground that his present belief might violate that oath. . . . I cannot agree that a state can bar from a semi-public position a well-qualified man of good character solely because he entertains a religious belief which might prompt him at some time in the future to violate a law which has not yet been and may never be enacted."[1] The decision may have had one salutary effect: Summers is now an eminent professor at Yale Law School and member of the New York Bar.

The militant as well as the pacifist has found himself burdened by the same rule. Some years after the *Summers* case, Illinois refused to admit a young air force veteran to the bar because he was foolish enough to affirm his belief in the Declaration of Independence. During the course of a required essay for admission to the bar, George Anastaplo wrote: "And of course, whenever the particular government in power becomes destructive of these ends, it is the right of the people to alter or to abolish it and thereupon to establish a new government." The Declaration of Independence declares in part: "Whenever any Form of Govern-

[1] In re Summers, 325 U.S. 561, 576, 578 (1945).

ment becomes destructive of these Ends, it is the Right of the People to alter or to abolish it, and to institute new Government . . ." Perhaps as a plagiarist he should have been denied admission but since the law thrives on plagiarism, that would have been incongruous.

There was not a shred of evidence inside the record or without that Anastaplo believed in violence, unless participation in the Armed Forces during World War II proved it; or that he was in any sense subversive, unless adherence to the Declaration of Independence and Bill of Rights is subversive; or that he was a member of any prohibited organization, unless the attempt to become a lawyer compelled the prohibition. But once again the Supreme Court upheld Illinois.[2]

Illinois is not the only state to raise such political issues. An equally baffling case arose in California and occupied the courts from 1954 to 1961. Rafael Koningsberg was qualified for the California bar in all respects but "good moral character." The Committee of Bar Examiners questioned him at great length about his political beliefs; he refused to answer the questions on the ground that the state had no business inquiring into his personal beliefs. The Committee denied his application and stated in a letter to the California supreme court:

"1. He failed to demonstrate that he was a person of good moral character, and

"2. He failed to show that he did not advocate the overthrow of the Government of the United States by force, violence, or other unconstitutional means."[3]

Koningsberg was then 43 years old; he had actively pursued other occupations until he decided to attend law school in the early 1950's. In support of his moral character, Koningsberg supplied letters from forty-two references, none of which were in the slightest adverse. No evidence of bad character was intro-

[2] In re Anastaplo, 3 Ill. 2d 477, 121 N.E. 2d 826 (1954), cert. den. 348 U.S. 946 (1954), 366 U.S. 82 (1961).

[3] Quoted in Koningsberg v. State Bar of California, 353 U.S. 252, 259 (1957).

duced by the Committee except for the testimony of one lady who claimed to be an ex-Communist. The Committee accepted her statement that, although she could not positively identify Koningsberg, she thought she recalled that in 1941 he had attended meetings of a discussion group which she said was a Communist Party unit and from which she inferred he was a member. Koningsberg denied knowing her and she herself admitted her only contact with Koningsberg, if indeed he was the man, was at the meetings thirteen years before. Koningsberg denied being a communist.

His real problem was one faced by others in democracies: Koningsberg was conceited enough to have opinions which he expressed in print in a local newspaper. He "severely criticized, among other things, this country's participation in the Korean War, the actions and policies of the leaders of the major political parties, influence of 'big business' in American life, racial discrimination," and several Supreme Court decisions.[4] He also appeared before the notorious Tenney Committee (the California Senate's Un-American Activities Committee) and said to members: "I pledge my word to use every democratic means to defeat you." That statement, said the Bar Committee, put his moral character in question because he had the temerity to disapprove the acts of government.

He repeatedly denied any belief in violent overthrow: "I answer specifically I do not, I never did, or never will," he had said. The Committee produced no evidence to the contrary and Koningsberg stated his readiness to subscribe to loyalty oaths supporting the United States and California constitutions. But, said the Committee, his belief in violent overthrow of the government was evident from language such as this: "Loyalty to America, in my opinion, has always meant adherence to the basic principles of our Constitution and Declaration of Independence — not loyalty to any man or group of men. Loyalty to America means belief in and militant support of her noble ideals and the faith of her people."[5]

[4] *Koningsberg*, at 268.
[5] *Koningsberg*, at 271, 275.

The Supreme Court reversed the California court decision denying Koningsberg admission to the bar. On the state of facts presented, the Court saw no inference of bad moral character that could be adduced and remanded the case to the state court in 1957. Three years had already elapsed. The state court in turn remanded the case to the Committee of Bar Examiners for reconsideration. The Committee went through the same routine and once again Koningsberg refused to answer political questions put to him. But this time the Committee made it a specific ground for refusal to certify Koningsberg that he declined to answer the questions. The issue of unanswered questions had not been a part of the original Supreme Court test and that Court had expressly declined to pass on the issue of whether a man could be refused admission to the bar for failure to answer questions. Now the issue was presented. Four years later the Supreme Court answered that sufficient grounds for denial did at last exist. The questions were relevant to the Committee's inquiry and the refusal to answer was enough of an "obstruction" to the investigation to warrant exclusion.

How had Koningsberg impeded the investigation? Only by refusing to answer whether he had ever been a member of the Communist Party; he had already specifically denied being a communist or an advocate of violent overthrow. Mr. Justice Harlan for the Court majority said that "as regards the questioning of public employees relative to Communist Party membership, it has already been held that the interest in not subjecting speech and association to the deterrence of subsequent disclosure is outweighed by the State's interest in ascertaining the fitness of the employee for the post he holds and hence that such questioning does not infringe constitutional protections."[6] Thus lawyers were equated with public employees, and neither the Committee of Bar Examiners, composed exclusively of lawyers, nor the California Bar, raised its voice in protest. Koningsberg was excluded.

[6] Koningsberg v. State Bar of California, 366 U.S. 36, 52 (1961).

Of course, Justice Harlan was disingenuous: The burden of proving good moral character was the Committee's, he said, and because Koningsberg refused to answer the questions put to him the Committee was obstructed in meeting it. He who does not speak is convicted by his silence. The short answer to the entire episode is that "obstructionism" was a doctrine manufactured for the case. The Court in its first decision noted that failure to answer was not a basis for denial under any California rule or law — and none was asserted in the second case.

As it happened, in a case decided the same day as *Koningsberg I* the Supreme Court had held that membership in the Party many years before would not by itself warrant denial of admission and certainly the suspicion of it would not.[7] In other words, Koningsberg was excluded for refusing to answer a question, an affirmative answer to which the Supreme Court had already said was no basis for exclusion whatsoever. For whatever proposition *Koningsberg I* and *II* may thus be cited as standing, it can be reported that by 1969 there were signs that the fog may be lifting from the Court.[8]

Lest the reader conclude that political opinions have a direct bearing on the fitness of lawyers only and thus these cases are of a kind, consider briefly the case of Dr. Edward K. Barsky. Con-

[7] Schware v. Board of Bar Examiners of New Mexico, 353 U.S. 232 (1957). In the state case, Schware v. Board of Bar Examiners, 291 P. 2d 607 (N.M. 1955), the state board had refused to certify the applicant for licensing because, among other reasons, he had been a member of the Communist Party during the 1930's, when membership was legal, and he had resigned before it became illegal. The Court further restricted the use a state can make of such membership in a series of cases standing for the proposition that members of the Communist Party cannot be convicted of a crime (or be ousted from a government job) unless they are active members, aware of the Party's principles, adhere to the doctrine that violent overthrow of the government is necessary and go about directly inciting others to action, intending overthrow. See Yates v. United States, 354 U.S. 298 (1957), Scales v. United States, 367 U.S. 203 (1961); Noto v. United States, 367 U.S. 290 (1961); Elfbrandt v. Russell, 384 U.S. 11 (1966).

[8] As this book was being written, the Supreme Court granted *certiorari* in Baird v. State Bar of Arizona, 394 U.S. 957 (1969), to consider anew the question raised in *Koningsberg II*.

victed in 1947 in federal district court for failure to provide Congress with papers when subpoenaed by the House Un-American Activities Committee, he was suspended from medical practice in New York State for six months following hearings conducted by the Department of Education's Medical Committee on Grievances.

Dr. Barsky was a key member of the Joint Anti-Fascist Refugee Committee, founded to help Spanish refugees after World War II. The Attorney General of the United States had cited it as a subversive organization, a listing which the Supreme Court subsequently found unconstitutional.[9]   When Congress subpoenaed Dr. Barsky and others to determine whether his organization was engaged in subversive propaganda, on advice of counsel that the subpoena was unlawful, he refused to turn his records over because he feared that the lives of people in Spain would be endangered were the names of contributors and their relatives to be made public. The Supreme Court refused to hear an appeal of his conviction — i.e., his attorney was wrong — and Dr. Barsky was jailed five months.

The New York Medical Committee on Grievances then held its hearings. That Committee consisted of ten licensed physicians, appointed by the New York Board of Regents to serve five year terms. The ten were chosen as follows: three directly by the Board and the other seven by the Board from lists prepared by the New York State Medical, Homeopathic, and Osteopathic Societies. The Board of Regents need not have suspended his license; but its decision was final and not subject to review by the Court of Appeals. When the Board suspended, it gave no reason. Most of the original hearings involved the alleged "communistic" activities of Dr. Barsky; none of the hearings related to his ability to practice medicine. The Committee on Discipline of the Board of Regents, a group intermediate between the Grievance Committee and the full Board, noting that the Supreme Court had struck the Anti-Fascist Refugee group from the Attorney General's list, rec-

9 Joint Anti-Fascist Refugee Committee v. McGrath, 341 U.S. 123 (1951).

ommended no suspension, but the full Board upheld it. Dr. Barsky was caught between the medical worriers on the Grievance Com mittee and the political neurotics on the Board of Regents and there was no escape, for the Supreme Court, now hearing an appeal from the Regents' decision, upheld the suspension.[10]

Political belief is not the only route to blacklisting. There has long been a more literal approach toward Negroes. For decades it has been the practice of southern state medical and dental societies to refuse admission to black physicians and dentists solely on the ground of race. Since the societies were deemed "private," there was no constitutional basis on which courts could compel membership. Without membership, the ability of these doctors to broaden their experience by professional contacts with a wide cross-section of the states' practitioners was denied, as were all-important affiliations with the white hospitals.

Characteristic of the prevalent attitude was the case of Dr. Reginald A. Hawkins, a Negro dentist licensed to practice in North Carolina. Membership in his district dental society was prerequi-site to his gaining admission to the North Carolina Dental Society. The district required two active members to sponsor each candi-date. Hawkins' district had no black members and he could find no willing sponsors. Blocked by the local rule, he sought relief in federal district court. The case was dismissed.[11] The district judge found no ties between the state and the society, noting espe-cially that the state society had no power to nominate members of the state board of dental examiners and that numerous other state medical agencies did not expressly require any affirmative action by the state society nor did it have an explicit veto power. That the dental society did have an explicit power to name the state dental examining board at the time Dr. Hawkins filed the suit was apparently irrelevant to the judge since the state legis-lature, moved by the court proceedings, had quickly amended the

[10] Barsky v. Board of Regents, 347 U.S. 442 (1954).
[11] Hawkins v. North Carolina Dental Society, 230 F. Supp. 805 (W.D.N.C. 1964), reversed 355 F. 2d 718 (4th Cir., 1966) (Haynsworth, J.).

dental code. What distinguished this case from countless others was the course of its appeal.[12] Yet the practice of many professions by blacks fortunate enough to acquire an education has been largely (and still is) restricted by attitudes and practices of the larger body of organized professionals.

The professional organization may thus be used as a mask to hide racial or religious discrimination. If an organization can successfully claim to be private, then the contemporary political dogma does not condemn it for refusing to admit or simply ignoring Negroes, Jews, Catholics, or foreigners. Some do-gooders may carp, but they are merely cranks. Obviously it is mere happenstance that no one practices in X hospital unless he belongs to the county medical association, which is private. No piece of writing will ever be found that determines the coincidence, which has always occurred.

2

If good moral and racial character requirements were overshadowed by disciplinary proceedings aimed at weeding out professionals unfit to practice on grounds related to their expertise or lack of it, perhaps we could accept this philosophically. But proceedings to inquire into professional competence are rare. Of the two hundred eight medical licenses revoked in 1967 in thirty-one states, only twenty-three cases related to professional practice, and these had to do with narcotics violations and abortions only.[13] Yet repeated studies of medical practice and surgery during the past few years have indicated that professional incompetence is nearing epidemic proportions in some areas. The Peterson study of North Carolina general practice indicated that "less than one physician in thirty carried out adequate physical examinations."[14]

[12] See Chapter 13.
[13] *Time Magazine*, February 21, 1969, p. 55.
[14] Quoted in Lasagna, *Life, Death, and the Doctor* (1968), p. 60. See Osler L. Peterson, *et al.*, "An Analytical Study of North Carolina General Practice, 1953–1954," 31 *J. of Med. Educ.* 22 (1956) (on the state of the art of

There is ample evidence that in significant numbers of cases inept medical decisions were made. But the doctors studied were not investigated with discipline in mind and presumably they continue to practice. The incidence of unnecessary surgery and prescriptions by doctors with an interest in performing operations or in pharmacies or pharmaceutical companies is high. Cases of lawyers who continue to practice in spite of unethical conduct directly related to the lawyer's function are legion.[15] It is worthy of mention that Illinois, the same state which prohibited Summers and Anastaplo from practicing law, permitted an attorney convicted of selling post office jobs and jailed for twenty-two months to "withdraw" from the bar and to be readmitted upon release from prison.[16] To be sure, it is questionable whether conviction, of itself, should be grounds for disbarment, but the Illinois Bar might be presumed to profit more from having men unafraid to speak their minds than one involved in the seamy side of federal patronage.

An isolated mistake may be dismissed, if not forgiven. But when mistakes occur rather routinely in twenty or thirty per cent of some kinds of operations, the citizen may well wonder whether the profession is doing an acceptable job of quality control. Professionals are given privileges to do a job — if they do not, it requires no taxing cerebration to see that privileges may be withdrawn and the public reassert some kind of control over the degree of expertise to which it is subject.

The failure of professional groups to act is sometimes due to

---

medical histories, physical examinations, laboratory aids, and therapy); John H. Knowles, ed., *Hospitals, Doctors, and the Public Interest* (1965); Ray E. Trussell, *The Quantity, Quality and Costs of Medicine and Hospital Care Secured by a Sample of Teamster Families in the New York Area* (1962) (hysterectomies and Caesarian operations); *JAMA* (January 1953), pp. 360–365 (hysterectomies and diagnostic curettage); J. Frederick Sparling, "Measuring Medical Care Quality," *Hospitals*, March 16, 1962, pp. 62–68 (appendectomies).

[15] See Murray Teigh Bloom, *The Trouble With Lawyers* (1968), Chapter 1.
[16] Bloom, *supra* note 15, p. 161.

the failure of the investigating boards to gather facts. Thus the state boards of pharmacy are manned by pharmacists, but the field force — the inspecting teams — are laymen.[17] This is precisely the reverse of the desirable arrangement. Laymen cannot pass on that which requires expert knowledge; experts cannot be expected to avoid those unfortunate conflicts of interest and desires that tempt those who judge themselves.

More often, the failure to act is due to a failure of will. I lived for a while in a rural Maryland county with a relatively small practicing bar. Within the space of a very few years, two prominent attorneys were indicted and convicted — one by the state for embezzling more than $100,000 from a bank of which he was a trustee and the other by the federal government for evading many thousands of dollars worth of income tax. These were not crimes of oversight. But in neither case did the bar association think it necessary to take any action at all, not even to consider whether to study the possibility of a short suspension. The state bar said that any recommendation to the courts to suspend or disbar should come from the local association. The local association was small enough to want to set a precedent to help the next errant member. The embezzler is still in jail, but the tax evader is back in practice without a lost day.

Often action is not taken because the existence of a grievance committee is not well enough known to the clients to bring forth complaints. This is true in the case of many medical and legal committees, and it is also apparently true of the Committee for the Improvement of Advertising Content (known as Interchange), a joint committee of the Association of National Advertisers and the American Association of Advertising Agencies. Interchange was established to discourage advertisements which mislead, disparage, or are in bad taste. As the number of cases coming to Interchange decreased, industry spokesmen concluded that bad advertising is "on the wane." But that is less likely than that most

17 Margaret Krieg, *Black Market Medicine* (1967), pp. 193–4.

people, even those in advertising, are unaware of the Committee.[18]

More times than any organization would care to admit, violations are deliberately buried in committee. The American Lumber Standards Committee, for example, hires inspectors to check marketable lumber against the grade stamps placed on it. The industry has been made uncomfortable by occasions of deliberately misgraded lumber. But the Committee has consistently refused to take action against any grading agencies found violating industry standards. "When violations are found they are promptly reported to the committee's headquarters. These reports are brought to the attention of a special subcommittee, denominated the Board of Review, which checks them and assigns them to the appropriate filing cabinet. . . . To assure that the problem does not disturb too many minds and consciences, the American Lumber Standards Committee has voted that its 5-man Board of Review, which examines the policing reports, must never reveal their contents to anyone, including any of the other members of the American Lumber Standards Committee. So the filing cabinets fill and without knowledge of the facts, the committee members, except for the unlucky five on the Board of Review, go with clear consciences."[19]

Burial in committee does not mean complete lack of enforcement. It has been argued by Oliver Garceau, a careful and noted observer of the medical profession, that discipline can take place at informal, unseen levels: "Suspension or expulsion are seldom

[18] *The New York Times,* July 12, 1966, p. 69.
[19] Rep. John D. Dingell (D.-Mich.), 112 *Congressional Record,* Pt. 21 (89.2), p. 28314 (October 20, 1966). The same charge has been made against lawyers' client security funds. These are funds privately established by bar associations to compensate victims of unethical practitioners. Bloom, *supra* note 15, p. 47, argues that lawyers' funds rarely pay out because no one knows about them or because (by implication) lawyers are not diligent in prosecuting members of the bar. By comparison an Arizona real estate brokers' fund with $300,000 in 1967 had yet to pay out any money at all; Bloom takes this as a sign of professional honesty. He wants it both ways to attack lawyers as excessively evil, missing the opportunity to note that the vice inheres in professionalism itself.

formally used against the unethical, the negligent, the overambitious, the exploitative, or the incompetent doctor. Doctors fear gossip. They fear countersuit. They proceed only with written statements and witnesses. They seldom proceed. But this by no means indicates that the machinery is otiose. Its availability in reserve allows proceedings by informal conversation, fatherly advice, preliminary warning. The good opinion of his professional colleagues is almost as necessary to a physician as hospital access. He can be frozen by lack of consultation, lack of referral, social ostracism, and informal advice to patients. So the formal record is no measure of the discipline exercised. At best, however, it is no sharp, all-seeing, alert enforcement."[20]

Danger inheres precisely in the informal approach. If a professional is not hurt publicly because there is no formal proceeding, he can be extensively damaged within the profession for lack of any public method of clearing himself. Informal boycott, like rumor, can spread quickly and maliciously.

3

Serious tensions exist in the opposing tug of professional grievance committee purposes. The committees serve ostensibly to discipline and deter wayward professionals. But the theory of discipline is also tied to the public image of the professions: Punitive action is necessary to demonstrate publicly that the organized profession does not support misfeasance. In fact, discipline is for any unorthodoxy of a public nature. Since the reputation of the profession is important to maintain public confidence, a tension necessarily arises: When the public does not know about the misdeeds of one of their fellows, there is no need to act since that would only call public attention to it. Nor is there reason to disbar

[20] Oliver Garceau, "The Morals of Medicine," in James C. Charlesworth, ed., *Ethics in America: Norms and Deviations*, 363 *The Annals* of the American Academy of Political and Social Science (1966), p. 65.

or eject a member permanently if the public is likely to forget.[21] Indeed, to the extent reputation is the desideratum, the mere *existence* of a grievance committee may suffice. Hence we may expect inactivity in the areas that count and activity in many areas irrelevant to any considerations but those of image. Thus, political opinions deviant enough from the popular view call for public rebuke; thus, racial minorities cannot be allowed to contaminate the inner professional core.

The concern for the profession's reputation and honor is a theme whose influence is felt in a hundred ways at all levels of professional behavior. In the military, "conduct unbecoming an officer and gentleman" is punishable as a court martial may direct. Included as an example of such conduct is *"public* association with *notorious* prostitutes."[22] It is not the crime that is forbidden; it is the damage that certain conduct will inflict on the public's impression of the military officer. The same fear is evident in the case of an attorney disbarred for pleading the Fifth Amendment in New York during an investigation into ambulance chasing. The Supreme Court reversed the state court, ordering a reinstatement.[23] Some lawyers and judges[24] were upset because it would now be more difficult to discipline errant members of the bar. The unstated premise of their concern is that the real crime — pleading the Fifth — tarnishes the reputation of the legal profession, and it is now beyond the reach of disbarment proceedings.[25]

---

[21] Thus a pharmacist who was sentenced to eleven months in prison for illegally substituting sulfa drugs in prescriptions at a cost of a 2000 percent markup and one human life found the state pharmacy board's action to his liking: "We reprimanded this fellow *very* seriously; we *really* chewed him out!" Quoted in Krieg, *supra* note 17, p. 185.

[22] Uniform Code of Military Justice, Article 133 (10 USC § 933). *Manual for Courts-Martial* (1969), Paragraph 212, p. 28–71 (emphasis added).

[23] Spevack v. Klein, 385 U.S. 511 (1964).

[24] See Bloom, *supra* note 15, p. 164; and Justice Harlan's dissent in *Spevack*, *supra* note 23, at p. 520.

[25] Cohen v. Hurley, 366 U.S. 117 (1961), which *Spevack* overruled, had held that a lawyer could be disbarred for pleading the Fifth Amendment in an official investigation. *Cohen* thus hinged the practice of law (and by implica-

The general "good moral character" requirement asked of almost every applicant for licensure is understandable in the same light, and is significant as the descendant of the original historical requirement that the professions be practiced only by "gentlemen." In ancient days when examinations were easy or nonexistent, the character of a man (*i.e.*, his family position) said a good deal about his ability to mingle with the class of people he was to serve professionally. The professions were originally the "gentleman's" occupation (when that term was restricted to relatively few); only a man of good character would have the common background necessary to the development of a relationship of trust.[26] Of course, the skill requirement implicit in modern professions undercuts the fear that the rude-born will be unable to discharge the professional function, but the moral character requirement lingers on, now to preserve the corporate image of the entire profession. What dangers lurk within its ambiguities have already been explored.

Codes of ethics and disciplinary committees are justified in large part as devices to protect the profession from the universal fear that the public will "lose confidence." The fear is unreasonable, applied to the practice of a profession as such. If the public should ever lose confidence in physicians it is hardly likely appendectomies will be performed by professional chefs. Nor is it any more likely that people will clamor for clergymen to litigate their claims in the courtroom should the bar lose its grip of respect on the hushed and reverent public.

There is, however, a real reason for the fear. If the public loses confidence, it does not discard professionals; it seeks to assure

tion, many other professions as well) on a willingness to forego a constitutional right. The dangers are manifest. For almost everything in our society can be construed as a "privilege": the carrying on of almost every occupation, the driving of a car, etc. It would be easy thus to operate a police state by the simple device of denying the amenities unless the people renounce their political rights.

26 W. J. Reader, *Professional Men: The Rise of the Professional Classes in Nineteenth Century England* (1966), p. 47.

itself that they will be motivated to perform their functions more capably.

Ethics and discipline serve a more important private goal — to promote professional autonomy and to guard against the imposition of public regulation. To the extent that professionals can ward off public inquiry by keeping their fellows bland and in line, the public, it is hoped, will not attempt to sneak its wants and whims into the nature and conduct of professional services. The practitioner is free.

8

The Theory
of the Professional Class (II)

The expert tends to make his subject the measure of life, instead of making life the measure of his subject. . . . Lord Kelvin was a great physicist, and his discoveries in cable-laying were of supreme importance to its development; but when he sought to act as a director of a cable-laying company, his complete inability to judge men resulted in serious financial loss. . . . Mr. Henry Ford is obviously a business man of genius; but, equally obviously, his table talk upon themes outside his special sphere reveals a mentality which is mediocre in the extreme. . . . Because a man is an expert on medieval French history, that does not make him the best judge of the disposition of the Saar Valley in 1919. Because a man is a brilliant prison doctor, that does not make him the person who ought to determine the principles of a penal code. The skill of a great soldier does not entitle him to decide upon the scale of a military armament; just as no anthropologist, simply as an anthropologist, would be a fitting governor for a colonial territory administered by native races.

— HAROLD J. LASKI, *The Limitations of the Expert*

1

Professionals and their organizations are plagued with a practical as well as a theoretical difficulty. To maintain public reputation and to serve the art, professionals must take actions which undermine both goals.

To be professional they must seem politically neutral; to preserve the public confidence, they demand strict adherence to a code of ethics. The code is enforced most often in cases where the public reputation would otherwise suffer — that is, in cases where political neutrality is breached. Only by so doing will autonomy — i.e., freedom from lay control — be secured. But autonomy has another aspect also: It is not enough to be free from control; the practitioner must also be free to act in many ways. Absolute freedom to perform a narrowly circumscribed task is not to be preferred to the freedom to perform broadly defined tasks. Both aspects of autonomy are reinforcing: Freedom from control allows the professional to assume a broader base; the assumption of a broader base makes it correspondingly more difficult to fashion lay power to control the profession. Thus ethics and discipline broaden autonomy on the one hand and the power to define unauthorized practice extends it on the other.

To extend autonomy, the professional through his organization must promote the assertion that all within his realm belongs to him. To defend against his core of interests, the boundaries of the realm must be increasingly expanded to encompass the social aspects of the discipline. But at this point the professional goes beyond his expertise. He holds his territorial conquests, however, as follows: (1) Only small numbers of professionals actually run the organizations, and they have become something more like professional managers with a corporate existence at stake and something less like the professionals they were trained to be. They can be expected to use the organization's resources of skill, mystique, and capital to increase the political leverage of the group. (2) Most professionals who might be inclined to disagree are deterred by a far more real and pressing interest in their work and a disinclination to fight a battle against the organization men who can inflict real damage in a showdown. Moreover, the usual practitioner is no more an expert on the social implications of his organization's political positions than his leaders, so he either agrees with his leaders or does not work up enough interest to interfere.

These considerations raise the practical and theoretical difficulties. The professional theory holds that the practitioner must appear neutral, yet to maintain the appearance of neutrality the profession must engage in exceedingly political acts. Usually they are shadowy maneuvers, but sometimes they are highly visible. In the case of medicine, the Knowles affair springs to mind: In 1969 the Secretary of Health, Education, and Welfare was forced to withdraw the name of his nominee for the Assistant Secretaryship of Health and Scientific Affairs, Dr. John Knowles of Boston, because of intense AMA antipathy toward his reported social beliefs. The effort to sustain neutrality may thus be self-defeating.

The theoretical difficulty is more subtle but accordingly more dangerous: The professions create organizations to protect the public interest; in extending the power of these organizations to perform this task, however, the organizations grow beyond the purposes for which they were formed and the power created effectively undermines the interests they were created to serve. The existence of an organized body of practitioners necessarily distorts the underlying art in which the profession purports to engage. Some examples may make the point more clear.

2

The distortion of legal theory — *i.e.*, the perversion of justice — is a commonplace within the legal profession. It has been amply illustrated that professionals who accept money to perform services have motives that keep them from seeking necessary reforms. Law deals with institutionalized conflict; any attempt of a reform group to change the institutions handling the conflict or to mute it altogether is likely to bring a storm of protest from some or all segments of the bar.

One of the most pressing problems facing the judicial system today is the congestion of court calendars. More than ninety per cent of cases on the civil dockets involve automobile accidents. Under prevailing concepts of the common law, the person at fault in an automobile accident must reimburse the injured victims. Usually, of course, the loss is covered by automobile insurance and the net legal effect of accidents is a proliferation of insurance company litigation in the courts. This is a costly, time-consuming procedure. In recent years it has been proposed, most notably by law Professors Robert E. Keeton and Jeffrey O'Connell (the Keeton-O'Connell plan)[1] that the fault basis of reimbursement should be shifted to a need basis. An overhauling of the basic system of tort liability with respect to automobile accident claims by shifting fault to need could be accomplished in a manner roughly similar to well-established insurance plans for medical needs, homeowners' and other theft and fire losses, and workman's compensation plans. A person responsible for his medical condition is not thereby denied the coverage of his insurance for surgery and medication. In all these areas, the victim collects directly from his insurance company; since premiums are presumably based on a broad set of statistics, the costs of operating comprehensive plans are allocated over a wide spectrum of society. The result is a less expensive, speedier method of compensation.

Some such reform is long overdue. But the organized bar has so far resisted the suggestions. The American Bar Association in its midwinter 1969 meeting opposed the non-fault plans because they are "not in the public interest." This conclusion was reached by a Special Committee on Automobile Accident Reparations, which reported to the ABA's House of Delegates that "the proposals violate our instincts and traditions that people should not

---

[1] See Keeton and O'Connell, "Basic Protection — A Proposal for Improving Automobile Claims Systems," 78 *Harv L. Rev.* 329 (1964); and Keeton and O'Connell, *Basic Protection for the Traffic Victim — A Blueprint for Reforming Automobile Insurance* (1965). See also James Marshall, "The Unreality of Automobile Litigation," 50 *ABAJ* 713 (1964).

benefit from their own fault."[2] Instinct and tradition are usually relied on as words with emotive power to stem change. Instincts and tradition argue against practically anything one would care to name. The instinct is, of course, the lawyer's job in operating the current litigation system and the tradition is one that pays large contingent fees to lawyers who win large suits in almost all branches of tort law.

The problem here is one of allocating costs more efficiently. The legal profession distorts it by finding it impossible to perceive a solution in any terms but those that encompass the profession.[3] The distortion is not simple or all-corrupting. Obviously there are "legal" functions to be performed, regardless of who performs them. These functions have costs. The problem is to remove the distortions which costs can introduce and to reduce extraneous costs which the distortions preserve. So long as the legal profession insists on the natural rights of lawyers to produce inconspicuously in many areas (including probate, divorce, tort, and many types of competency and criminal hearings), legal theory will be kept unsound. For justice requires that rules, regulations, and methods of proceedings should apply to all, regardless of race, religion, creed, or income.

The distortion of legal theory is not caused simply by lawyers requiring themselves in proceedings where others might do as well at lower costs. The very existence of the legal profession and the common law adversary system sets a minimum limit on the economic size of claims that can be recovered. The lawyer's fee

<hr />

[2] Quoted in *Trial Magazine*, February/March 1969, p. 3.

[3] Thus, during the 1966 New York State Surrogate's Court (probate) campaign, the charge was made that the Surrogate's Court was scandal-ridden, that for years judicial patronage was used to enable lawyers practicing before it to take in enormous and highly unwarranted fees. A supporter of the court answered by observing that "the unanimous opinion of attorneys who practice in the court and who observe its conduct on a day-to-day basis" was that the court conducted its business expeditiously and that its judges were competent. See *The New York Times*, June 12, 1966, p. 43. Lawyers who profit from existing institutions are not likely to criticize them nor to perceive them in any light other than of indispensability.

plus the trouble and nuisance of litigation make it unlikely that even a simple claim for anything less than $500 or $1000 will be satisfied. In moderately complex cases, involving the interpretation of contracts, for instance, this minimum limit may be as high as $5,000 or more.[4] New ways of securing rights must be devised; perhaps binding arbitration. In any event, recognition of the problem must precede solution.

The problem is coëxtensive with the legal system. Not merely monetary claims are at stake. The quality of service is as important as costs, yet it is almost impossible to insist on a particular level of competency since the theory holds that all lawyers in practice are better than the minimum acceptable level. Malpractice suits are difficult to initiate and to win; the courts adhere to a rarely justified conclusion that an attorney cannot be liable for an "error of judgment."[5] But this theory assumes the conclusion in a malpractice suit, since the question is always whether the attorney was negligent. To be sure, a lawyer may make a mistake for which he should not be held liable, but to draw a distinction between the honesty of judgment and the quality of the lawyer's

---

[4] *Cf.* Mrs. Virginia Knauer, Special Assistant to President Nixon for Consumer Affairs: "We know one of the consumer's major problems. When he gets illegally taken at the marketplace the loss is generally lower than a lawyer's fees." *The New York Times*, August 24, 1969, p. 30.

[5] See, *e.g.*, Lucas v. Hamm, 56 Cal. 2d 583, 364 P. 2d 685 (1961), cert. denied, 368 U.S. 987 (1962). In this case, the intended beneficiaries of a defective will sued the attorney who drafted the document for the deceased, alleging negligence on the part of the attorney in overlooking salient features of the Rule Against Perpetuities, which has been described as a "technicality-ridden legal nightmare" and a "dangerous instrumentality in the hands of most members of the bar." W. Barton Leach, "Perpetuities Legislation," 67 *Harv. L. Rev.* 1349 (1954). So the California Supreme Court, one of the nation's best courts, declined to hold the erring lawyer liable, since negligence means failure to use the skill, prudence, and diligence that ordinary lawyers would use. Ordinary lawyers, the court concluded, err frequently where the Rule is concerned. It might fairly be asked why the Rule is entrusted to lawyers at the expense of clients and their intended beneficiaries. It might also fairly be asked why this preposterous Rule Against Perpetuities is perpetuated by lawyer-dominated legislatures and courts.

other duties reflects murky logic. The client pays for judgment as well as the knowledge that a suit, to be timely, must be filed within so many days or years of the injury for which recovery is sought.

On the criminal side of the law, the professional distortion has been sanctified by an ancient rule that everyone is entitled to his day in court. This old and highly precious legal saw is made dull only by insistence that that is *all* a man is entitled to: If his lawyer is sloppy or unartful, it is the client who must suffer. Here is a serious distortion. For if the practice of law is a learned mystery and clients are at the mercy of their hired experts, lawyers' mistakes ought not be chargeable against the client. The usual justification for saying a lawyer's mistake can deprive a client of a right is the assumption that an attorney is an agent and that a "master" is bound by his agent's acts when done within the scope of the employment. But the usual sterile dialectic of the law fails here as it so often does in other areas — here, because in the nature of the case the client is forced to hire this class of agent to pursue his remedies or his defenses. The client must either retain an attorney or forego a defense. Some courts have struck back at the theory that the client is entitled to one day and one lawyer only. Although federal law permits a defendant to protest his conviction and sentence if the quality of representation was very poor (merely poor is not enough to win a new trial), the tests for reversal are difficult to meet.[6]

---

[6] Under 28 U.S.C. § 2255, a defendant can have his sentence and conviction vacated if he can show "gross incompetence" of counsel which has made a fair defense impossible. As one Court of Appeals has noted, "the cases are rare and extraordinary." Bruce v. United States, 379 F. 2d 113, 116 (D.C. Cir. 1967). Interestingly, federal military law is more vigorous in securing the criminally accused "effective assistance of counsel," since the Court of Military Appeals decided in United States v. McMahon, 6 U.S.C.M.A. 709, 21 C.M.R. 31 (1956), that denial of "effective" assistance is prejudicial error requiring reversal. The Court of Military Appeals since then has indicated by specific reversals that it is more willing to second-guess military lawyers and find them at fault than are other federal courts. Whether this is because military lawyers are not as highly regarded is difficult to say.

The fact that the existence of a profession is sometimes a bar to strict adherence to the underlying discipline can be taken one step farther. Sometimes the profession is directly opposed to the interest it is supposed to serve. One of the attributes of a profession is rationality,[7] a devotion to faith in the power of critical reason, a disinclination to allow the past to rule the future for the past's sake; a disinclination, that is, to be mired in tradition. The legal profession conjures tradition as one of the most sacred social values for which it is organized to uphold. The judicial system depends on precedent, as any critic of the Supreme Court will readily declaim. Society can change, but slowly. So there is tension within the legal profession, and this is a continuing source of instability which has a decided impact on society.

This same self-generating tension exists in the relationship between the profession and the professional organization which speaks for it. Medicine may be based on a rational science, but the American Medical Association is not rationally organized to serve that science. It is tradition oriented; its managers are part of an administration, and their allegiances to the profession change when they accept as a large part of their own daily routine the characteristics of another profession — management. To the fear of "deterioration of medical service" the professional managers of the medical profession bring the reality. We have seen it in the case of Group Health Association of Washington, D.C., and I call it to mind only to note that it was not an isolated example of the medical society's tendency to prescribe belladonna in large rather than small doses, reasoning that if a small amount is a helpful drug, then larger amounts must necessarily work faster. They do, but only as poisons to hasten the decline. Thus the Health Insurance Plan of Greater New York (HIP) was formed to permit prepayment for physicians' fees in order to lower the cost of medical care. HIP does not cover hospital costs; the member is required

---

[7] See Greenwood, "The Attributes of a Profession," in Sigmund Nosow and William H. Form, eds., *Man, Work, and Society* (1962), p. 209.

to join some hospitalization plan. Three Staten Island hospitals refused to permit HIP doctors not already associated with them to use their facilities during 1958–1960, not because the doctors were incompetent but because the hospitals disliked HIP and thought they could kill it. This is "deterioration of services" compelled by doctors, not because the non-participating physician was paid too little but because he feared what others were doing. Health care was there sacrificed to the needs of the medical profession, as it still is sacrificed today.[8]

The conflict between client and professional needs is everywhere apparent. Privately practicing psychiatrists have managed to incorporate into their theory two peculiar rationalizations: (1) High fees are necessary to cure since by putting the patient to a high financial sacrifice he will be encouraged to regain his wits sooner. That assumes that the one rule of rationality none of us avoid, even if we are "mentally ill," is that we are better off with money than without it. (2) Patients are better off, at least in the metropolitan New York area, without their psychiatrists during one month so that they can gain in self-reliance. It is probably only a coincidence that most psychiatrists choose the same month — August — and take their vacations then.[9] The theory of psychiatry at the service of partisanship was vividly portrayed at the trial of Sirhan Sirhan for the murder of Senator Robert F. Kennedy. Prosecution and defense psychiatrists had radically different stories to tell of their tests. Expert tests, whose results just happen to coincide with the interest of the side paying for them, are common occurrences within the experience of all trial lawyers.

Real estate associations are another example of groups which strive to achieve the public interest in bits and pieces. Many

---

[8] For numerous other examples of organized medicine's hostility to social needs, see Elton Rayack, *Professional Power and American Medicine: The Economics of the American Medical Association* (1967), pp. 180 ff.; Richard Carter, *The Doctor Business* (1961); and James Howard Means, *Doctors, People, and Government* (1953).

[9] *The New York Times*, July 31, 1967, p. 29.

associations draft "standard" leases and purchase agreements; real estate brokers and salesmen, on behalf of landlords and sellers, "agree" to adhere to them. They turn out to be documents artfully drawn to avoid responsibilities put on landlords by law. It is not the brokers' fault that everyone is not a landlord. Moreover, "realtors commonly believe it is unethical to sell or rent to a Negro in a predominantly white or all-white neighborhood."[9a]

The list of distortions could be indefinitely extended. Accountants certify the books of most corporations in America. The "generally accepted accounting principles" are adopted by accountants and changed only slowly to reflect the changes in commercial enterprises that frequently occur. The principles do not overtly sanction the approval of misleading financial statements, but that they do in practice is undeniable. A member of a large accounting firm testified in a legal proceeding not so many years ago that his firm was not required to make known to the stockholder the fact known to him that the principal officer of a company whose books the firm certified was draining the company's funds through an affiliated company. Insolvency, according to the accountant, had nothing to do with the health of the company. It was unfortunate, he agreed, that the company shortly went bankrupt, much to the distress of stockholders who sued the accounting firm. Accountants do not like to raise as an excuse the possibility that the business corporation can fail to retain the accounting firm that does not coöperate. Accounting is a plastic art.[10]

[9a] Douglas, J., concurring in Reitman v. Mulkey, 387 U.S. 369 (1967), citing U.S. Commission on Civil Rights, *Civil Rights U.S.A., Housing Washington, D.C.* (1962), pp. 12–13.

[10] *The New York Times,* January 9, 1967, p. 19. See also, March 27, 1966, p. III-1, and October 18, 1966, p. 61. According to Abraham J. Briloff, Professor of Accountancy at City University of New York, in testimony before the Senate Subcommittee on Antitrust and Monopoly, generally accepted accounting principles (GAAP), are "a rather amorphous, at least highly flexible, body of alternatives which were developed throughout our profession's evolution by academicians, practitioners, advisers to government and management. These principles find their way into the ambit of respectability sometimes through our professional literature and sometimes

If the lawyer and doctor may lose money by the introduction of competing forms of service, so may many others be tempted to minimize performance by maximizing temptation. The architect, for example, "working on a percentage basis, may find his pecuniary advantage at variance with his professional duty to secure the best service for the least cost."[11]

The professional need not be independent to distort the underlying theory. Sometimes, as in the case of social work, the institutional setting of the social work agency is apparently necessary to subvert its own ends. Dr. Eric Berne in his *Games People Play* notes an excellent example of how inconspicuous production can become the mainstay of an agency's job and thus distort the goal it was created to serve in his story of Miss Black, the right-thinking social worker who believed it her duty to help her clients find work ("rehabilitate" them). She discovered that the agency staff was not apparently interested in losing its clientele to private industry because it was more interested in playing the game of "I'm Only Trying to Help You." The agency was government supported. Miss Black began questioning her clients to see what efforts they were making toward seeking employment. When she found some whose efforts were self-defeating, she threatened to cut off their welfare checks unless they realistically sought work. Many found jobs "almost immediately." Unfortunately for Miss Black, the agency supervisor threatened to terminate her job because of the "undue pressure" she was putting on her clients, whom the supervisor felt were not rehabilitated, the fact that they were now self-supporting notwithstanding.[12]

Dr. Berne seeks the psychological explanation for the agency's

just because they are applied and practiced. *Antitrust and Trade Reporter*, No. 488, February 10, 1970, p. A8. Moreover, the balance sheet is like a bikini, he noted: "What each revealed was interesting, while that which was concealed was vital" (at p. A9).

11 Robert MacIver, "The Social Significance of Professional Ethics," 297 *The Annals* of the American Academy of Political and Social Science 118 (1955); reprinted in H. M. Vollmer, *Professionalization* (1966), p. 54.

12 Eric Berne, *Games People Play* (1967), pp. 147–9.

behavior. The economic one is patent. But it should be noted that many professionals adhere to a cult that prescribes ritual and procedure which may not be entirely explainable on economic or political grounds. Thus lawyers prepare briefs and annotate cases for judges who will never look at their work,[13] and psychoanalysts are as interested in "historical reconstructions of the troubles of their patients" as the cure to those troubles.[14] The cult exists because standards of success are imprecise, because rituals of relevance in one sphere are irrationally extended to others and the practice lives on, and because the professionals' goals are often at odds with the clients' needs.

3

So far we have been considering only the theoretical difficulty which occurs when the professional practice undermines the interest it was created to protect. This difficulty is related to the search for profit as well as for autonomy. Each serves the other.

The practical difficulty remains to be explored. That, it will be recalled, is met when the profession in its search for autonomy must go beyond neutrality and enter the political realm. The extension of autonomy carries the professional beyond his claim to knowledge and it also acts, ironically enough, as perhaps the only cause by which the public genuinely does come to lose its confidence in him.

It is necessary first to note that the search for autonomy involves more than simply the fixing of "unauthorized practice" boundaries. The search ultimately involves the hope that the profession will come to be regarded as synonymous with the theory: The lawyers are the law and the doctors health.

To illustrate: A special committee of the Association of the Bar of the City of New York recommended particular changes to the

---

[13] David Riesman, "Toward an Anthropological Science of Law and the Legal Profession," 57 *Am. J. of Sociology* 121 (1951).

[14] Everett C. Hughes, *Men and Their Work* (1958), p. 94.

loyalty-security programs that were rampant in the land during the 1950's. Commenting on the suggested reforms — and none can deny they were reforms — the Committee said: "Some may think it presumptuous for private citizens to take upon themselves the responsibility for proposing to our government far-reaching changes in this field. We deem it appropriate that members of the Bar should do this. Indeed, as we conceive it, our duty as lawyers requires us to do so. The Bar of the United States has always been, and must always be, alert in the protection of the liberties on which our country was founded as well as of other measures essential to national security. It is so, in fact, with lawyers in every other country where freedom exists or is emerging. It is only in the countries where freedom is rejected that the right and duty of the Bar to protect the liberty of the citizens are denied or suppressed."[15]

That is exceedingly coy, even for lawyers. Even in 1956, no one was disputing the right of a bunch of lawyers to publish their select and solemn opinions on a subject that touched a national nerve. That does not need justification. What does lies beneath the surface — the lurking suggestion that the Bar alone should be heeded in matters of liberty, for liberty is of the law, and lawyers, perforce, are the law. The Special Committee did not say this and would doubtless deny it, but denials sometimes serve to uncover meaning as well as to mask it: Were it not so the apology of citizens proposing and the ringing declaration of lawyers' duty to do the same would be meaningless.

Those who find this merely literary artifice should ponder a more pedestrian consideration: If the question of what the law is can be answered in terms of the staffing of law-making jobs, then the lawyers long ago achieved in practice what their theory holds. For there is hardly a court in the land that is not staffed entirely

[15] *Report of the Special Committee on the Federal Loyalty-Security Program of the Association of the Bar of the City of New York* (1956), pp. 24–5. Quoted in Countryman, "The Scope of the Lawyer's Professional Responsibility," 26 *Ohio S.L.J.* 66, 71–2 (1965).

by lawyers and rare is the legislature whose majority is not comprised of attorneys. The traditional argument justifying the heavy preponderance of lawyers in state legislatures, in Congress, and at all levels of every executive department is that the lawyers' special "training in analysis, flexibility of mind, diversity of experience and professional skills"[16] make them ideal for the job. We may disbelieve it: These skills and the training may even be irrelevant, equipping the lawyer to be more a staff aide than a public official. Indeed, in the theory of most enterprises the lawyer is staff, not line; his function is to advise, not lead; he is a specialist, not a generalist; and he is no better equipped than many other kinds of specially trained people to be a leader or a manager. Yet at the highest levels of public government the lawyer sheds his "staff" coat and becomes the policymaker. And because this is so we ought to be as worried about lawyers who go in and out of government as some are about military officers who go from the military to the industrial end of that particular "complex." We ought to be more aware than we seem traditionally to have been that legislatures are slow to advance needed changes in the legal order that strike at the organization of the profession, because it is their profession.

The same reluctance is true of all too many judges. The appointment of lawyers to the bench rather than others reflects the commonly held belief that judging requires not merely a wise and honest mind, but one possessing a special technique. Thus Al Smith, in supporting the appointive system of judicial selection, condemned their election because it "means the selection of judges by political leaders and the ratification of their selection by an electorate who are not really in a position to pass upon the legal and other abilities of the individual."[17] Thus the American Bar Association decades ago drew up canons of judicial ethics.

[16] The phrase, though not the sentiment, from Countryman, *supra* note 15, p. 84.
[17] *The Citizen and His Government* (1935), p. 86; quoted in Countryman, p. 73.

Though it cannot enforce them, it can apply them to save the reputation of the "profession": Not until Justice Abe Fortas resigned from the Supreme Court did the ABA's Committee on Judicial Ethics venture the opinion that the Justice had violated the canons by presenting an "appearance of impropriety." The Justice was spared that official knowledge before he resigned because it was unclear whether or not in fact he would, and it would not do to have a sitting Justice deemed unethical; once he had left, it would not do to have a resignation under such circumstances be for any but unethical conduct. The ABA has declined to pass on the ethics of some sitting judges who do not seem likely to resign.

The belief that the underlying professional functions are to be completely identified with the licensed practitioner is capable of much mischief. The identification can lead to an emphasis on certain values and a complete sacrifice of others. Lawyers and judges are insistent that the "dignity" of courts be upheld. Not merely do judges assert the power to hold in contempt those who disrupt judicial proceedings (and this means to fine or to jail without jury trial the person who offends the judge for a variety of reasons), the bench often seeks to impose a uniform standard of dignity by using the contempt and other powers to deter those who have the temerity to criticize judges out of court.

A woman lawyer was suspended from practice for one year for making a speech about the course of an on-going trial in Hawaii at a meeting held on a Sunday morning 182 miles from the court. She was defending a Smith Act case, and in her speech she lashed out at the philosophy of political conspiracy trials. She recounted the tactics of the prosecution in seeking convictions, charging the government attorneys with putting in testimony they knew conflicted with early testimony of the same witnesses, and with operating under the rule that "conspiracy means to charge a lot of people for agreeing to do something you have never done." She claimed that the Government took two days to read Communist books into evidence because it was alleged that one of the defendants had espied them in a duffel bag. There was much more. The Legal Ethics Committee and the Hawaii Supreme Court found that she had impugned the integrity of the trial judge and ordered her suspension. The Supreme Court reversed the suspension order, noting that her speech did not deal with the judge's handling of the case. The Court held that an attorney may "litigate by day and castigate by night" so long as a judge is not impugned during a pending case.[18] The Supreme Court's decision, welcome on the facts in the particular case, was itself ominous: It was a 5–4 decision and it suggested strongly that the line of permissible criticism is vague and must ultimately be construed by the judges themselves.[19]

Despite the right of attorneys and the public to speak out against judges, the bar continues to see attacks on courts as personal insults. A typical example was the coöperative manner in which Maryland courts and the local bar instilled in the citizenry a proper respect for the state judiciary. A Maryland circuit judge in 1969 asked a grand jury to investigate the *Washington Free Press*, a local "underground" newspaper, for alleged violations of the state anti-subversive law. The paper responded by printing a five-page attack on the judge, including a cartoon of a naked judge masturbating. Another judge subsequently decided that the cartoon was obscene and sentenced one of the *Free Press* distributors to six months in jail for selling the paper. The Montgomery County Bar Association promptly issued stern criticism of the *Free Press,* calling the article and cartoon, a "scurrilous and scandalous attack upon one of the judges of the Circuit Court

[18] In re Sawyer, 360 U.S. 622 (1959).

[19] The Court seems to have eased the danger in more recent decisions, notably New York Times Co. v. Sullivan, 376 U.S. 254 (1964), in which it was held that except for statements made in deliberate disregard of the truth, anyone is constitutionally permitted to criticize public officials; and Garrison v. Louisiana, 379 U.S. 64 (1964), holding that a district attorney cannot be convicted under a criminal defamation statute for charging that judges are responsible for court calendar congestion because they are lazy and inefficient.

Bench." Both bar and bench evidently overlooked the fact that by current legal standards the cartoon was not legally obscene.[20] Another state judge denounced newspapers and citizens who criticized the sentence; he indicated that they were "perilously close to contempt of court."[21] The Montgomery County Bar Association president elaborated on his group's proclamation by stating that "the children of this community [the *Free Press* was distributed to students at some schools], as well as the adults of this community, must accord our courts, our judges, and the officers of our courts [attorneys are usually considered by the courts to be their "officers"] the respect intended them by the men who founded this Nation and all the men and women who subsequently gave their lives in defense of the values upon which this country is built." The bar association is not noted for any statements deploring those who urged in prior years the impeachment of the Chief Justice of the United States. Shortly after the young peddler was sentenced (pending appeal he was required to post $5000 bond), still another Maryland judge was convicted of assaulting and threatening to kill a 39-year-old woman friend. That judge was sentenced to a $300 fine. In accordance with its policy of promoting respect for the courts, the Montgomery County Bar Association respectfully did not comment.

Other professions are not as well situated as the bar to promote autonomy. It is obviously more difficult to link themselves so intimately with so many agencies of government. But that does not mean that other professions lack the ability to respond to suggestions of reform. When laymen do suggest such a possibility —

[20] By current standards, a work must, among other things, be "utterly without redeeming social value" to be judged obscene. Memoirs v. Massachusetts, 383 U.S. 413 (1966). Political criticism, *per se*, implies a redeeming value. *The Washington Post* aptly commented that "the *Free Press* cartoon, ugly and unjust as it may have been, excites no lustful thoughts, stimulates no libidinous desire, appeals to no prurient interest. Its purpose was to arouse political, not sexual, excitement. It lampoons a judge. That may be scurrility but it is not obscenity." April 8, 1969, p. A10.

[21] Quoted in *The Washington Post*, April 10, 1969, p. A1.

when autonomy is threatened — the professions may respond by invoking similar patriotic symbols. Often this means calling the reformer a communist.

Since laymen will not usually propose changes to a professional mystery they are presumed to know nothing about until the need is very pressing, the professional may have no alternative but to impugn his opponents' motives. During the worst days of the Depression, when the delivery of medical care was a costly proposition, reform talk was in the air. The AMA countered by suggesting that sinister forces were at work. "The alinement is clear," *JAMA* editorialized in 1932 following publication of the independent Committee on the Costs of Medical Care report, which recommended group payment insurance and tax incentives for meeting medical care costs, "— on the one side, the forces representing the great foundations, public health officialdom, social theory — even socialism and communism — inciting to revolution; on the other side, the organized medical profession of this country urging an orderly evolution guided by controlled experimentation which will observe the principles that have been found through the centuries to be necessary to the sound practice of medicine."[22] Doctors are not alone. When spokesmen for the funeral industry responded to *The American Way of Death*, the danger of subversion was duly noted.[23]

The ease of overlooking the merit of reform proposals to find communism hidden inside attests to the laziness of patriotic professionals. It is likewise too easy to say that because professionals do so respond they are merely sick or frauds; since they identify their nation's goals with the maintenance of their own autonomy, any subversion of their power necessarily weakens the nation. And no one, of course, would weaken the nation but a communist.

The organized bar, a bit more sensitive to the political problem

---

[22] Quoted in Rayack, *supra* note 8, p. 149; from *JAMA*, December 3, 1932, pp. 1950–2.

[23] See David Finn, "The Businessman and His Critics," *Saturday Review*, September 12, 1964, p. 60.

of declaring anyone with his eyes closed a communist[24] has, at least lately, found other means to fend off attacks which might lessen autonomy. For example, the ABA "persuaded" a large text-book publisher to delete material it considered offensive. "A widely used high school text-book entitled *Occupations Today* by Brewer and Landy and published by Ginn and Company, might appropriately be called 'comic' in its weirdly inaccurate and mis-leading portrayal of the legal profession," said the ABA Report for 1953. "After receiving a number of complaints from various parts of the country, the writer called them to the attention of the publishers, who responded with notable promptness and vigor. Wherever possible the books were withdrawn from circulation or sale, and the authors instructed to re-write the offending section on The Occupation of Lawyers so as to conform with the facts."[25] The Ginn and Company authors had said in part: "Though the lawyer is a professional worker, and many of our greatest and most valuable men are lawyers, yet the profession as a whole has far to go before it can be said to live up to its ideals and possibili-ties. Perhaps the reason for this is the temptation which comes into the work of the lawyer. . . . The lawyer is faced with the temptation of helping those whom he knows to be wrongdoers to keep out of jail. . . . Before you choose a vocation in which thousands of young men are not succeeding, you should ask your-self, 'Am I especially well equipped to push past those men and make good in law?' This means, for one thing, are you able to resist temptations and keep your record honest?"[26] These passages were excised in the subsequent edition. And this is but one instance of a continuing course of contact and pressure that the

---

[24] Except for the Southern bar; see, for a discussion of the Southern bar's approach to judicial change, Frankel, "The Alabama Lawyer, 1954–64: Has the Official Organ Atrophied?" 64 *Col. L. Rev.* 1243 (1964); Leon Friedman, ed., *Southern Justice* (1965).

[25] 78 *ABA Report* (1953), pp. 263–4: quoted in Countryman and Finman, *The Lawyer in Modern Society* (1966), p. 387.

[26] Brewer and Landy, *Occupations Today* (1949), pp. 219–20: quoted in Countryman and Finman, *supra* note 25. p. 387.

American Bar Association has directed toward the press, television, and the film industry.[27]

This crude "image policing" might be dismissed if such books were not an important way by which the public can monitor the state of the professions. It may fairly be held a truism that what the censor blue pencils is close to the mark. Not even the censor has yet advocated the embargo on lay writing about the law suggested by a correspondent in a letter to the ABA *Journal.* "As long as the Committee on Professional Ethics persists in its curious view that the publishing of law does not constitute the practice of law, it will be difficult to bring ethical considerations to bear on these professional activities," he says.[28] When only lawyers can write about law, the takeover is complete.

The search for autonomy involves a high cost for the professions, however. Inevitably, to create and exercise the power necessary to sustain autonomy requires professionals to become politically active. Though censorship activities may be carried on relatively free of front-page coverage, concerted lobbying activities make news. The professional vow of neutrality becomes merely idle talk. The most obvious example of partisanship is the campaign against "socialized medicine," carried on by medical organizations since the 1920's. Shortly before Congress finally enacted Medicare in 1965, there was talk of boycott. The official position of the AMA was its usual one that Medicare would lead to a disintegration in the quality of medical services. The AMA House of Delegates had provided a contingency plan four years before: In 1961 the House by majority vote declared it "ethical" to resist.[29] Later events, ironically enough, bore out the medical conclusion, noted before, that when someone else pays the bill, the doctor grows unscrupulous: As the Government paid out money, a significant number of professional men proved that they were more anxious for the dole than they were to perform a service. Unhappily,

[27] See Countryman and Finman, pp. 386–91.
[28] See letter, 55 *ABAJ* 700 (1969).
[29] *The New York Times,* May 13, 1965, p. 27.

the AMA does not oppose Medicare because it is "temptation legislation." Opposition is based on the more primitive fear of government control. Thus the intense fight waged to prevent the nomination of Dr. John Knowles as Assistant Secretary of Health, Education, and Welfare for Health and Scientific Affairs. Thus also the millions of dollars poured into the campaigns of conservative office-seekers and lobbying activities over the years.[30]

The very intensity of the campaign has only led to reaction against organized medicine, from inside the ranks as well as from the outside public.[31]   Much of the ineptitude of the AMA's public relations effort could have been avoided.   But this is only to say that the practical difficulty professionals have in maintaining autonomy — the reach for autonomy bringing a corresponding threat of loss in autonomy — is organic: Doctors in politics are quacks. Other professionals are also.   By that is simply meant that when the question is one of relating their discipline to the needs of the public, professionals are no longer experts.   We tolerate political and economic quacks because the Constitution recognizes no official party line, but that does not mean we must believe in their piety or sincerity.   A former president of the AMA says: "We are faced with the concept of health care as a right rather than a privilege. . . . What is our philosophy?   It is the faith in private enterprise.   We can, therefore, concentrate our attention on the single obligation to protect the American way

---

[30] In 1949–50, the AMA spent twice as much money for lobbying in Washington as any other lobbying organization; during the first quarter of 1965, it spent $950,000, an amount topped — by *annual* expenditures — only twice before, and both times by the AMA itself. See Rayack, *supra* note 8, p. 11; *The New York Times*, June 23, 1965, p. 63.

[31] For an example of criticism in the popular press, see Charles and Bonnie Remsberg, "Is Your Doctor a Profiteer?" *Good Housekeeping*, November 1968, pp. 94 ff. Doctor-owned drugstores, office dispensing, dispensing glasses, "rainbow pills," doctor-owned drug companies, misuse of medical laboratories and tests, unnecessary surgery, unnecessary hospitalization, surgical "overreaching," fee splitting, and inflated fees are devastatingly discussed in turn.

of life. That way can be described in one word: Capitalism."[32] Yet another has said that medical care for the aged is a "hoax and a fraud" that spells the "end of democratic government in this country."[33] We may take these sentiments for what they are worth and discard them accordingly, noting while we do how blatantly impolitic they are.

4

The professional asserts that he is engaged in non-profit endeavor. The assertion is justified in part by the making of it, in part by noting that the basic charge is for time. Since there is no raw material to show a markup on, no profit can ever be visible. That there is a fee is understood, but it is said to be merely the worth of time.

Because professionals take themselves to be motivated by the spirit of service they can ask the consumer for tolerance — tolerance of the skill or lack of it used, the amount of time the job takes, the permanence of the cure, or the lasting quality of the service performed.

The demand for tolerance is an enviable one, if met. It is one which businessmen would like very much to claim. It entitles *JAMA* to claim tax immunity for drug advertising, for example.[34] The moral superiority of professional over profit-oriented activity is the rationale for benefits; not all poor people, obviously, are entitled to subsidy. Since governmental largesse and autonomy are as desirable for profit-oriented activity as non-profit enterprises, we should not be surprised to find the ideology of non-

---

[32] Dr. Milford O. Rouse; quoted by Ashley Montagu in a letter to *The New York Times*, July 13, 1969, p. IV-13.

[33] Dr. Edward R. Annis; quoted in *The New York Times*, October 18, 1964, p. 76.

[34] Charges that *JAMA* has been lax in reporting on drug deficiencies cast doubt on the professionalization of *JAMA*, if not on the merits of U.S. tax policy.

profit work[35] espoused by "private enterprise." Thus it is the current corporate philosophy that large businesses are as much "charitable," "educational," or "socially responsible" enterprises as they are productive. We should expect to find the theory of the professional class most readily advanced by those industries which sell time, taste, or knowledge. And if we look we will find it among morticians, advertisers, public relations men, barbers, cosmetologists, and even dry cleaners.

The theory of the professional class — that responsible conduct is to be maintained by a code of ethics that reinforces group autonomy without which responsible conduct is impossible — is embraced by a large number of professional associations and groups in America. These groups fete the theory as one indispensable to the maintenance of free enterprise and democracy. In fact, as we must next observe, the theory cuts quite the other way.

[35] See Joseph Bensman, *Dollars and Sense: Ideology, Ethics, and the Meaning of Work in Profit and Non-Profit Organizations* (1967), pp. 72–5.

9

The Decline of the Consumer

People of the same trade seldom meet together even for merriment and diversion, but the conversation ends in a conspiracy against the public, or in some contrivance to raise prices.

— ADAM SMITH, *The Wealth of Nations*

My six-year-old son can aspire to be the President of the United States, but he cannot reasonably aspire to become a watchmaker in Wisconsin. Of course, if he can pass the examinations that they have managed to get the Wisconsin legislature to legalize, then he can have a license. If, for example, he can learn to make watch parts which watchmakers for a generation have bought in wholesale lots from large manufacturers, and can perform other minor miracles that very few of the watchmakers now comfortably in business can do, then he too can get into the trade.

— RUTH B. DOYLE, "The Fence-Me-In Laws"

1

Since the end of World War II, an awareness has been steadily developing in American social and economic thinkers that a vast change has occurred in the life of the nation. *The Organization Man* provoked business executives, professional management, sociologists, and countless workers to an understanding that the old

135

days of rugged individualists were gone. The organization had taken hold, demanded an oath of obeisance (to offset the concomitant vow of riches), and compelled a belief in the moral superiority of group activity. Though its author, William H. Whyte, Jr., challenged the organization man to foresake his complete capitulation to group values, there is little evidence that the organization has lessened its hold on its vassals. Even student strikers tend to channel their actions through organizations, which are every bit as demanding as those they repudiate; there, as in all organization, is bleated the smugness that the group knows all and does best.

The social transformation of the individual has been translated directly to the economy. "Free enterprise," is now practiced least by those who confess to loving it most. The Organization Men have discovered how to escape the market system at last. Though the "market system," considered impersonally over the course of the past two centuries, might be thought a marvelous vehicle for economic progress, the threat of its continued existence makes most management uncomfortable. Who could relax and enjoy a system that tells you circumstances beyond your control may cause your enterprise to be remembered (or forgotten) as one which dropped between supply and demand curves to bankruptcy? It is not so surprising that men who conform to their organizations and are known as "management men" should not also attempt to manage the consumer and the state as well as their own workers.

An honest belief in free enterprise is dying. Though the words are mouthed by most who speak to the public, whether in a private capacity as a stockholder representative or in a public capacity as a government official, few believe it. Not the shipping magnates who receive yearly shipping subsidies, nor the airline moguls who receive airline subsidies, nor the many salesmen whose only customer is the Department of Defense, nor again the gentlemen farmers in the United States Senate who receive large cash allotments for not cultivating their land, nor most traders and industry exponents of import tariffs on their particular commodities. To hide the fact that it pursues goals of growth and stability, corporate America masks itself in a cloak of "free enterprise" rhetoric.

Despite his occasional ringing declaration in the eternal verities of capitalism, the professional stands outside this tradition. He claims not to be motivated by money or the market system; he pays respectful homage to his codes of ethics; he says over and over again that he is not a mere businessman engaged in a commercial enterprise; he is ever alert against the "commercialization" of his profession. If the businessman professes a belief in capitalism to hide his real aims, the professional scorns the practice of capitalism in order to practice it faithfully. This is not as much a paradox as it sounds. For while the professional claims to serve the public interest and to be concerned not one whit about his own interest (the private self-interest of the classical theorists), and while the professional is respectable, responsible, and redoubtable, he is actually behaving in a remarkable capitalistic manner. The professional is the last of the entrepreneurs; like the robber barons before him, he is merely trying to work through the market to monopoly.

Both legal and economic theory assume the economy flourishes by the competitive actions of unrelated producers. What is good for the economy is not necessarily good for the individual enterprise, however. In 1958, automobile dealers sought from Congress a special exclusion from the antitrust laws to allow the manufacturers to assign and control specific territories to retail outlets. In the Oriental phraseology so common to American businessmen, the dealers appealed for "equality of competitive opportunity."[1] Obviously a dealer who tried to make a buck in someone else's territory by unethically selling an automobile to an innocent consumer is unprofessional. Congress did not authorize the exemption.

Professionals are achieving by indirection what the same anti-

---

[1] Quoted in Henry S. Kariel, *The Decline of American Pluralism* (1961), p. 41.

trust laws prohibit. Professionals cannot privately get together to limit the number of competitors by refusing to employ them or by making it difficult for the competitor to compete, so they procure laws from state legislatures which authorize them to achieve remarkably similar effects by quasi-public regulation.[2] To this end they are aided even by the federal government. In 1968, the National Funeral Directors Association signed a consent decree in federal court, enjoining members from agreeing to restrict the advertising of funeral prices. The decree contained a significant exception for state laws which make such price advertising unlawful; nothing in the antitrust laws do or can prohibit associations or anyone else from inducing state legislatures from passing such laws.[2a]

Legal regulations permeate the American economy. Anyone who denies the usefulness of regulation must be taken as either daft or at his word: We all admit, in theory, that "naked power" must be controlled; the man who generally decries regulation of any type in the economic sphere is either lacking in mentality altogether or happens to have a personal interest in a business which someone seeks to regulate. That is why in those industries composed of a few giant companies, strong exponents of "free enterprise" are to be found: Invoking the magic words is a short-hand expression for the desire to be left alone by the government as well as by the market; in short, to be free of any restraints at all.

---

[2] Governor Sam Goddard of Arizona has written that in his state "there is one dentist for approximately every twenty-three to twenty-four hundred residents. I believe I am correct in stating that the national average is one dentist for each eleven hundred citizens. Much of this is due to the licensing procedures as established by occupational licensing laws." Letter to the author, dated September 29, 1965.

[2a] See United States v. National Funeral Directors Association, *1968 CCH Trade Cases*, ¶ 72,529 (E.D. Wisc. 1968). The so-called *Noerr* doctrine, from Eastern Railroad President's Conference v. Noerr Motor Freight Co., 365 U.S. 127 (1961), permits any concerted effort to induce legislation, even if the statements in the promotional campaign contain deliberate and knowing falsehoods.

This is understandable, but we should understand what it is we are understanding: No one in power ever has power enough.

Of course, businessmen have not been left alone. There are two theoretical systems for controlling economic power: classical competition and modern countervailing power. These have technical definitions, but it is sufficient to say that the one means enough producers that none can control prices in the marketplace and the other means a consumer large enough to stare down a producer who tries to make an unreasonable deal. The economic theory of the professional class is that both these types of control can be — and are — avoided.

The position of the consumer in a modern economy is weak. The only market device by which consumers can indicate their preferences is money, and money is an ambiguous indicator, at best. For years Henry Ford was able to satisfy consumer wants by providing his customers with any color they wanted so long as it was black. In an age that proclaims necessary and desirable an infinite variety of goods and services the consumer must spread himself thin. In an age dominated by large organizations, the consumer stands small. Consumers of some commodities can protect themselves by banding into organizations like agricultural coöperatives, but only when their interest with respect to the commodity is the same; usually the consumer coöperative is effective only at the wholesale level. What power retail consumers — the general population — have is diffused: In an industrial system, many buyers have no power against few sellers.

If consumers cannot force prices down, they will attempt to join together to bid wages up. This is the achievement of the union. The professional movement can be viewed as a similar attempt by many groups to endow themselves with power as producers that they do not have as consumers. Scores of occupations have taken this route: The transformation of the mere day laborer to the ranks of professional means the consumer is everywhere becoming a producer. In a modern economy the course is natural: All consumers are producers in some sense; the work done on their daily job is narrow and usually far removed from the task of satisfying biological needs. To survive one must fill a slot somewhere in the social machine.

To promote a healthy return to his services, the professional must reduce the level of competition wherever possible: He accredits the institutions which train his fellow practitioners (controls supply); he establishes rules of conduct and admission (control over intra-professional competition); he blocks out an exclusive specialty (control over inter-professional competition). He must also thwart the formation of centers of countervailing power because otherwise the producer orientation is reduced.

The consumer orientation weakens even more in the due course of producer strengthening, for two reasons. First, where the producer orientation prevails, there is no time for a slack pace. To achieve the goal of producer, a long and hard technical battle must be waged. After the position is consolidated, constant effort to prevent backsliding is necessary. Producing is literally a full-time job. There is no time to worry about one's moments as a consumer.

Second, to achieve professional status it is not good to wade into another fight: All others struggling for the same goal must be left alone, not merely because your own job is full time, but because to attack another's right to professional status is to undercut the legitimacy of your own claim. This is not to say there are never battles at the margin: Lawyers do not fight barbers, but barbers and beauticians have long been at it, and many medical specialties are still in flux. But the tendency is always to harden the line, to divide up the jobs that are to be done in order to end the fighting and get back to producing. It is always desirable to have a wider yard to play in, but it is even more desirable to be able to play at all.

The rush to professionalism is identical with the increase in specialization: Each is an indispenable aspect of the other. The specialist could not operate without a complex industrial system to buttress his claims and a professional ethos to attest to his specialty; the professional could not provide an ethos were it not for the claim that he does something invaluable that no one else can. The techniques of economic control have been more than broadly hinted at so far. Yet it will be necessary to bring them into sharper focus to see how the professional operates in an industrial society.

2

In a competitive economy as it is usually described, no producer can be sufficiently large enough to fix prices. These are set impersonally by the market: Consumer demand fixes the price of the producers' output. It is evident that professionals can remove themselves from the market system by establishing licensed monopolies. By defining the boundaries of the profession and specialties within professions, the experts can eliminate competition among different types of professionals. By setting standards of conduct, they can restrict members of the same profession from competing with each other.

The increasing tendency for occupations of all sorts to seek licensed status has already been noted.[3] When the right to practice a particular trade or profession depends not on personal initiative but also on the approval of some agency — be it public or private — and the official approval is based on factors related to the occupation (that is, not merely on the payment of a tax), the industry has laid the foundation for the exercise of monopoly power. No longer may anyone perform legal, medical, accounting, architectural, or other tasks. The first condition for a competitive industry — freedom of entry — is gone.

Restrictions on entry come in many forms. Long apprenticeship periods in engineering, architecture, and many trades make the initial investment so high that the commitments to certain occupations necessarily are lifelong. There is no easy mobility among professionals.

[3] See Chapter 2.

Often the admission to a given profession depends upon the ability of an individual to perform feats largely unrelated to the profession he is about to enter. Thus watchmakers in Wisconsin are faced with a battery of tests that have little to do with modern watchmaking; dentists in California must do gold foil placements to be licensed, a technique largely abandoned in practice by most dentists, including Californians. Cosmetologists in New York are apparently faced with equally obsolescent requirements. Vidal Sassoon publicly denounced the state hairdressers' test in 1965 on the grounds that it is "asinine and obsolete." Said the British beautician: "The test requires that I do finger waving, reverse pin-curling and a haircut in which you thin as you cut — things that haven't been used since Gloria Swanson was in silent movies." *The New York Times* further reported:

"It's not that I don't know how to do a finger wave — I do," said Mr. Sassoon, who had been working in New York on a temporary license that expired yesterday. "But if you do a set like that today anywhere in the world — with bobby pins, metal clips and all that junk — your customer would be laughed off the street."

He said one of his best hairdressers failed the test three months ago because she did not know how to do the finger wave properly.

"But the finger wave will come back — it always has," protested Mrs. Marge Dreckmann, supervisor of the examination.

"No, no, no," the slender, dark-haired hairdresser exclaimed. "We all admire Christopher Wren, but nobody builds houses like his any more, do they?"

Michael Kalman, a tall burly examiner who looked more like a policeman, said the purpose of the test was to see if a hairdresser was acquainted with the rudiments of hairdressing, "and not the advanced stylings that Mr. Sassoon does."[4]

4 *The New York Times*, September 20, 1966, p. 51.

It is evident how far from the pretense of protecting the public health the New York cosmetologists have gone.[5]

A logical step for the licensed profession to take is the obtaining of power to control the supply of new professionals indirectly by placing limitations on the schools in which they must necessarily be trained. This is an old technique with doctors. By the fifth year of the Depression, the mean net income of the American physician had fallen from $5524, what it had been in 1929, to $3382, or forty per cent.[6] In 1932, the Final Report of the Commission on Medical Education of the Association of American Medical Colleges discovered a nationwide oversupply of 25,000 physicians and declared somewhat contradictorily: "An oversupply is likely to introduce excessive economic competition, the performance of unnecessary services, an elevated total cost of medical care, and conditions in the profession which will not encourage students of superior ability and character to enter the profession."[7]

The spirit of the times led to such ringing proclamations as that of Dr. Dean W. Lewis, President of the AMA in 1933: "One is forced to the conviction that more doctors are being turned out than society needs and can comfortably reward"; and that of his successor, Dr. Walter L. Bierring: "Whether the problems of the new day in medicine will be met by a limitation in the number of existing institutions or the number of students cannot be foretold, but it will require real courage and tenacity to bend the educational processes to the urgent social and economic needs of the changing order. A fine piece of educational work could well be done if we were to use only one-half of the 70-odd medical schools in the United States."[8] That piece of work was accom-

---

[5] Sassoon apparently recanted. He studied for the exam after all and later denied calling it "obsolete." *The New York Times,* March 22, 1967, p. 34.

[6] Elton Rayack, *Professional Power and American Medicine: The Economics of the American Medical Association* (1967), p. 73.

[7] Quoted in Rayack, p. 73; from *Final Report of the Committee on Medical Education* (1932), p. 89.

[8] Both quoted in Rayack, p. 75.

plished: The AMA Committee on Medical Education and Hospitals made a survey of eighty-nine medical schools from 1934 to 1936, found too many students than could "properly" be "cared for" and the medical schools acceded. For the 1932-1933 academic year, 7,357 places were tendered to 12,280 applicants. In 1937–1938, of 12,207 applying, only 6,410 were accepted. By 1949–1950, the medical school acceptances had climbed to only 7,150 of 24,353 applicants.[9] The lack of adequate facilities contributed greatly to the failure of medical schools to meet the demand for entrance. And this was in spite of the fact that 7,000 extra physicians were turned out during the war in accelerated medical programs. The facilities of medical schools were kept in check by virulent AMA opposition to federal aid for medical educational construction and for operating expenses, a fight waged successfully until 1958 when it pressed less vigorously because it had by that time precipitated a crisis-proportion shortage of physicians throughout the country. During the same time the AMA consistently supported federal aid for research and other measures that would increase the demand for medical services.[10]

Despite projections in 1948 by the U. S. Public Health Service that a medical shortage would be apparent by 1960 without action, the AMA counseled calm. Its demurrer was in spite of the position of the American Association of Medical Colleges, which now saw a positive need for federal aid, "provided the educational and administrative policies can continue to rest in the hands of the medical colleges without political interference and with the maintenance of academic freedom."[11] By 1969, the AMA's position had blown up in its face. Health, Education, and Welfare Secretary Robert H. Finch issued a report predicting a "massive crisis" without affirmative steps by organized medicine. The report pin-

---

[9] Figures from Rayack, p. 79.
[10] See Rayack, p. 99.
[11] Quoted in Rayack, p. 3. See his Chapter 3 for the misrepresentation and tactics of the AMA officialdom in forestalling federal aid to increase the supply of doctors and improve the quality of education.

pointed the problem as follows: "Expansion of private and public financing for health services has created a demand for services far in excess of the capacity of our health system to respond. The result is crippling inflation in medical costs, causing vast increases in Government health expenditures for little return, raising private health insurance premiums and reducing the purchasing power of the health dollar of our citizens."[12] The irony of the situation — that the crisis had been induced by the failure of organized medicine to practice the economic principles it says are indispensable to the maintenance of the American system — has so far escaped the AMA.

The AMA is not the only professional group capable of wielding great power over professional schools. To cite only one of many other available examples: The American Council on Pharmaceutical Education accredits pharmaceutical colleges. In 1959, of the ten council members, three were members of the American Pharmaceutical Association, three represented the National Association of Boards of Pharmacy, three were members of the American Association of Colleges of Pharmacy (each of whom was a dean of a pharmacy college), and one represented the American Council on Education.[13]

[12] *The New York Times*, July 11, 1969, p. 1. Others would like to cash in on AMA techniques. The salary of civil engineers ranges from the beginners' $9500 to the twenty-year veteran's $15,000, not an encouraging spread, as an article in *Civil Engineering*, the magazine of the American Society of Civil Engineers, notes. What to do? "The first corrective measure that must be undertaken . . . to revitalize our profession is to change the general salary range. . . . We all recognize that salaries, like commodities in a free market, obey the laws of supply and demand. The question can then be asked, 'If higher salaries attract more people to engineering, won't there be a glut on the market and won't salaries then become depressed?' Here we might learn from the doctors and establish truly professional returns. If necessary, professional engineering salaries should be scheduled and rigidly controlled by our professional societies." David Carsen, "Civil Engineering Today: A Profession in Crisis," 40 *Civil Engineers* 48, 50 (1970).

[13] G. Lester Anderson and Merton W. Ertell, "Extra-Institutional Forces Affecting Professional Education," in Nelson B. Henry, ed., *Education for the Professions* (1962), p. 243.

The AMA has long assumed — or at least its editorialists have — that the only concern of the doctor is money. The profession, the AMA has warned so often it seems to have become an automatic reflex, will be incapable of providing proper service if any controls are placed on physicians or any steps are taken to lighten the public's economic load. Hence the dire predictions of doom against physicians who work for a salary; hence the blandishment that the public should be "absolutely free" to choose its physicians and hospitals. Such statements can only remind the drowsy peruser of the bombast and rhetoric of the ancient days when industrialists insisted that nothing must interfere with the sacred right of the worker to contract for his working conditions — so long as he did it singly and not in unions and so long as these conditions included the right to work twelve-hour days. Did the public really have freedom to choose its physicians and hospitals, the AMA would doubtless protest equally vigorously, since that would presuppose the knowledge to discriminate among doctors, which the theory of the professional class expressly disallows. When a highly specialized group speaks out in a matter that directly concerns its economic well-being by saying that it has the public's interest at heart, it is engaging in the highly developed American art of bombast — a subject worthy of far more serious study than it has been given.

Control over supply is not the only method of limiting competition. The normal market system can also be impaired by subdividing the practice of a single profession. There are more than 300,000 licensed attorneys in the United States, but not all of these are in private practice, and this group is further subdivided into various specialties: corporations; taxation; securities; antitrust; estates; general commerce; public administration; and criminal, domestic, real estate, and personal injury law are among the chief branches. By the time the subdividing has petered out, the ratio of specialty lawyers to population is not very high.

No legal certification separates the criminal lawyer from the real estate specialist, the tax man from the tort litigator. By contrast, many segments of the medical profession have long been engaged in intense battles for the exclusive legal or institutional right to carry on the given specialty. Opticians, optometrists, and ophthalmologists have been attempting to scratch each others' eyes out for years. Dentists have likewise been protesting the claim of dental technicians in laboratories to competence in the repair of dental prosthetics: Several states have forbidden laboratories from advertising directly to the public; at least eighteen states prohibit all contact between dental laboratories and the public.[14] There may be legitimate grounds for regulation — obviously the repair of prosthetics, which involves fittings on patients' mouths, is related to the public health. But as far back as 1953 a dental survey concluded that the dentists' single most profitable activity was the sale of prosthetics.[15] In some states, dental laboratories have pushed for separate licensing. The experience in Great Britain, which licensed technicians in 1921, was interesting: The standards for licensing were raised until the technicians became dentists and both dentists and "public dental technicians" took to farming out work to unlicensed technicians anyway.[16] Dentists in the United States have hit on an alternate plan: In some states (e.g., California, Florida, New York, North Carolina, and Ohio) the state dental society accredits laboratories and pressures practitioners to patronize those only. But whether licensed or accredited, dental laboratories do not significantly compete with dentists for prosthetic work. Once their numbers are sufficiently reduced, the laboratories along with organized dentistry become privileged sanctuaries immune from consumers who might like to pay less.

Restrictions on competition by substitute services is common to all professions. To cite but one more example, cemetery owners have preserved their economic immunities in California, Alaska,

[14] See Note, "Dentists, Dental Laboratories, and the Public Interest," 51 Nw. U. L. Rev. 123 (1956).

[15] 29 Dental Survey (1953), p. 1620.

[16] Supra note 14, p. 130.

Indiana, and Washington State; there cremated remains cannot be scattered but must be buried.[17]

Competition can be further reduced by restricting practice to those who live within the state. The consequent limitation on interstate competition can be extended fairly far. Florida accountants, for example, may not practice their profession if they work in branch offices of out-of-state firms. No person may practice accountancy in the state unless all partners are licensed Florida accountants. Price Waterhouse & Company, a New York firm with more than 150 offices, is therefore precluded from doing business in Florida, since the alternative to residence of all its partners is for each of them to take the accounting test, prerequisite for which are academic courses not given when many of the partners studied accounting.[18]

It is uncharitable to deny that the possibility of competition still exists within professions. The logical substitute for the doctor is still another doctor; in the wide areas of overlap among dozens of medical specialties, competition might occur. One can quite well visualize, however, the animated cartoon in which doctors rush to the patient, grab him (or her) by all extremities and tug for control — until the throat somehow slips out and the otolaryngologist and the thoracic surgeon toss for it, the intestines slither to the ground and the proctologist and gynecologist fight over pieces of it, the patient screams and the psychiatrist wonders whether something is wrong until the brain pops into the air with the neurosurgeon standing underneath; suddenly the patient gives a convulsive shudder and the coroner comes in to be displaced at last by the policeman who says "all right now, don't nobody move." That is not precisely the kind of competition the patient had in mind, but it does exist and it can lead rather to more than less expense, because specialists want a closed shop as intensely as medicine generally wants the public kept out.

The classical market system is more directly abandoned by

17 Jessica Mitford, *The American Way of Death* (1963), pp. 168–9.
18 *The New York Times,* October 24, 1967, p. 35.

controls on prices than by limitations on competition, however. Price regulation would seem to follow as a necessity once a group is granted monopoly status; it is not unreasonable to expect price-fixing to guard against monopoly power. In fact, the price-fixing power is used to set *minimum* prices. Monopolists, even oligopolists, are not traditionally thought to require such powers, but professional monopolies have it.

Price-fixing is a fact of life in many professions, but perhaps in none other is it as strictly maintained as in law, because the courts are willing partners in the crime. Lawyers are able to administer prices more efficiently than in the oligopolistic industries because to deviate from minimum fee schedules in many states is a breach of ethics. Obviously no judge would require a lawyer to violate his code of ethics, even if the code sanctions a system that in all commodity-producing enterprises would in turn be a clear violation of state and federal antitrust laws. More than half the states and some eight hundred counties and cities are under bar association set price fixes.[19] The method works well: If all lawyers must charge at least so much for each kind of legal effort, on pain of being disciplined for a sustained breach, the public will pay to maintain all lawyers in a style to which they can quickly become accustomed.

Some occupations have achieved statutory price-fixing powers. In many states, self-regulation of the dry cleaning industry has been permitted and, with it, the power to set retail prices. The Oklahoma Supreme Court has upheld the state law empowering a State Board of Dry Cleaners, composed exclusively of dry cleaners, to supervise the industry.[20] The Board's power extends to matters relating to the "proper control" of the industry; it can make rules enforceable in court to support its supervision, and it can grant and revoke licenses for failure to follow these rules. In 1945, six years after the original enactment, the Oklahoma

---

[19] According to Bloom, *The Trouble With Lawyers* (1968), p. 194.
[20] Jack Lincoln Shops, Inc. v. State Dry Cleaner's Board, 192 Okla. 251, 136 P. 2d 332 (1943).

Legislature delegated to the Board the power to approve minimum price schedules when supported by seventy-five per cent of the state's licensed dry cleaners. This power was also upheld.[21]

In support of this pricing authority, the dry cleaners argued variously that (1) safety measures required by the original act cost more than could be afforded at income levels set by competition; (2) since fire insurance was unavailable, more money was necessary to enable cleaners to become self-insurers; and (3) it cost money to prevent misleading advertising.[22]   When a state representative introduced a bill in 1951 to rescind the licensing and pricing power held by dry cleaners and barbers, hundreds of cleaners and barbers turned out for hearings; the bill was tabled in committee.[23]

There is no evidence that the Board operates as a political screening agency. The cost of required capital equipment is high, but fees and taxes are relatively low, and the Board, at least by statute, does not concern itself with the moral character of the applicant. But the Board does set and enforce an extremely detailed set of prices: More than 100 items of clothing are subject to these minimum prices. A dry cleaner who offered customers free storage was held to have violated the price regulations.[24] Thus the Board effectively prevents hidden price decreases.

The alternative to regulated prices as an excuse to maintain safety standards is to institute a mandatory safety program with an adequately financed inspection force. Now it may be that the public will pay in any event—through taxes for an inspection force or through higher prices if regulated. But it is not necessary to conclude that regulated prices are the sole answer, as launderers, airlines, and others insist. For the regulated price may well work out to entail greater private expenditures in the aggregate than

[21] State Dry Cleaner's Board v. Compton, 201 Okla. 284, 205 P. 2d 288 (1949).
[22] Plott, "Occupational Self-Regulation: A Case Study of the Oklahoma Dry Cleaners," 8 *J. of L. and Econ.* 195, 199 (1965).
[23] Plott, p. 200.
[24] Plott, p. 204.

the public tax expenditures required by inspection protection; and higher regulated prices are in themselves no guarantor of safety. Besides, if safety is the object, we may desire an adequate inspection whatever the cost, in which case regulated prices are superfluous (at least under the market system usually praised in this country).

There are indirect means of price-fixing, as well. The legislative or customary proscription of price advertising is the most important example. To preserve "the economic independence of a profession serving public health needs," regulations prohibiting dental laboratories from advertising to the public have been upheld by the courts.[25] Similar restrictions have been placed on optometrists and opticians.[26] Morticians, through their national and state associations, decry price advertising (though not other forms of advertising) as unethical.

Federal antitrust enforcers are principally concerned with corporate activities and do not usually investigate or institute proceedings against professional groups because it is assumed that professional activity is not a business in interstate commerce (the constitutional basis for antitrust legislation). But occasionally a professional organization with interest in corporate enterprises will engage in deliberate restraint of trade and the Justice Department will take cognizance. The College of American Pathologists is one such group. In 1969 it signed a consent agreement with the Department, signalling its acceptance of guidelines to prevent what the Department had charged as a conspiracy to fix prices. Included among the list of illegal practices (which the College did not admit having engaged in) were attempts to keep non-member owned laboratory advertising out of medical journals and

---

[25] See People v. AAA Dental Laboratories, Inc., 8 Ill. 2d 330, 337, 134 N.E. 2d 285, 290 (1956); see also Perlow v. Board of Dental Examiners, 332 Mass. 682, 127 N.E. 2d 306 (1950); Board of Dental Examiners v. Jameson, 64 Cal. App. 2d 614, 149 P. 2d 233 (1944).

[26] See Fisher v. Schumacher, 72 So. 2d 804 (Fla. 1954); Roberts Optical Co. v. Department of Registration, 4 Ill. 2d 290, 122 N.E. 2d 824 (1954).

boycotts against doctors patronizing non-member laboratories. Prices for services charged by automated laboratories, the Justice Department said, were fixed at artificially high levels in order to permit less efficient, old laboratories to remain in business. The nationwide pathology bill is greater than $3 billion annually.[27]

3

Corporate business can stabilize prices and costs without resort to overt agreements among firms. Solo practitioners of service-oriented occupations cannot because they do not accumulate capital and a large work force; their only way to escape competitive enterprise is to "professionalize," to license, and to develop a community interest among themselves.

If competition is forestalled by this community of interest, there still remains another kind of economic control — countervailing power, that set of "restraints on private power" that appear "not on the same side of the market but on the opposite side, not with competitors but with customers or suppliers."[28] If consumers could join together to form a bargaining power roughly the match of the professional estate, this control would be operative. Unfortunately, they very largely cannot.

Countervailing power will not develop, according to Professor

[27] United States v. The College of American Pathologists, *CCH 1969 Trade Cases,* ¶72,825 (N.D. Ill 1969). See *The New York Times,* June 15, 1969, p. 1. Professional and trade groups have skirted the antitrust laws for decades. As long ago as 1917, the Justice Department succeeded in obtaining a consent decree against the National Association of Master Plumbers, its constituent associations, and all individual members. They were "perpetually enjoined" from refusing to install equipment which they did not sell and from other activities designed to hinder competition and, no doubt, to preserve the welfare of master plumbers. United States v. National Association of Master Plumbers of the United States, Equity No. 151 (W.D. Pa. 1917). See *Antitrust Consent Decrees, 1906–1966* (American Enterprise Institute for Public Policy Research 1968), Abstract 23, p. 245; and *passim* for other cases.

[28] John Kenneth Galbraith, *American Capitalism* (1953), p. 111.

Galbraith, whenever economic demand outruns supply.[29] That is because the supplier — the professional here — will always have other consumers — clients — to whom he can turn. It is not necessary to rehearse at any greater length than has already been done the power of professionals to limit their own supply.

Countervailing power requires what it says — power. When consumers are weak it has often been necessary to substitute governmental power for economic power in order to equalize the bargaining position. Unions are supported by a host of laws and regulations. But consumers — as opposed to workers — are rarely organized to compete with producers for the capture of governmental power; as already noted, the consumer's interests are too diffuse to permit him to lobby effectively, especially when he is working hard all day at his own specialty.[30]

Professionals have far outdistanced consumers in the race to power. The few consumer attempts to develop countervailing power show how difficult the prospects are, at least without governmental support. Codes of ethics make it unprofessional for many types of practitioners to associate with the enemy, who is familiar to us as a joiner of consumer coöperatives in the shape of group health associations and union legal assistance programs. Government power, far from equalizing the struggle, is used as a shield to insulate the professionals from any control.

Typical of the practical power involved in establishing countervailing power in an area where expert skills are called for is the funeral industry's bewildered battled against burial or funeral societies.[31] These associations are devoted to insuring that their members can have the kind of funeral they desire — the

---

[29] Galbraith, pp. 128 ff.

[30] Cf. Milton Friedman, *Capitalism and Freedom* (1962), p. 143: "We are much more specialized and devote a much larger fraction of our attention to our activity as a producer than as a consumer . . . those of us who use barbers at all, get barbered infrequently and spend only a minor fraction of our income in barber shops. Our interest is casual. Hardly any of us are willing to devote much time going to the legislature in order to testify against the iniquity of restricting the practice of barbering."

[31] See Mitford, *supra* note 17, pp. 266 ff.

associations, in contracting with funeral homes, are able to control fees, maintain simplicity, prevent expensive embalming, encourage cremation and the willing of the body for research or the vital organs to the living in need of them. An editor of *Mortuary Management* did not see their purpose as solely to drive down prices: "Equally strong is the desire to change established customs. It can be focused on funerals today and on something else tomorrow. The promulgations of these outfits hint at Communism and its brother-in-arms, atheism."[32] The signs of desperation are apparent; it is significant that as burial societies have sprung up they are quick to force down the price and perversity of funerals.

The practical response of the industry is to boycott funeral directors who coöperate with burial societies[33] or to secure legislation to cancel their effectiveness. Michigan law prohibits reduced prepayment group agreements between burial society and funeral directors.[34] It was once argued that legislation could not regulate the working hours of bakers[35] because this would violate their right to contract. This belief is no longer held. It is evident, however, that the argument has been altered: People (in Michigan, at any rate) are not to be able to contract for preneed burial service because the freedom to choose their funeral directors is circumscribed.[36]

It is not inappropriate to digress briefly to point out that the function of the union is different from that of the professional

[32] Quoted in Mitford, p. 272.
[33] *Antitrust Aspects of the Funeral Industry*, Hearings Before the Senate Antitrust and Monopoly Subcommittee, 88th Cong., 2d Sess. (1964), p. 187.
[34] Michigan Statutes Ann. §14.509 (12).
[35] See p. 182ff.
[36] Hearings, *supra* note 33, p. 150. Of course the analogy is bad and the suggestion is puerile, since all contract implies a restriction of future options. But something like this thinking lies behind medicine's traditional rejoinder that nothing must interfere with the "patient–doctor relationship," which is more tolerable than one commentator's more cumbersome equivalent "price discriminating monopolist without the barrier of a 'third-party' intermediary." Rayack, *supra* note 6, p. 175. The familiar is less troublesome.

association; the two should not be confused. The union represents a concerted effort by a combination of laborers to force concessions from highly organized business firms. No such parallel can be found between professional organizations and the employers of professionals — the public. The public as client of the professional is unorganized. The power of professional associations is "original," not countervailing; the true analogy would be that between laborers and consumers.[37]

4

The lack of effective restraints on the economic power of the professional class has serious consequences. The ancient craft guilds imposed or were bound to abide by fee, weight, and measure schedules motivated in large part by the fears of some that unless artisans showed a single face to the town in which they worked, the misdeeds of the individual might prove harmful to the assembly of craftsmen. There can be small doubt they were motivated also by the understanding that they were thereby a monopoly. But there was a context in which the guilds flourished, which we have quite lost: the Catholic belief that there was a just price above which a seller accepted money literally at the peril of going to a fire-filled hell. And in those days, that was no trifle (though we may imagine that men were then as wont to sell their souls as now; today, however, the soul brings in more but is worth much less).

Inflation has been a principal economic effect of the transformation from a moral to an ethical basis. Most professional incomes have climbed more rapidly than the growth in the average national income. Highest among these are the doctors. Between 1949 and 1964, the median net income of non-salaried physicians (who

---

[37] Cf. Galbraith, *American Capitalism*, p. 140: "[The distinction between original and countervailing power] would make restrictive practices of master plumbers or plasterers a proper object of interest by the Department of Justice while the absolutely (though not relatively) far more powerful unions in steel or automobiles who impose no similar restrictions on the supply of their labor would not be."

account for eighty per cent of all M.D.'s) rose from $8,744 to $28,380. During the same period, the median wage or salary income of managers, officials, and non-farm proprietors rose from $3,345 to $7,560.[38] Since the advent of Medicare and Medicaid, the pressure has become even more intense. The consumer price index reflects an eleven per cent increase for the cost of all items between 1966 and 1969. The comparable rate for physicians was twenty-one per cent; for hospital service charges, fifty-two per cent.

The inflationary tendency has not been confined to the highly skilled. By virtue of their minimum price schedules, the Oklahoma dry cleaners have benefited in the same way, one careful analyst has concluded.[39] The price-fixing power has "caused a larger number of plants per capita, more expenditures per capita, a greater proportion of per capita personal income to be spent for dry cleaning and more employees and proprietors per capita" than in similar non-price fixed areas. In return for their extra margin of profit, they tend to deliver more often and "offer the additional service of rug cleaning," a bonus the people of Oklahoma might be disposed to do without at least at the option of lower prices generally.[40]

The motivation of the funeral industry has similarly led to unjustifiable price increases. The rationalizations for each facet of the items and services sold dovetail neatly with the highest possible profit. Morticians resist the lowering of funeral prices because the plain fact is there are too many professionals among them who would be wiped out. In 1880, 993,000 people died in the United States and had to be disposed of by 5100 undertakers; in 1960, 25,000 morticians had to divide the 1,700,000 corpses among them.[41] If funeral directors were merely businessmen, we could tolerate the loss since what accords with supply and demand is

---

[38] Figures are from Table 25, Rayack, *supra* note 6, p. 110.
[39] See Plott, *supra* note 22, pp. 213–14.
[40] Unfortunately the dry-cleaning study did not examine whether fire and safety precautions were lacking and deceptive advertising was significantly higher in the non-regulated nearby state of Kansas. One suspects not.
[41] Mitford, *supra* note 17, p. 52; and Hearings, *supra* note 33, pp. 184 ff.

obviously efficient in a business operation (unless it is a Big Business, and there is ample indication that, to the suppliers of coffins and other devices, it is). But those who might be bankrupted successfully resist by transforming themselves into professionals who can legitimately foreswear competition.

To be sure, there is an undersupply of physicians, and an oversupply of morticians and Oklahoma dry cleaners. This seeming paradox can be resolved by noting the inelastic demand for funeral directors' services and the enormous educational requirements for doctors. (Dry cleaners are legislatively protected.) But both situations are responsible for prices higher than they would be were traditional economic restraints in force. If the public is convinced that the services of different specialists are not fungible, there can be no effective competition and monopoly prices will be easy to administer and receive.

As more groups enter the professional estate, the general price level will be bid higher than any increase in productivity will warrant. This is especially true where inconspicuous production is the rule. When highly skilled specialists arrogate routine chores to their exclusive competence, the client pays a high price for a low-grade service. To the contention that all members of the profession should be up to the highest standards of competence it has been argued that in an imperfect world to train and maintain Grade A professionals means that many people will receive no professional care at all.[42] This misconceives the problem slightly — what is really wrong with legislatively protected or inconspicuous production is that paraprofessionals cannot form to do the subprofessional task at a fairer price. In medicine, the lack of paraprofessionals has reached a crisis state: "Nearly all hospitals that lack adequate house staff are now letting registered nurses perform many services once performed only by doctors despite the fact that this is a practice barred by a number of state laws."[43]

---

[42] See Friedman, *supra* note 30, p. 153.
[43] Rayack, *supra* note 6, p. 127.

We should not be so sanguine as to hope that prices will readjust accordingly.

Inflation is not the only effect of the economic theory of the professional class. There is also a tendency toward a deterioration in the quality of services, or at least against improvement. Neither doctors nor plumbers make night house calls any more, and lucky is the person who can cajole either to come over in the day. Many case studies have shown medical examinations and care to be extremely low in quality.[44] We might be thankful that dry cleaners, at least, are not overworked, and so I thought until one day my local laundry shredded an expensive handloomed tablecloth. To my suggestion that the laundry could reimburse me, the manager responded that the American Institute of Laundering (Laboratory Division) would have to pass on the cause of the damage. The tablecloth was duly mailed off. In its wisdom, the Institute subsequently declared that the laundry could not have been the causative agent because although a too-concentrated bleach of the type laundries use might be responsible, no laundry would use a concentration strong enough to do such damage. The manager endorsed the report, despite the lack of any inquiry into whether in fact the laundry's bleach-allocating machine was temporarily deranged when it encountered the tablecloth. That would have been quite beyond the range of the Institute's competence. When, after my insistent queries as to what did cause the damage, the manager declared that the holes had obviously been carved by "leaking battery acid," I knew I had found another cause of inflation and decided I never liked the tablecloth anyway.

The market system is historical, and its evolution today is clearly toward a process in which the traditional economic restraints of competition and countervailing power are on the decline. The control of power being a felt necessity of a democratic people, we must next inquire whether the means to such control exist through politics.

[44] *Supra* p. 104, note 14.

10
The Abrogation
of the Democratic Dogma

Not fear, but caution, comes from the realization that democracy's destruction in other nations has been less a consequence of an incumbent government's tyranny than of some private group's uncontrollable ascendancy.
— W. WILLARD WIRTZ, "Government by Private Groups"

When two elephants fight, it is the grass that suffers.
— African proverb

1

Power has long been regarded as a fundamental concept in the discipline of the political scientist. Yet one large segment of power in America — corporate — has been left to the economist. That is because the economist can pretend that the business firm is part of the "economic system," and that, besides, when a corporation exercises power it is manifesting aberrant behavior; the monopoly, after all, is supposed to be cut to size by antitrust laws. Lawyers turn to economists, not political scientists, when they need antitrust advice. Economic power is somehow not quite power.

But of course it is. When an economist places economic power

159

in perspective, his work no longer seems very comfortably within the economic tradition,[1] for the economic tradition is derivative. If we are really interested in the quality of man's life and how he orders his existence, we should be less concerned about dividing power into economic or political categories than we are with the impact upon us of institutional decisions of all types. If we are to understand the full significance of the professional evolution, it will be necessary to consider the political side of professional power as well as its economic manifestations.

The simplest image of representative government — that voters, informed on the issues, come to the ballot box to elect representatives to enact laws in accordance with the express wishes of the constituency — broke down at the end of the nineteenth century when it became evident that certain sinister "interests" often prevailed on the peoples' choice in Washington or the state houses. From these observations grew a political theory of democracy that, with few dissents,[2] has become the accepted model of our governmental process.

This theory — pluralism — is not unlike classical economic doctrine. The "perfect competition" model of classical capitalism minimized the danger of power by defining it out of the system. No firm, in the model, was large enough to control prices or demand. So, in pluralism, it is assumed by definition that the multitude of factions or "pressure groups" will be sufficient to prevent any one of them from gaining control of the legislature. But this is a large assumption and depends on two less-frequently stated assumptions: (1) like the economically competitive firm, the group is small; and (2) there are others like it which will contest for power in the public arena. To test these assumptions against the current reality, it will first be necessary to present the theory in greater detail.

---

[1] Witness the evolution of Professor Galbraith's thinking from *American Capitalism* (1953) to *The New Industrial State* (1967).

[2] For well-documented dissents, see Henry S. Kariel, *The Decline of American Pluralism* (1961), and Theodore Lowi, *The End of Liberalism* (1969).

2

In 1835, Alexis de Tocqueville recognized that "no countries need associations more — to prevent either despotism of parties or the arbitrary rule of a prince — than those with a democratic social state."[3]   In 1852, John C. Calhoun understood that the basis of "sectional and interest compromise is both the distinctly American form of political organization and the cornerstone of practically all major political institutions of the modern U.S.A."[4]   But the possibility of a more complete understanding of pressure groups had to wait the development of modern tools, techniques, and methodologies.   Before the advent of the survey and other techniques, the role pressure groups play in the political process was incompletely seen.   Before the pressure group could have a maximum impact on American society it was also necessary that a new society emerge, different in quality from the Revolutionary agrarianism.

At least seven forces are at work remaking society since those days: growing technology, interdependence, complexity, specialization, a proliferation of alternatives that may be taken in any given possibility of action, increasing pluralism, and an accelerating process of institutionalized change.[5]   The way these forces have changed society from its medieval inheritance is no less startling for its much remarked upon nature.   Whereas in past centuries the numbers of different kinds of occupations were relatively low (and most people did not have jobs so much as they farmed to maintain life), today the individual American works within a highly specialized economic system, performing a specialized task to earn sufficient purchasing power to buy food and other commodities.   If one part of the society is disrupted

---

[3] Alexis de Tocqueville, *Democracy in America* (Mayer and Lerner, eds., 1966), p. 177.

[4] Drucker, "A Key to American Politics: Calhoun's Pluralism," 10 *Rev. of Politics* 412 (1948).

[5] See J. P. Corbett, *Europe and the Social Order* (1959).

or ceases to function for some reason, the rest of society is soon disrupted also. In feudal days, such interdependence was non-existent. Functions were repeated from fief to fief and from town to town. There was no market system, so a disturbance in one town did not cause repercussions in another. Moreover, goods produced centuries ago were of extremely narrow range. Sons tended on the whole to continue in the craft of the father, thus limiting innovation and the desire for change. In our age the specialization of technology has led to a wide diversity of goods and services. Increasingly, the social dictum which ordered sons to follow fathers is disappearing and the desire and drive for change and innovation is becoming vastly greater.

On the institutional level, complexity is reflected in the growth of a myriad of professional and trade associations, unions, business corporations, retail and wholesale operations, banking and financial and insurance institutions, political associations and parties, governmental bureaucracies and regulatory commissions, and transportation and communication systems. This proliferation of activities allows an individual an increasing host of alternative ways to accomplish his purposes — and gives him a host of new alternative purposes. The need for an accommodation among these different groups and purposes is imperative — thus an infinite number of smaller societies have formed, all of which intermingle, overlap, supplement, complement, and contrast with each other in the great complex of the general society.

The American political desideratum has become this: That government is best which (1) guarantees a certain minimum to its people, (2) rests on the consensus of the people that the minimum is the correct one, rather than on force or manipulation to maintain it (or to establish it), (3) allows for change of the society as a whole, as well as changes in individual desires and preferences, and (4) prohibits any majority from forcibly halting a minority's becoming itself a majority. The American striving for democracy can be viewed as the conjunction of a system of due process of law that allows for change and a social democracy that is the total process of guaranteeing livable conditions and the chance for each individual to improve his conditions and to enjoy his human dignity.

The problems which arise in order to fulfill the requirements of this kind of society are immense. The complexity of issues demands increasingly that important and far-reaching decisions be made, always without knowledge of all the factors which should influence the decision and always without knowledge of the full consequences of any decision. Every action, every issue, depends upon every other. The people cannot make the decisions because they have neither the time nor the resources and because there is no practical way whereby so many issues could be referred to them.

A unique system of political compromise and control by the people over the decision-makers has had to evolve. This is pluralism, the system of "minorities rule."[6] The existence of the polity rests on a consensus about the norms of society, on the belief that the government should be maintained and that certain rights should be guaranteed the people. Consensus is fundamental. "Prior to politics, beneath it, enveloping it, restricting it, conditioning it, is the underlying consensus on policy that usually exists in the society among a predominant portion of the politically

---

[6] See Robert A. Dahl, *A Preface to Democratic Theory* (1956). "Minorities rule" is to be contrasted with two earlier models of democratic government. The writers of the *Federalist Papers* sought, as Dahl puts it, "to bring off a compromise between the power of majorities and the power of minorities, between the political equality of all adult citizens on one side, and the desire to limit their sovereignty on the other." (p. 4.) The theory of "Madisonian democracy" holds that tyranny can be restrained by the separation of governmental powers, by the control of factions through the operation of the "Republican principle," by popular elections, and by diversifying the interests of the electorate. The other model is the "Populistic" theory of democracy. That theory seeks to show how to maximize popular sovereignty and political equality by an application of the majority principle to allow that governmental policy to prevail which is most preferred by the citizens, whose preferences are each given equal weight. As Dahl shows, neither of the traditional democratic models adequately describes the activities of our governmental process.

active members."⁷   There must be a consensus among all (or
almost all) members of the society that the general rules will be
followed. In America, this means that people must respect the
rule of law and believe in the permissibility and possibility of
changing the laws when necessary.

To provide the initiative and decision-making responsibility
which a constantly changing society requires, the people elect
their public officials. The two-party system serves to make these
officials responsive to the populace (as they are unresponsive
where it does not exist). Parties present candidates between
whom the people choose their officers at regular intervals. Since
generally only the candidates of the two major parties can hope
to win, each party selects a candidate who can hopefully attract
the majority of all the people. Extreme positions are eliminated
(in general) in favor of middle-of-the-road ones. Strife is eliminated in favor of compromise. Citizens remain peaceful because
the candidate is "the peoples' choice" (and only when he is their
choice). They will "go along" with the man they have elected.
The candidate is kept from extreme positions because he must be
their choice; in order for him to win and stay in office through the
next election, he must appeal to the widest number of people,
thus excluding extremes on either end of the political spectrum.

In the American democracy the people determine the bounds
within which decisions can be made and then leave the specific
decisions in the hands of those whom they elect to and remove
from office. In this kind of election, the vote cannot settle issues.
It acts as a means to pick a compromise between issues. Empirical
studies show that there is not much more than a "trace of 'ideological' thinking" in a large proportion of the electorate and that
"there is a great deal of uncertainty and confusion in the public
mind as to what specific policies the election of one party over
the other would imply."⁸   That elections do not define issues has
been concisely argued, as follows:

⁷ Dahl, p. 132.
⁸ Angus Campbell, et al., The American Voter (1960), p. 542.

The popular election is a device of control. It is much else, too, but in the practice and normative theory of democracy elections are important largely as a means by which the acts of government can be brought under the control of the governed. And yet, as a formal matter, the electorate does not vote on what the government shall do. Referenda on public laws, either statutory or constitutional, have not been more than ancillary features of popular elections. The public's explicit task is to decide not what government shall do but rather *who shall decide* what government shall do. If the two decisions are bound together, as they are in the practice of every democratic state, it is because candidates for public office are judged partly for the position they take on public policies, while policies arc judged partly for the impact they have on the electorate's choice between candidates.[9]

It is apparent that the public is not the group that dictates the specific direction of government. The question, then, is how the public enables leaders to decide what to decide. The answer is clear: Leaders determine policy on the basis of the conflicting claims and interests of groups. Although the individual may not reason ideologically, he has desires which can be expressed by group leaders. Because groups can be collections of thousands or millions of people, leaders have money and bargaining power and can deal effectively with public officials. The groups make agreements, take actions, strike contracts, and are victims or beneficiaries of accidents and circumstances that daily occur. They buy or do not buy, criticize or encourage, threaten, cajole, argue, support, persuade, attend, strike, boycott, organize, construct, and praise. They exist because they have some special interest to protect and they fight either to gain it or to preserve it. Their political efficacy is dependent upon their size, their cohesiveness, and their formal structure. They represent economic, political, ideological, religious, moral, reform, social, business, financial,

9 Campbell, pp. 542–3.

industrial, military, agricultural, scientific, technological, trade, and professional interests.

What prevents the most powerful group from becoming the oppressors is that there is no one "most powerful" group. People belong to many groups, have many cross interests, and realize that to accomplish anything they must bargain and compromise. These groups provide a mechanism for determining public consensus and public policy. Relationships are formed between individuals, groups, parties, factions, and cliques; private deals are made in the marketplace and at the bargaining table.

The fundamental contention of current pluralistic theory is that the actions of the multiude of private groups limit the capacity of government to be arbitrary, and contrariwise, government acts as a brake on private power because it can function by mediating disputes that arise in the private sector. The interplay between private and public spheres is supposed to keep in check power that would otherwise oppress the individual. Neither majorities nor minorities can tyrannize.

The organized pressure group is assumed to act at specific points in the legislative, executive, and judicial processes and serve as a buffer between the individual and the government. So long as there is no one majority but rather several thousands of constantly shifting minorities, the group theory presumes an equilibrium in public policy will at least roughly satisfy the vague criterion that the public interest be preserved.[10] The assumption made by current theory is that the equilibrium is disturbed only at the margins. The hundreds of majorities and thousands of minorities when confronted with complex and interdependent issues make it impossible for themselves to remain permanent; none can long dominate, if indeed any can dominate at all. Groups help shape issues and push individual interests, but they cannot vote for them in their corporate status; because voters

[10] See, e.g., Earl Latham, The Group Basis of Politics.

have overlapping interests and belong to many groups, ever-changing coalitions of issues and political compromise rule — not specific ideology, not an identifiable majority.

The federal system, the undisciplined two-party system, pressure group participation, and frequent elections are thus the crucial instruments of American democracy: They inhibit dictation, provide a method for interests to be made known, encourage compromise, discourage widescale strife (confining it instead to local areas where it changes constantly from issue to issue and is rarely in danger of developing into a national conflagration). They hold down the workload for any small set of politicians and keep the powers of decision-making in the hands of local officials who know their own problems and who therefore do not have to waste others' time and resources.

All this is the theory.[11]

3

Economists have long thought it more important to consider how goods were produced than what were produced. Because production — a process — is the goal, the content can safely be ignored.[12]   Political scientists have heeded the same dogma.   Because the process of pluralism seems to offer a maximum possibility of political freedom, the actual content of the compromises arrived at within the legislative halls has been conveniently ignored.   But we ignore substance for form at our peril.

Throughout much of the previous chapters, the content of legislative decisions has been explicit.   It will not strike the reader who has progressed this far as novel that within the field of professional interests, little is legislated in the way of compromise and much is legislated without effective opposition.   The reasons should be clear: The interests of experts are not politically overlapping; they do not contest the right of other groups to have

[11] See Lowi, *supra* note 2.
[12] *Cf.* Galbraith, *The Affluent Society* (1956).

their legislation enacted, because the character of professionalism demands that only the expert is competent to take a stand on proposed legislation affecting his area of interest. Adherence to this policy is widespread because each group is willing to admit that it is less well-equipped to judge another specialty and its relation to the public interest than are the practitioners of that specialty.

Pluralism, which was to rest on the mutual interests of members of many groups, is now degenerating into a series of discrete, specialized, non-related monopolies. These groups are neither small nor similar in purpose. The mass of citizenry is losing its identity and force because each individual neglects his role as consumer when he seeks to become a producer. So a new American consensus is developing: The general welfare is the sum of various specialist interests.

When legislatures become agencies for ratifying policies of separate groups, there is reason to expect that private groups will seek at some point to impose their own policies on the public directly. That this in fact is the situation for many professional groups has already been demonstrated. When North Carolina decided to change its dental code to stave off judicial defeat at the hands of Dr. Hawkins, the law was amended to permit all state dentists – and no one else – to elect the state dental board, presumably a public agency. Lawyers and laundrymen set minimum fees. Medical associations have the power to define which diseases are to be treated by which specialists. Overt legislative delegation of authority to private groups combines with the acquiescence of legislatures and courts in the customary power of other groups to enforce private standards; in either case, traditional controls postulated by the theory of pluralism are unavailing. Laymen do not have access to the decision-making process of "private" groups.[13] Legislatures grant medical associations accred-

[13] *Cf.* William Kornhauser, *The Politics of Mass Society* (1961), p. 81: "A plurality of groups that are both independent and non-inclusive not only protects elites and non-elites from one another but does so in a manner that

itation power: "Expertise may justify the granting of power to a professional association to certify those medical schools whose graduates may be licensed in a state."[14] Legislatures go farther; they authorize private groups to fix standards to which individual practitioners must conform. This power may be exercised in the future: The association, that is, may change the rules after the legislature has delegated rule-making power without the necessity of having the rules adopted by the legislature. Many courts have explicitly upheld the power of professional organizations to promulgate ethical standards; thus the National Chiropody Association was held entitled to fix standards for Arizona[15] and the American Veterinary Medical Association has issued regulations for Rhode Island veterinarians.[16]

Often the legislature defaults even on the threshold question of defining the profession subsequently given rule-making power. Osteopathy has been defined as that which is taught in "recognized" osteopathy schools,[17] and drugs have been defined in part as things listed in the U.S. Pharmacopoeia,[18] which is issued by private pharmaceutical groups. Even industrial standards have

permits liberal democratic control. Liberal democratic control requires that people have *access* to elites, and that they exercise *restraint* in their participation. Independent groups help to maintain access to top-level decision-making by bringing organized pressure to bear on elites to remain responsive to outside influence. Each group has interests of its own in gaining access to elites, and has organized power not available to separate individuals for the implementation of those interests. These interests require not only that elites pay attention to the demands of the group but also that other groups do not become so strong as to be able to shut off this group's access to the elite. Since independent groups seek to maintain their position by checking one another's power as well as the power of higher-level elites, the interaction of these groups helps to sustain access to decision-making processes in the larger society."

[14] Note, "The State Courts and Delegation of Public Authority to Private Groups," 67 *Harv. L. Rev.* 1398, 1400 (1954).

[15] State v. Hynds, 61 Ariz. 281, 148 P. 2d 1000 (1944).

[16] Allen v. State Board of Veterinarians, 72 R.I. 372, 52 A. 2d 131 (1947).

[17] Beck v. Gleason, 148 Kan. 1, 79 P. 2d 911 (1938).

[18] State v. Walgeen, 263 Wisc. 401, 57 N.W. 2d 364 (1953).

been issued and enforced without apparent public interference. The lumber industry, for instance, extensively manages — or mismanages[19] — the grading of lumber. The industry has the power to reduce the size of lumber unilaterally; "2 inches dimension" lumber is currently 1⅝ inches thick. The idea of delegating power to specialists is so ingrained that the United States Immigration and Naturalization Service has even deferred from exercising its statutory duty of deciding which alien musicians and singers should be given working visas to perform in the United States. Popular singers have been barred, not by INS, but by such groups as the American Federation of Radio Artists. Since the standard for permission has turned in the past on whether or not the singer is of "distinguished merit and ability" or whether "unemployed persons capable of performing such services or labor cannot be found in this country," the performers' unions have significant power to impose cultural tariffs.[20]

The power of these guilds to compel membership has already been remarked on. As a practical matter, most professionals must maintain ties with the national and state associations. Contributions in the form of dues are in effect compelled contributions to lobbying funds which can be used to tighten the association's grip on public policy-making. The degree to which members can control disbursements from their association treasuries is limited. The fifteen-man Board of Trustees of the AMA, elected by the House of Delegates (who are twice removed from the general membership in the medical electoral process), has the power to spend AMA money for any purposes it chooses.

Occasionally a profession can persuade a public agency to compel membership by law. The most notable example is that of the "integrated" bar; there are no racial connotations in the term, for it means simply that all licensed lawyers must belong to a statewide bar association. More than half the states have

---

[19] See "Lumber Misgrading: Builders Beware," *The Washington Post*, November 18, 1968, p. 1.
[20] *The New York Times*, April 25, 1965, p. 1.

"integrated" their bars in this sense. The New Hampshire Supreme Court, acting on a private petition, integrated the bar for a three-year trial period beginning in 1969, declaring that integration would create a "unified bar" and would "require that the costs of improving the profession be shared by its members, the lawyers admitted to practice in the state."[21]

To the extent that professionals are required to belong to associations, the associations cannot be considered "private" in the traditional sense. Even where the state does not overtly require membership, the pressure to join is strong. These associations hardly square with the traditional notion of private organizations composed of willing participants struggling in the public arena for legislative votes. We are led to the danger foreseen by James Madison two centuries ago: "In *The Federalist No. 51*, Madison expressed the hope that the individual in America would be guarded against the oppression of his governors and against his own presumptuous groups. This hope is being frustrated as pluralism runs its course under modern conditions, when private law-making groups operate under color of public ones — or, conversely, when public instrumentalities are obliged to find their sole source of support in private ones. To allow public policy to be shaped only by such a pluralism is to present a radical challenge to the ultimate aspirations of pluralism itself."[22]

---

[21] In re Unification of the New Hampshire Bar, 248 A. 2d 709 (N.H. 1968). The court said: "It is also argued that under voluntary association discipline and requiring observance of ethical standards is ineffective as to its members and impossible with regard to non-members, who have caused many of the serious disciplinary problems. A unified bar will permit the imposition of ethical standards on all the lawyers admitted to practice in this State and provide an effective means of enforcing their observance which is not the case today under the voluntary association. This will facil-·itate and improve supervision by this court to protect the rights of the public against unethical activities of members of the bar" — at 713. This is specious, since the court will still be the agency considering disbarment and suspensions from practice, a power unaffected by unification.

[22] Kariel, *supra* note 2, p. 187.

4

It has been argued that a new system of political representation is necessary in the modern age; rather than geographical representation, the people should appoint their legislators on an occupational basis. New York and New Jersey should no longer be a dividing line, for what separates these states but a river long ago spanned by many bridges and connected by many tunnels? Better to give to Congress and the state legislatures a doctor from the doctors, a merchant from the merchants (and presumably a criminal from the criminals).[23]

Though this position may have a surface plausibility, it is questionable whether we should commit to formal political institutions what informal ones are already effecting. The problem with such representation is great. It is the nature of occupational services that we need very many of them; that the survival of local communities depends on them all. But the serious problems of each geographic area — the meat of politics — cannot be solved simply by summing occupational specialties. Slum conditions, sewage disposal, utility distribution, pollution, transportation, land development, health care, and public recreational facilities are not to be cleaned up, efficiently provided for, effectively controlled, developed or established by councils made up of one doctor, one lawyer, one merchant, one farmer, and an occasional politician.

"Government by experts," Harold Laski has said, "would, however ardent their original zeal for the public welfare, mean after a time government in the interests of experts. Of that the outcome would be either stagnation, on the one hand, or social antagonism, upon the other."[24] History bears out this analysis. In medieval Liége, the craft guilds succeeded so well in their fight with merchants for control of the powers of municipal administration that the city after 1384 was directed by a council composed of representatives from each of the city's thirty-two craft guilds.

---

[23] See, e.g., letter to The New York Times, July 29, 1964.
[24] Harold J. Laski, The Limitations of the Expert (1931), p. 14.

The result was an unworkable government that fell near to collapse and long floundered until the craft guilds were reduced in power by Ferdinand of Bavaria in 1649.[25]

We drift in that direction.   In an interdependent society, "functional" political representation is dangerous; territorial representation imperative.   This is true not only because it is impossible to find the one most significant concern of any man to classify him for voting purposes.   Is a lawyer who is the executive vice president of a brewing company's retail sales division to be catalogued as an attorney, a businessman, bureaucrat, manager, beer master, or salesman?   When he retires, does he join a different electorate?   Functional representation is dangerous also because broad questions of public policy cannot be answered by adding up specialist solutions.   The generalist synthesis is indispensable.

5

The specialist's power to shape public policy poses serious problems.   We would surely balk if printers were to announce that henceforth they would set in type and print only those topics of which they approved and that any printer who refused to abide by a national association of printers ruling as to acceptable subjects would not be permitted to purchase type.   The function of printing plants, we would surely observe, is not to pass on the merits of that which it linotypes.

Precisely this kind of policy-making is indulged in by various specialist groups.   Longshoremen have been known to strike because they would not load or unload ships plying the Communist trade route; longshoremen, in other words, have taken it upon themselves to conduct foreign commercial policy of the United States.   Insurance companies have begun to deny necessary insurance to those whose homes are not neatly kept or whose home

25 Sigmund Nosow and William H. Form, eds., *Man, Work, and Society* (1962), pp. 165-6.

life is otherwise "inadequate"; whether the irrelevance of the fact is more dangerous than that most of that kind of information is based on faulty hearsay is difficult to say. The military has long been recognized to present the threat of the misuse of expertise: The advice of generals on military matters has often been mistaken for advice on whether military force should be used. It has only lately been recognized that the police, too, have begun to substitute their expert judgments for the larger political judgments they are in no way qualified by any particular training to make.[26] The power of private professional organizations intensifies the problem. When professional groups can promulgate private ethics that are acceptable by public agencies there is enormous potential for translating private whims into public ways.[27]

It is unavailing to refurbish the democratic dogma by showing occasions on which the public interest seems to have triumphed over the cries of professionals. That Congress in 1965 could pass comprehensive medical care assistance programs in the face of AMA opposition is not to argue that organized medicine is powerless in significant ways. Tendencies are not disproved by showing they are not everywhere complete. Furthermore, the AMA opposition withstood attack for more than thirty years, and it may be plausibly argued that the AMA lost in 1965 only because it had been too successful in exercising its more important power to

---

[26] Cf. Report of the National Commission on the Causes and Prevention of Violence (1969); quoted in The New York Times, June 15, 1969, p. IV-2: "The police tend to view themselves as society's experts in the determination of guilt and apprehension of guilty persons. Because they also see themselves as an abused and misunderstood minority, they are particularly sensitive to what they perceive as challenges to 'their' system of criminal justice — whether by unruly black Panthers or 'misguided' judges."

[27] Cf. Beatty v. State Board, 352 Pa. 565, 43 A. 2d 127, 128 (1945): "As to what constitutes 'misconduct' in the carrying on of the business of undertaking, a large measure of discretion must necessarily be left to the State Board of Undertakers and to the Court of Common Pleas of Dauphin County on appeal, for misconduct may consist of the breach of any of the generally accepted canons of ethics and propriety governing the respectful and reverential burial of the dead."

limit the production of doctors, thus driving costs to a point beyond the ability of citizens to pay. Moreover, the argument against Medicare — against "socialized medicine" — though not ended yet was no more than a sham; most doctors were quick to realize once government assistance in financing health care became a reality that it represented a "gold mine"[28] not a loss of autonomy.[29]

"Were the functions of the state admitted to be an accommodation to the needs of the industrial system, it would no longer be possible to regard the latter as an independent entity," says Professor Galbraith.[30] Professionals have long had to admit that they are not independent of the state: This is explicit, after all, in licensing requirements and in the very notion that they serve a public interest which the state may reasonably regulate. But there is no need for doctors to fear interference by the state in the affairs of medicine (say) because, to a significant degree, organized medicine, in its relation to medical problems, is the state.

On the whole the professions have managed to avoid the question whether the state accommodates itself to the needs of the professions. They have avoided it and hoped the issue would not be raised because accommodation is a two-way street; an admission would jeopardize autonomy. The issue is easily avoided by asking for — and getting — self-regulation. That there is regulation quiets fears because the public sees the professions as subservient to the state. What the public does not see is the agency of regulation, and this suits the professions.

It is instructive that morticians cause no injury when they are professionally negligent, except possibly to the sensibilities of the excessively squeamish. Yet morticians are almost everywhere licensed, and automotive mechanics, whose negligence can cause

[28] The New York Times, July 6, 1969, p. IV-10.
[29] Cf. John Kenneth Galbraith, Economics and the Art of Controversy (1959), pp. 82–86. Professor Galbraith notes that all the while organized medicine bitterly fought off government assistance schemes, it was approving comprehensive care plans for large segments of the population in private industry and through such agencies as the Veterans Administration.
[30] Galbraith, The New Industrial State (1967), p. 232.

grisly death, are almost nowhere licensed.[31] The fact that garage mechanics are not licensed, when the benefits to them should be manifest, can be explained only by the assumption that there are many incompetent and dishonest practitioners among them who are worried enough to block such legislation or not interested enough to press for it. This is a paradox arising from their own ignorance, since licensing legislation is certainly no guarantee of honesty or competence. But at the outset, a licensing board which could suspend the dishonest and incompetent from practice could disturb the industry; that problem, too, could be obviated with the usual grandfather clause. It must be that the repairman's coefficient of laziness is too large: With a licensing board he could no longer be open about his practices; he would have to be surreptitiously incompetent and slyly dishonest.

Garage mechanics, along with television repairmen, perhaps have their reasons, but they are anomalies among those who perform or purport to perform basic services. For the instinct toward self-regulation is well-nigh universal. "In some states," Miss Mitford relates, "the regulation of perpetual care funds is placed under the benign authority of a board composed entirely of cemetery owners."[32] In 1968, the American Retail Federation, through the administrative vice president of Gimbel Brothers, told the Federal Trade Commission that "we feel that business can successfully regulate itself in its own best interests and that of the consumer."[33] But what the businessman wants, the professional seems to get. It has been many decades since any business could claim to be self-regulating; it has been just as many decades since many professions could claim not to be. Yet busi-

---

[31] Testimony before the Senate Antitrust and Monopoly Subcommittee indicated that in the Denver, Colo., area, ninety-nine per cent of all automobile repair work would be inadequately performed if done at all. *The New York Times*, December 4, 1968, p. 1.

[32] Jessica Mitford, *The American Way of Death* (1963), p. 145.

[33] Quoted in *The New York Times*, December 3, 1968, p. 22.

nessmen are not commonly supposed to be politically impotent.[34] We are seeing laissez-faire at its last outpost. That wispy "principle" is applied to private associations and the government is deterred. Not only is there economic justification for leaving the professions to themselves, there is a political one, they say, and nothing is more sacred in America than that combination. But it is a short step from piety to blasphemy and it has already been taken. For laissez-faire was always grounded on the belief that no one man or group could significantly influence price or production in the economic realm. That this assumption is untenable in the professional sphere is manifest. And the right to be free of political intervention by public government similarly rests on the premise that the group does not have governmental power over the public. This power the professionals do hold. So however pleasant the abstract principle, it has no bearing on the way things are in the world we know. All power must be held in check — regardless of whether men choose to call it public, private, absolute, or relative. But until this is recognized, the democratic dogma will have been abrogated by the very forces that were to assure its survival.

[34] Businessmen have, however, been able to adapt their modes of business to the state in such a way as to exercise a high degree of self-regulation in some areas. But this is self-regulation achieved through economic power, not through legal right. They do not have outward legal control over supply and they must manufacture demand. Furthermore, businessmen do not usually claim they have the power to regulate themselves; professionals are not shy in admitting it.

11
The Rise of Undue Process

Neither the [Fourteenth] Amendment — broad and comprehensive as it is — nor any other amendment, was designed to interfere with the power of the state, sometimes termed its police power, to prescribe regulations to promote the health, peace, morals, education, and good order of the people, and to legislate so as to increase the industries of the state, develop its resources, and add to its wealth and prosperity.
> — MR. JUSTICE FIELD, *Barbier v. Connoly* (1885)

1

Regulation is freedom.

On this Orwellian equation rests the foundations of both democratic and totalitarian societies. Jean Jacques Rousseau, James Madison, and Josef Stalin all knew this formula and understood that there was more than one practical use that could be made of it. Democratic majorities, elitist minorities, and dictators have all asserted their competence at regulating in the public interest; but in neither open nor closed societies is there a pretense that regulations are dispensable; quite the contrary, they are a necessary ingredient in the matrix of freedom — whether for all, many, some, or one.

If the day is past for competition and countervailing power to act as economic restraints on professional pricing and for the public to regain control over professional policy-making by the

178

ordinary political techniques, the question remains whether resort to the courts would result in any weakening of the professional muscle. When politics fails, Americans invoke the Constitution. It will not be surprising to learn, therefore, that as licensing legislation gained in frequency, it was brought under judicial scrutiny. A society formed of pioneering virtues would not let restrictive legislation survive unquestioned. Especially was this true of courts to which the questions were presented, jealous as they were of their own prerogative to fashion the common law. Legislation was not usual during the early nineteenth century, and the courts were quick to construe narrowly much of the social legislation that came before them.[1]

The states asserted the power to regulate private affairs to preserve and promote the health, safety, and public welfare of their citizens. This legislative prerogative became fashionably known as the "police power" of the state. A classic definition of this power was early put forth by the Oklahoma Supreme Court as "an attribute of sovereignty, inherent in every sovereign state, and not derived from any written constitution nor vested by grant of any superior power. The term 'police power' comprehends the power to make and enforce all wholesome and reasonable laws and regulations necessary to the maintenance, upbuilding, and advancement of the public weal and protection of the public interests."[2]   Chief Justice Roger B. Taney put it more succinctly when he wrote that the police powers "are nothing more or less than the powers of government inherent in every sovereignty . . . that is to say . . . the power to govern men and things."[3]

Against the police power was arrayed the freedom of the individual to engage in his ordinary pursuits as he sees fit. Since the police power was so broad as to encompass every conceivable

---

[1] Whenever a statute altered the common law, such as legislation regulating the railroad industry, the courts solemnly declared it "in derogation of the common law" and often did their best to emasculate it.

[2] Ex parte Tindall, 102 Okla. 192, 229 P. 125, 126 (1924).

[3] License Cases, 46 U.S. (5 How) 504 , 583 (1847).

activity of man, it was natural for a litigious people to look to the courts for the vindication of their freedoms. The ensuing battle between the legislatures and courts lasted fifty years and had a profound impact on the development of the professional class and the growth of licensing. It will be necessary to examine this struggle in some detail.

2

In 1868, the Fourteenth Amendment became part of the United States Constitution. In pertinent part, it denied the states what the Fifth Amendment denied the federal government as early as 1791: the power to deprive any person of "life, liberty, or property without due process of law." Although it was expected that this section of the Amendment would effectively bar the states from discriminating against the recently freed slaves, it became instead a method by which business corporations could prevent governmental encroachments on the market.

The first important judicial construction of the Fourteenth Amendment due process clause came in 1873 in the *Slaughter House Cases*,[4] in which the Supreme Court construed the word "persons" to mean not merely the natural inhabitants of the states but corporate bodies brought to life by legal fiction. The *Cases* arose from the establishment by Louisiana of the Crescent City Live-Stock Landing and Slaughter House Company, which was given a monopoly to conduct its business throughout the New Orleans area. Butchers who were suddenly put out of business appealed, but the Court disappointed them. The due process clause, it said, did not prevent a state from regulating the slaughtering business in that manner. Indeed, why should it?

This decision was ringingly reaffirmed three years later in *Munn v. Illinois*.[5] The state had enacted legislation pursuant to a mandate in the Illinois Constitution, requiring proprietors of grain

4 83 U.S. (16 Wall.) 36 (1873).
5 94 U.S. 113 (1877).

warehouses in cities of more than 100,000 population to be bonded, licensed, and to adhere to published rate schedules with stated maximum prices. When the Chicago proprietors Munn and Scott refused to comply, charging storage rates higher than the maximum set by law, they were convicted and fined. They appealed, but the Court found the regulatory scheme reasonable in light of the conditions in the industry. The Court noted that Chicago grain elevators then held between 300,000 and 1,000,000 bushels at once. The grains of thousands of producers coming by rail and water were necessarily mixed on arrival; grain necessarily had to be inspected and receipted for. Since nine firms controlled all elevators, constituting a monopoly, the state sought to impose controls. Finding common carriers, innkeepers, millers, ferrymen, wharfingers, bakers, carmen, and hackney-coachmen having been held to public regulation in the past, the Supreme Court upheld the Illinois law by analogy. Of course, a businessman may find oppressive the legislative power to regulate business. "We know that this is a power which may be abused; but that is no argument against its existence. For protection against abuses by legislatures the people must resort to the polls, not to the courts."[6]

The police power was judicially recognized in the professional field at least as early as 1888 with the conviction of "Doctor" Dent, who had procured a diploma from the "American Eclectic College of Cincinnati, Ohio." The West Virginia State Board of Health denied him a license on the ground that his school was disreputable. Dent practiced medicine anyway and was convicted. He appealed to the Supreme Court, arguing that the West Virginia law unconstitutionally interfered with his "vested right" to carry on a profession. The Court affirmed his conviction, holding that skill and knowledge being necessary to medical practice, the law was reasonably related to the legitimate end of insuring high competence among physicians.[7]

[6] Munn v. Illinois, *supra* note 5, at 134.
[7] Dent v. West Virginia, 129 U.S. 114 (1888).

The first of a series of cases testing the power of a state to regulate the number of hours a day a man could legally work came to the Court in 1898; the Court persevered in its adherence to the doctrine that the states may regulate industrial conditions without offending due process. The case, *Holden v. Hardy*, concerned the legitimacy of the Utah mining law, which limited to eight the hours miners in underground mines, smelters, and "all other institutions for the reduction of refining of ores or metals" could work, excepting only "cases of emergency where life or property is in imminent danger." When Holden, the employer, required a workman to spend ten hours one day in the Old Jordan Mine with no emergency, he was arrested and jailed for fifty-seven days. He contested his way to the Supreme Court, which decided that "these employments, when too long pursued, the legislature has judged to be detrimental to the health of the employes, and, so long as there are reasonable grounds for believing that this is so, its decisions upon this subject cannot be reviewed by the Federal courts."[8]   *Munn* was not adverted to.

As late as 1900, the Court stuck to this principle, despite hints that its thinking was becoming affected by the wealth of antitrust and other regulatory legislation aimed at curbing the excesses of large corporations.[9]   A Minnesota law which required barbers to close up shop on Sunday was upheld in that year. In the *Barbers' Sunday Closing Case*, the Court noted that since barbers tend to stay open in the evenings it was a proper object of the law "to protect the employees by insuring them a day of rest."[10]

The reverse came dramatically in 1905 in a decision that hampered economic legislation for more than thirty years. A public investigation in New York State into conditions in the baking industry had resulted in recommendations to the legislature that

---

[8] Holden v. Hardy, 169 U.S. 366, 395 (1898).
[9] In the Minnesota Rate Case, 134 U.S. 418 (1890) and Smyth v. Ames, 169 U.S. 466 (1898), the Court took positions that, if they did not overrule *Munn*, foreshadowed its demise.
[10] Petit v. Minnesota, 177 U.S. 164, 168 (1900).

the hours of bakers in "biscuit, bread, cake, bakery, or confectionery establishments" be limited to sixty per week and ten per day, with certain exceptions. As usual, an employer, Lochner, wishing to squeeze the last crumbs from his dilatory employees, required a baker to work more than sixty hours, in the face of the legislative proscription against "requiring or permitting" such excess. The conviction was appealed, and this time, in *Lochner v. New York*,[11] reversed.

Lochner was grounded on a single premise: that the liberty of the *baker* to contract for as many hours as he pleased was infringed, in violation of his right under the Fourteenth Amendment. Could there be any clearer deprivation of a man's liberty than to limit the hours he could work? asked Mr. Justice Peckham, for a 5–4 majority which took it to be rhetorical. Justice Peckham proceeded by way of *reductio ad absurdum*: There must be a limit to the police power, he said, because if not then the state could regulate everyone under the pretext of health. "A printer, a tinsmith, a locksmith, a carpenter, a cabinetmaker, a dry goods clerk, a bank's, a lawyer's, or a physician's clerk, or a clerk in almost any kind of business, would all come under the power of the legislature, on this assumption."[12]   But, as Mr. Justice Holmes epigramatically dissented: "General propositions do not decide concrete cases."[13]   For the opposite assumption was open to the Court: It could equally be argued that if there is a limit on the police power at all, the courts should never permit regulation of any sort; yet some restrictions on work had clearly been allowed. Justice Peckham knew that he had to distinguish *Holden v. Hardy* (in which he had dissented) since the Court in those days was not disposed to overrule itself. The "emergency clause" in the limitation of miners' hours was contrasted with the lack of an escape clause in the bakers': *Holden* did not cover *Lochner*, said Justice Peckham. A more specious distinction would be difficult

[11] 198 U.S. 45 (1905).
[12] *Lochner, supra* note 11, at p. 59.
[13] *Lochner,* at 76.

to find. Despite the wealth of evidence that conditions in bake-shops were unhealthy, New York was denied the power to alleviate the dangers.

The *Barbers' Sunday Closing Case* was ignored altogether. Perhaps too great embarrassments are better forgotten. Perhaps, too, the distinction between bakers and barbers inheres in the regularity with which judges frequent barbers and the infrequency with which they talk to bakers. The scientific difference between resting on Sundays and stopping after ten hours seems too shallow to support the difference.[14] It may also be that state commissions and public investigating bodies smacked a little too much of socialism. In the *Barbers' Case* and in at least one state case upholding the power of the state to regulate the practice of barbering,[15] the political muscle of barbers — a free people asking the legislature for help to protect the public — outshone the efforts of public bodies making inquiries. Noble motives will go for naught when not disguised by public relations men. Good-hearted laws, like good-hearted women, are likely to be ignored if they are unattractively packaged.

What was extraordinary about *Lochner*, however, was that the decision rested on a protection of a person not a party to the case. If there was anything sacred about constitutional litigation in 1905, it was that a litigant must raise only those issues which affect him. As the Court pointed out in the earlier mining case, the defense of the employer was "not so much that his right to contract has been infringed upon, but that the act works a peculiar hardship to his employees, whose right to labor as long as they please is alleged to be thereby violated. The argument would certainly come with better grace and greater cogency from the latter class."[16]

The issue at the bottom of *Lochner* was the state's legislative

---

14 The Court observed in *Petit* that "one day in seven is the rule, founded in experience, and sustained by science." *Supra* note 10, at 165.
15 State v. Walker, 48 Wash. 8, 92 P. 775 (1907).
16 *Holden, supra* note 8, at p. 397.

attempt to make more nearly equal the bargaining power between employer and employee. The real question for decision was whether New York had sought a reasonable method in achieving that goal. That question was dismissed out of hand.

So the proposition of *Lochner* was that the Supreme Court would decide whether a regulation was reasonable, not on the basis of what the legislature might find reasonable but according to the intense, personal, and very partisan standards of the Justices themselves. For many years thereafter the Court fashioned an inconsistent doctrine; no one could ever say what regulation might be reasonable and thus upheld because the Court itself had no standard but its murky intuition.[17]

Thus in 1908 the Court began to see-saw. The Court first wrestled with the politically explosive issue of the labor union. Congress had outlawed a common railroad practice of threatening employees with discharge or discrimination if they continued their membership in a union. Established in the same act was a procedure to mediate and settle railway labor disputes. The necessity for the law, said the Senate committee which drafted the bill, "arises from the calamitous results in the way of ill-considered strikes arising from the tyranny of capital on the unjust demands of labor organizations, whereby the business of the country is brought to a standstill and thousands of employes, with their helpless wives and children, are confronted with starvation. . . . It is our opinion that this bill, should it become law, would reduce to a minimum labor strikes which affect interstate commerce." But the Court saw the law as an infringement on the liberty of

---

[17] *Cf.* Friedman, "Freedom of Contract and Occupational Licensing, 1890–1910: A Legal and Social Study," 53 *Calif. L. Rev.* 487 (1965): "If a workman had a constitutional and God-given right to contract to work eleven hours a day in a bakeshop or to be paid in kind instead of cash, he should have had a similar right to contract with an unlicensed barber or to buy a laxative from a druggist without a certificate on his wall. Similarly, the right of the barber to sell his services without 'paternal interference' from the state might seem as cogent as the right of a bakery owner to buy labor unimpeded."

the employer to offer employment on whatever terms he desired — a premise, of course, but hardly a conclusion — and the practical ability of men to join unions was mooted by the vindicated liberty of the mighty companies to discharge any employee who did so.[18]

Yet 1908 was also a year for the economic protection of women, and a personal triumph for Louis D. Brandeis, who won an important case. Oregon had enacted a law limiting employment of women to ten hours a day "in any mechanical establishment, factory, or laundry." The $10 fine against Muller, convicted of violating the statute, was appealed to the Supreme Court, which held that the distinction between men and women was sufficient to justify the distinction between *Lochner* and the decision in *Muller v. Oregon*.[19] The Court was evidently awed by the "Brandeis brief": a document with three pages of legal argument and ninety-seven pages of social facts and statistics "diagnos[ing] factory conditions and their effect on individual workers and the public health."[20] Taking "judicial cognizance" of the commonly held "belief that woman's physical structure and the functions she performs in consequence thereof justify special legislation restricting or qualifying the conditions under which she should be permitted to toil," the Court upheld the law. "As healthy mothers are essential to vigorous offspring, the physical well-being of woman becomes an object of public interest and care in order to preserve the strength and vigor of the race." What of the liberty of the menopausal woman to contract her hours as she saw fit? Lost in the golden fog of Mr. Justice Brewer's declamations that such legislation is justified to protect womankind "from the greed as well as the passion of man."[21]

For nearly thirty years thereafter, the Court weaved a wobbly course, creating uncertainty on the infrequent occasions when

[18] Adair v. United States, 208 U. S. 161, 187 (1908).

[19] 208 U.S. 412 (1908).

[20] See Attorney General Biddle's remarks at the Proceedings to Honor the memory of Mr. Justice Brandeis, 317 U.S. xxxviii (1942).

[21] *Muller* v. *Oregon, supra* note 19, at 420, 421, 422.

it would find it possible to uphold economic legislation. In 1915 it voided a Kansas law forbidding yellow-dog contracts: Employers refusing to hire workers unless they agreed to drop out of their unions were subject to fines under the law.[22]   In 1917 the Court seemed to repudiate *Lochner* when it upheld an Oregon law limiting the hours of factory, mill, and manufacturing hands, except for emergencies and for a permissible three hours a day overtime, for which time and half was required to be paid. Against the claim that it was a "wage law" which took employers' property without due process of law, the Court avowed that "the Constitutional validity of legislation cannot be determined by the degree of exactness of its provisions or remedies."[23]   But in 1918 the Court invalidated the federal child labor law, whose purpose was to keep out of interstate commerce goods produced in factories by children under fourteen years of age.[24]   Congress responded by enacting the Child Labor Tax Law, imposing a ten per cent tax on the net profits of any employer using the labor of children under fourteen for the production of goods traveling in interstate commerce.   The Court struck that down too.[25]   In 1923 the Court voided a law establishing minimum wages for women in the District of Columbia.[26]   And in 1924 a complex Nebraska bakery law, regulating weights of bread and establishing maximum sizes to prevent fraud, was undone with these words: "A state may not, under guise of protecting the public, arbitrarily interfere with private business or prohibit lawful occupations or impose unreasonable and unnecessary restrictions upon them. . . . It is the duty of the court to determine whether the challenged provision . . . really tends to accomplish the purpose for which it was enacted."[27] To this approach, Justice Brandeis responded in dissent at length,

[22] Coppage v. Kansas, 236 U.S. 1 (1915).
[23] Bunting v. Oregon, 243 U.S. 426, 438 (1917).
[24] Hammer v. Dagenhart, 247 U.S. 251 (1918).
[25] Child Labor Tax Case, 259 U.S. 20 (1922).
[26] Adkins v. Children's Hospital, 261 U.S. 525 (1923).
[27] Burns Baking Co. v. Bryan, 264 U.S. 504, 513 (1924).

meticulously describing bread conditions in Nebraska to show that "the provision as applied is [not] so clearly arbitrary or capricious that legislators acting reasonably could not have believed it to be necessary or appropriate for the public welfare."[28]

Occasionally the minority philosophy would command the Court. Thus, a New York law prohibiting the sale of eyeglasses at retail stores unless a licensed physician or optometrist was in charge of the counter was challenged as usual on the ground that it violated the liberty of work protected by the due process clause. The law covered the sale of ordinary magnifying spectacles; it did not require the optometrist to examine the eyes before selling the glasses. A professionally-inspired monopoly, charged the challenger, who lost. Assuming that the optometrist would naturally examine the eyes when he thought necessary, Justice Holmes for the Court upheld the law: "A statute is not invalid under the Constitution because it might have gone farther than it did, or because it may not succeed in bringing about the result that it intends to produce. . . . We cannot say, as the complainants would have us say, that the supposed benefits are a cloak for establishing a monopoly and a pretence."[29]

But the Court did not usually allow even professionals to meddle with the market. A Pennsylvania requirement that drug stores be owned by licensed pharmacists only and not by corporations unless all stockholders were pharmacists, was struck down,[30] as was an Oklahoma law that closely regulated the manufacture, sale, and distribution of ice. Ice making, the Court averred, was an "ordinary business," not a "paramount industry upon which the prosperity of the entire state in large measure depends."[31]

On the basis of the Court's economic due process doctrine, many state courts took a dim view of the scope of their state's police power. A Kentucky law requiring moral fitness for the

28 *Burns*, at 534.
29 Roschen v. Ward, 279 U.S. 337, 339, 340 (1929).
30 Liggett Co. v. Baldridge Co., 378 U.S. 105 (1829).
31 New State Ice Co. v. Liebmann, 285 U.S. 262, 277 (1932).

issuance of a real estate license was undercut by the state court when it directed the state licensing board to issue a license to a broker accused of fraud and misrepresentation. "If occasional opportunity for fraud is to be the test, then there is no reason why every grocer, every merchant, every automobile dealer, every keeper of a garage, and every manufacturer, and every mechanic who deals more frequently with the public in general and whose opportunities for fraud are far greater than those of the real estate agent or salesman, may not be put on the same basis. If that be done, then only those who, in the opinion of certain boards or the courts, have the necessary moral qualifications, will be permitted to engage in the ordinary occupations of life."[32]

Similarly, the Oklahoma Supreme Court struck down an accountants' licensing law on the ground that it denied the hiring businessman the liberty to contract with anyone he pleased for the carrying on of his private business. The court assumed that the "accountant has to do with what is recognized as an exact science. The correctness or incorrectness of the conclusion reached is subject to proof or disproof to the exactness of an absolute demonstration."[33] However wrong the court may have been about the state of the accounting art, its reasoning admitted a significant exception to the standard due process argument; those trades and professions which "are of such nature that the result of the services rendered cannot always be definitely known or determined, but reliance must be had upon the knowledge and skill of the one performing the service" could be constitutionally regulated.

Increasingly during the 1920's, doctors, lawyers, dentists, pharmacists, accountants, beauticians, barbers, and others were licensed and held to standards determined by public and private agencies. Always these regulations were justified by an appeal to the precarious position of the public health in an unregulated, but nevertheless complex, modern society. In many instances, courts upheld the regulations. In even more instances, cases never reached the

[32] Rawles v. Jenkins, 212 Ky. 287, 279 S.W. 350, 352 (1926).
[33] State ex rel. Short v. Riedell, 109 Okla. 35, 233 P. 684, 687 (1924).

courts: Professionals, after all, had sought their own regulation; and it was not the consumer or worker who had challenged regulations on the belief that it restricted the right to contract.

The confident '20's gave way to the crisis and despair of Depression. The election of Franklin D. Roosevelt and a New Deal Congress committed to experiment, precipitated in turn a first-class judicial crisis. For the Court's interpretation of due process ran head-on into the attempts of Congress and the Administration to deal with complex, disturbing, and mysterious problems. In rapid succession in 1935, the Supreme Court struck down the Railway Pension Act, the Farm Mortgage Act, providing bankruptcy relief for farmers in debt, the National Industrial Recovery Act. These decisions were followed the next year by the voiding of the Agricultural Adjustment Act of 1933, the Bituminous Coal Conservation Act of 1935, and a New York woman's minimum wage law.[34]

With the National Labor Relations Act, the Tennessee Valley Authority Act, important provisions of the Social Security Act, and the Public Utility Holding Company Act, among others, nearing the Supreme Court docket, the Administration announced its "court packing" plan. The President sought the power to appoint additional judges to the Supreme Court. In a radio address in 1937 President Roosevelt called attention to the need for "new blood": "We must have Judges who will bring to the Courts a present-day sense of the Constitution — Judges who will retain in the Courts the judicial functions of a court, and reject the legislative powers which the Courts have today assumed."[35]

The attack failed but it so unnerved the Court that the battle was won. The threat of legislation aimed at controlling the Court

[34] Railway Retirement Board v. Alton R.R., 295 U.S. 330 (1935); Louisville Joint Stock Land Bank v. Radford, 295 U.S. 555 (1935); Schechter Poultry Corp. v. United States, 295 U.S. 495 (1935); United States v. Butler, 297 U.S. 1 (1936); Carter v. Carter Coal Co., 298 U.S. 238 (1936); Morehead v. Tipaldo, 298 U.S. 587 (1936).

[35] Quoted in Freund, Sutherland, Howe, and Brown, *Cases on Constitutional Law* (1961), p. 244.

produced the remarkable "switch in time that saved nine."[36] Shortly after limited reforms — such as the provision extending retirement privileges to the Justices for the first time — were enacted by Congress, the Court utterly reversed its due process decisions. With Senator Hugo Black taking the place of the first of the retiring Justices in 1937, the Court quickly upheld the Washington State minimum wage law for women, the National Labor Relations Act, the Social Security Act old-age benefits provisions, and the Social Security Act employer tax.[37] The old cases were dead; many of them expressly repudiated. The position of the Court became that which had been urged upon it for so long by Holmes and Brandeis, dissenting: The question to determine in due process cases from then on was not whether the legislation under attack would reasonably achieve the ends for which it was designed, but whether the legislature reasonably thought so. For the remedy against unreasonable economic laws, the people were directed to the polls, as *Munn v. Illinois* had prescribed sixty years before.

The ramifications of the Court's decision to abstain in economic due process cases were yet to become clear. The same Depression that killed the doctrine of economic due process also proved a fertile creator of licensing legislation that prevented further reductions in already meager incomes. By the time specialty legislation became galvanic, the Supreme Court had switched, and the new economics soon reached the state courts. Economics is a complex subject, difficult enough for economists; there was nowhere near sufficient time for harried judges to ponder the impact of economic doctrine on legal thought. So economic due process was abandoned just at the time a refined version was growing necessary.

Constitutionality is often mistakenly confused with legislative

---

[36] For an entertaining and enlightening discussion of the great reversal, see Alpheus Thomas Mason, *The Supreme Court from Taft to Warren* (1958).

[37] West Coast Hotel Co. v. Parrish, 300 U.S. 379 (1937); National Labor Relations Board v. Jones & Laughlin Steel Corp., 301 U.S. 1 (1937); Helvering v. Davis, 301 U.S. 619 (1937); Steward Machine Co. v. Davis, 301 U.S. 548 (1937).

wisdom. When the Supreme Court finally withdrew itself from the economic throne, its philosophical change had three important effects: (1) The Court itself, as we shall shortly see, was impelled to go as far in abdicating its responsibility to decide the reasonableness of state regulations as it had formerly been in error in assuming that power. (2) State courts could have decided that the due process required by state constitutions was of somewhat different character from the due process mandated by the federal constitution. But the Supreme Court position was sufficiently influential to make most of them follow the leader most of the time. (3) Because it was well known that state legislation would not be upset — in many cases no matter how outrageous — legislators forgot to ask themselves whether the methods of regulation they established were wise and whether it was prudent to choose the professionals as regulators. The Court's position and its effects have given rise to what I call "undue process," which must next be explored.

3

The case that reduced the due process inquiry in the economic realm from a question of purpose to an inquiry about the fairness of the procedures used to achieve the now concededly lawful purposes was *West Coast Hotel Co. v. Parrish.*[38] Washington State had enacted a "minimum wages for women law," which established an Industrial Welfare Commission to investigate conditions in various industries and empowered it to set minimum wages. West Coast Hotel refused to pay Elsie Parrish the full $14.50 per forty-eight-hour week the Commission had fixed for hotel chambermaids; but the State supreme court upheld the legislation and awarded Mrs. Parrish the money. The hotel challenged the decision in an appeal to the Supreme Court, basing its attack on the direct precedent settled by the Court fourteen years before in

[38] *Supra* note 37.

Adkins v. Children's Hospital,[39] in which it was held that Congress had no power to fix minimum wages for women in the District of Columbia. To the hotel's surprise, that case was expressly overruled. "Liberty of contract" in the context of hour and wage legislation was seen to be a hoax: "The exploitation of a class of workers who are in an unequal position with respect to bargaining power and are thus relatively defenceless against the denial of a living wage is not only detrimental to their health and well-being but casts a direct burden for their support upon the community."[40] Whether the minimum wage law adequately solved the problem was not for the Court to say; it was enough for constitutionality that legislators had ample grounds to believe it might. The police power was returned to the station house.

It became apparent that an unfettered police power could prove an effective aid to underprivileged peoples. A Michigan statute forbidding any female from being a bartender unless she were wife or daughter of a male bar owner was upheld by the Court in 1948. The law prohibited issuance of licenses to women bartenders in cities with populations greater than 50,000. Though there was no express prohibition against a woman owning a bar herself, she would not be permitted under this law from selling in it, even if her husband were around to maintain order. Yet under the same law, a woman whose husband owned the bar could dispense drinks from the bar all day though her husband be separated from her and living across the continent. Even more curiously, the law permitted women to act as waitresses in bars. Evidently the law was a method of restricting the competition with male bartenders. But the Court, speaking through Mr. Justice Frankfurter, could not bring itself to believe that there were no reasonable grounds for the enactment: "Michigan evidently believes that the oversight assured through ownership of a bar by a barmaid's husband or father minimizes hazards that may confront a barmaid without such protecting oversight. The Court is cer-

[39] *Supra* note 26.
[40] *Supra* note 37 at 399.

tainly not in a position to gainsay such belief by the Michigan legislature."[41]

The next year the Court considered a South Carolina law prohibiting life insurance companies from engaging in undertaking. Only one undertaking establishment in the entire state also sold life insurance and it complied in every detail with the state insurance code. A lower state court, concluding that the legislation was passed at the behest of the company's competitors to put it out of business, voided the statute. The highest state court reversed, and on appeal the Supreme Court agreed. The legislation was not clearly unreasonable, said the Court, since the South Carolina legislature may have concluded that the possibility that the insured's premiums might go partly for funeral expenses was an evil to be avoided, just as the state had for years proscribed the "payment of insurance proceeds in merchandise or services." The insured, because he went monthly to the funeral home to pay his insurance, might get the idea that he should avail himself of an expensive funeral someday from his own insurance company.[42]

In 1955 the Supreme Court went the limit in its repudiation of the old economic due process doctrine. An Oklahoma law forbids opticians from fitting frames or grinding lenses without a prescription from a licensed ophthalmologist or optometrist. Advertising the sale of frames was also outlawed. A three-judge federal district court issued an injunction against enforcement of the law, finding it particularly unreasonable that an optician would need a prescription in order to fit frames alone to the face, and perceiving no relation between advertising frames for sale and the public health. On direct appeal, the Supreme Court reversed. Said Justice Douglas for the Court: "The Oklahoma law may exact a needless, wasteful requirement in many cases. But it is for the legislature, not the courts, to balance the advantages and disadvantages of the new requirement. . . . The legislature might

41 Goesaert v. Cleary, 335 U.S. 464, 466 (1948).
42 Daniel v. Family Life Ins. Co., 336 U.S. 220 (1949).

have concluded that the frequency of occasions when a prescription is necessary was sufficient to justify this regulation of the fitting of eyeglasses. . . . To be sure, the present law does not require a new examination of the eyes every time the frames are changed or the lenses duplicated. For if the old prescription is on file with the optician, he can go ahead and make the new fitting or duplicate the lenses. But the law need not be in every respect logically consistent with its aims to be constitutional."[43] Justice Douglas also noted, with respect to the ban on solicitation, that "an eyeglass frame, considered in isolation, is only a piece of merchandise. But an eyeglass frame is not used in isolation . . . ; it is used with lenses; and lenses, pertaining as they do to the human eye, enter the field of health. Therefore, the legislature might conclude that to regulate one effectively it would have to regulate the other.[44] That is only one notch more persuasive than banning the advertisement of empty glass spice jars on the ground that dangerous poisons might be put inside them once they were bought.

If the remedy for legislative abuses is not to be gained from the Supreme Court, it is not likely the state courts will provide relief either. In an important Depression case upholding the power of the Oklahoma Board of Barber Examiners to fix minimum prices, the state supreme court in 1938 rejected as irrelevant the argument that the litigant seeking an injunction against enforcement of the minimum price had built up a substantial business by charging low prices but nevertheless meeting sanitary regulations. Under the law, the Board could impose a minimum price after seventy-five per cent of the duly licensed barbers of any city of greater than 1000 population agreed that such a limitation would be helpful. The court approved the scheme and did not consider alternatives that might have equally maintained health conditions.

[43] Lee Optical Co. v. Williamson, 348 U.S. 483, 487–8 (1955).
[44] Supra note 43, at 490.

For this was Depression, and minimum prices were more valuable than sanitation.[45]

This decision was the basis for upholding in 1949 the power of the same state's Dry Cleaners' Board to fix minimum prices. Again, seventy-five per cent of the licensed dry cleaners had to agree to request the Board's imprimatur. "All of the testimony introduced at the hearing was to the general effect that the minimum prices sought and stipulated in the agreement were necessary to afford efficient labor, proper sanitation, the best and least injurious solvents, the best and least dangerous equipment, and best protection against fire hazard," said the court.[46] That health codes with sufficient enforcement provisions could do a better job of protection was undebated; that "efficient labor" meant nothing more than that the dry cleaners would pay their employees more — and doubtless make them more comfortable — if they could do so with the assurance that they would not be undercut by anyone else was an exceedingly roundabout approach to a minimum wage law.

It was a bad time to recall the old liberty of a man to engage in his calling unhampered by moral qualifications and doubts as to his competency. The Kentucky court, which years before had ordered the Real Estate Commission to award a license regardless of the applicant's moral qualification, emerged into the new era. When a real estate broker sued for his commission in 1948, the defendants answered that the salesman did not have a real estate license, without which, under Kentucky law, no court could award him his commission. The broker claimed the law was unconstitutional. The court disagreed: "There is much buying and selling of property through real estate brokers, and it certainly concerns public morals and welfare to have such brokers and agents identified and regulated by the State and required to execute a bond that they will conform to sound business practices,

[45] Herrin v. Arnold, District Judge, 183 Okla. 392, 82 P. 2d 977 (1938).
[46] State Dry Cleaners' Board v. Compton, 201 Okla. 284, 205 P. 2d 286, 286–7 (1949).

the violation of which will cause a revocation of their licenses."[47] So intent on upholding the law was the Kentucky supreme court that it ignored altogether the case that had been squarely to the contrary two decades before.[48] Five years later, the same court ringingly affirmed the power of the state to require licensing examinations for real estate brokers, banishing all doubts that the state's police power encompassed professional regulation. The old case was clearly repudiated, but *sub silentio*, for there was no citation of the earlier case, even to show how error-ridden it had been.[49]

The net effect of the vast extension of the police power was to abrogate the sensible policy that men did have the right to work as individuals and not as part of a larger body of fellow workers bound together in guilds. When any conduct that touched on the public health, safety, and welfare could lawfully be regulated, it was inevitable that the practice of any trade or profession would become a privilege to which the state could attach whatever standards of "responsible" conduct it desired. The Michigan Supreme Court spoke typically for the countless other cases in all other states when it upheld the State Optometry Board's power to deny a license to an Illinois-qualified optometrist who had attended a college not accredited in Michigan, and which did not provide a long enough course of instruction. "The rule [denying entry] does not deprive plaintiff of any personal property rights. His right to practice optometry is a privilege granted by the State and is subject to the statutory law and the reasonable and proper rules of the Board."[50] The rule that whatever is "affected with a public interest" may be regulated has been repeated so often it is

---

[47] Shelton v. McCarroll, 308 Ky. 280, 214 .W. 2d 396, 398 (1948).
[48] See p. 188f.
[49] Sims v. Reeves, 261 S.W. 2d 812 (Ky. 1953).
[50] Coffman v. State Board of Examiners in Optometry, 331 Mich. 582, 50 N.W. 2d 322, 326 (1951). Although the statutory accreditation provision was declared unconstitutional, the Court upheld the State Board's promulgation of a rule requiring twice as much schooling as the statute required. "It does not follow that the Board cannot within reason adopt higher standards than the minimum set up in the legislation."

now trite that a "legitimate" occupation may not be suppressed but may be regulated whenever the regulation bears a reasonable relation to the public health, safety, or welfare. Since that rule is so large it includes all possible cases, the courts apply it with a simple abandon: Rarely is an occupation unrelated to the well-being of the public.

4

So much for the regulatory aspect of self-regulation. It must next be inquired why and how the professionals came constitutionally to be the regulators.

The professional association in its bid for public power has consistently shielded itself behind the ancient fiction that it is a "private" organization entitled to the full panoply of constitutional protections afforded natural citizens by the Fourteenth Amendment. From the very series of Supreme Court cases during the 1870's and 1880's that held businessmen could be regulated despite the Amendment came the doctrine, astonishing in some ways, that except for voting and political representation the corporation is a "person" entitled to the protections of constitutional due process. From this position it was easy twenty years later to find the state depriving these "people" of their property in unconstitutional ways. In 1898, for example, the Court declared in *Smyth v. Ames*[51] that valid railroad rate regulation depended upon a company's earning a "fair" rate of return on the value of its land. This doctrine has been termed the "fair value fallacy,"[52] for the value of land was determined by the rates railroad companies had been able to charge. If just compensation requires the giving back to a company the value of what had been limited by regulation precisely because the rate was exorbitant, then regulation was self-defeating. Yet so it was held for more than forty years.[53]

---

[51] *Supra* note 9.
[52] See Robert L. Hale, *Freedom Through Law: Public Control of Private Governing Power* (1952), pp. 462 ff.
[53] The doctrine was finally rejected in Federal Power Comm. v. Hope Natural Gas Co., 320 U.S. 591 (1940).

Professional associations have managed to avoid public regulation because public scrutiny has been limited by an acceptance of the associations' assertions that they are "private." The Fifth and Fourteenth Amendments prohibit federal and state governments from depriving persons of life, liberty, and property without due process of law; they do not prohibit "private" persons from effecting such deprivations. As early as 1833 the Supreme Court fixed the doctrine that the Fifth Amendment is a limitation on the power of the federal government only. State governments remained free to take property without due process[54] until the oversight was corrected by ratification of the Fourteenth Amendment thirty-five years later. But the judicial opinions construing these amendments have consistently held since the time of the *Civil Rights Cases*[55] in 1883 that the Fourteenth Amendment does not limit private power (although, as we shall see, it does permit Congress to enact laws that restrict private acts).

That private associations license, discipline, and regulate professionals — or have a decided impact on their licensing, disciplining, and regulating — is rarely considered an act of the states for the purpose of bringing the associations within the scope of the Amendment. In case after case, expulsions from professional associations have been treated merely as the highhanded and unreviewable actions of private clubs.[56] The judicial attitude may be changing as reality begins to intrude into the lawyers' brief; yet despite the fact that Dr. Hawkins' case was overruled on appeal, the attitude that professional groups are private is widespread and they remain hostile to judicial scrutiny.

The return to guilds — private associations whose controls over members affect the public aspect of the professions — is not, as

---

[54] Barron v. Baltimore, 33 U.S. (7 Pet.) 243 (1833).

[55] 109 U.S. 3 (1833).

[56] See "Equitable Jurisdiction to Protect Membership in a Voluntary Association," 58 *Yale L. J.* 1000 (1949); "Judicial Control of Actions of Private Associations," 76 *Harv. L. Rev.* 983 (1963); "Legal Responsibility for Extra-Legal Censure," 62 *Col. L. Rev.* 475 (1962); "Exclusion from Private Associations," 74 *Yale L. J.* 1313 (1965).

we have seen, merely theorctical. So far has the concept spread
that membership in some private associations has become legislatively mandatory with nary a constitutional whimper. In 1956
the Supreme Court of Wisconsin ordered the integration of the
state bar[57] imposing on all lawyers as a condition to practicing
law the obligation to pay $15 dues to the state bar association.
Trayton L. Lathrop, a practicing attorney, protested. He claimed
that the state could not constitutionally compel him to join and pay
dues to an association which included among its activities the
formulation of opinion purporting to represent that of all state
lawyers in order to promote certain legislative policies. Lathrop
lost at the state level and appealed to the Supreme Court. Although
a majority could not agree why, the Court by a 7–2 vote sustained
the compulsory payment.[58]

Lathrop claimed that his freedoms of speech and association
were abridged by the integration order. The state proclaimed
the power to compel payment on the ground, as the Wisconsin
court put it, that "the general public and the legislature are entitled
to know how the profession as a whole stands on such type of proposed legislation."[59] The payment was also justified on the ground
that since there is no constitutional right to be a lawyer, the state
may declare by way of regulations what duty the lawyer owes to
the public. Although there is a line of doubtful Supreme Court
cases to this effect,[60] the usual starting point for this justification
was then Chief Justice Holmes' pungent remark in dismissing a
suit by a policeman who had been discharged by the mayor of

[57] Re Integration of Bar, 273 Wisc. 281, 77 N.W. 2d 602 (1956) (two-year
trial period); Re Integration of Bar, 5 Wisc. 2d 618, 93 N.W. 2d 601 (1958)
(continued indefinitely).

[58] Lathrop v. Donahue, 367 U.S. 820 (1961).

[59] Lathrop v. Donahue, 10 Wisc. 2d 230, 102 N.W. 2d 404, 409 (1960). Cf.
the dissent of Justice Black, *supra* note 58, at 874: "I feel entirely confident
that the Framers of the First Amendment would never have struck the balance against freedom on the basis of such a demonstrably specious
expediency."

[60] Beginning with Bradwell v. Illinois, 83 U.S. (16 Wall.) 36 (1873).

New Medford, Massachusetts, after a hearing in which the police-man was apparently found to have solicited money for political purposes and to have been a member of a "political committee" in violation of city regulations. Chief Justice Holmes said, "There is nothing in the Constitution or the statute to prevent the city from attaching obedience to this rule as a condition to the office of policeman, and making it part of the good conduct required. The petitioner may have a constitutional right to talk politics, but he has no constitutional right to be a policeman."[61]

The plurality opinion[62] dismissed Lathrop's contentions on the authority of a markedly dissimilar case[63] in which the power of a union to compel payment of dues was upheld. No claim was made that the union engaged in political activities; in fact, the question whether such activities would make compulsory payment a violation of the First Amendment was explicitly reserved. In the course of that case, the Court said, "On the present record [no political activities] there is no more an infringement or impairment of first amendment rights than there would be in the case of a lawyer who by state law is required to be a member of an inte-grated bar."[64] This became the sole precedent supporting Lathrop; the circularity of the reasoning should be apparent.[65]

[61] McAulifee v. Mayor of New Bedford, 155 Mass. 216, 29 N.E. 517 (1892). This position has been greatly circumscribed by such cases as Keyishian v. Board of Regents, 385 U.S. 589 (1967) but because Justice Holmes said it, the thought continues to haunt the halls of legislatures and the pages of constitutional law.

[62] Joined in by Chief Justice Warren and Justices Clark and Stewart. The opinion itself was written by Justice Brennan. Justice Harlan, though con-curring in result, disagreed with these four, who held that no constitutional issues were raised. He thought the case raised such issues and was prepared to settle them against Lathrop. Justice Frankfurter concurred with Harlan. Justice Whittaker concurred in the result. Justices Black and Douglas saw the constitutional issues and dissented. Thus four of the seven Justices who voted against Lathrop saw no constitutional issues; but five of the nine did see them. What the case actually stands for is in doubt.

[63] Railway Employees Dep't v. Hanson, 351 U.S. 225 (1955).

[64] Railway Employees, at 339.

[65] The dictum in Hanson concerning the integrated bar, an issue neither

Even if this bootstrap method of reasoning is not fatal, the circumstances of the cases are entirely different. *Lathrop* raised the question which the union case specifically reserved.[66] Furthermore, the one involved a forced payment to a union; the other, to a professional association. If there is any justification for compulsory payment to a union engaged in political activities, it is far from obvious that it automatically carries over to the professional association. The professional association does not serve the countervailing power function of the union; professionals in their business dealings face an unorganized body of consumers, not an amassed, resisting power.[67]

The legislative matters concerning which the state bar took a stand contrary to Lathrop's political opinions ("technical" matters: administration of justice in Wisconsin, court reform, legal practice, divorce reform) were not related to the end of serving lawyers as a professional group, except in an unexpected way.[68] But in any event, the integration of the bar was not ordered to enhance the working conditions of lawyers. Union payments can

briefed nor argued, is said to support the result in *Lathrop;* yet in fact *Hanson* follows *a fortiori* from *Lathrop;* that is the very reason for the *Hanson* Court's example of the integrated bar.

[66] The plurality opinion said the political activity issue was not raised since Lathrop did not *specify* in what way he disagreed with the state bar's political position. This disavowal of the free speech issue is disingenuous; if the facts of this case do not raise the issue it is difficult to see what set of facts would. And, as noted, *supra* note 62, a majority of the Court did see the issue in a constitutional light.

[67] "The notion," said Justice Frankfurter, "that economic and political concerns are separable is pre-Victorian. . . . It is not true in life that political protection is irrelevant to, and insulated from, economic interests. It is not true for industry or finance. Neither is it true for labor." Dissenting opinion in International Association of Machinists v. Street, 367 U.S. 740, 814–15 (1961) (companion case to *Lathrop*). So conceived, the argument misses the point when applied to the professions. Professional associations do not exercise countervailing power against the employers of their members; when the associations are given regulatory power, it is ostensibly for the purpose of *curtailing* the power of individual practitioners to engage in unscrupulous conduct, not to enhance their power to bargain.

[68] See Chapter 6.

be justified only because they support the cause and promote the purposes of the unions and labor itself — the workers are forced to help the general good of the workers; society, the legislatures have determined, has an interest in giving workers the means to develop bargaining power equal to that of their employers. Professional payments, on the other hand, fall in a substantially dissimilar category; society may have an interest in giving lawyers the means to promoting the general public welfare, but it should not have an interest in giving them a magnified bargaining power used against clients and society. Logic does not require the compulsion rule in the case of the union to extend to the case of an integrated bar.

If the state has an interest in technical law reform, it may tax all the people and form a law revision commission not controlled by private attorneys. Or the state legislature may vote itself a higher staff budget so it can appoint qualified counsel to give technical advice. In short, the state's method of obtaining advice on substantive legislation is unreasonable when compared to the policies inherent in the First Amendment. Alternatives are open to the state which do not violate these policies.

The grounds on which Lathrop was defeated are untenable. No constitutional provision or even any case construing any doctrine was cited which "entitles" the public to know the lawyers' views on legislation of any sort. It is doubtful, furthermore, that the state will get any representative expression (the explicit goal), since actual control of private associations almost always goes by default to a small number of active leaders.[69] Nor are cases cited which support the proposition that the lawyer has a "duty to the public." In a concurring opinion, Justice Whittaker simply stated that the practice of law is a "special privilege."[70] The danger of conditioning the exercise of the "privilege" on the waiver of constitutional rights may not be obvious but it is critical, for

[69] See McConnell, "The Spirit of Private Government," 52 *Am. Pol. Sci. Rev.* 762 (1958).

[70] *Lathrop, supra* note 58 at p. 865.

when everything is a privilege, all rights are gone.[71] Finally, no reasons were advanced to suggest what makes the legal profession different from all other professions; indeed, none are apparent and no limits on the state's regulatory power are suggested. It is arguable that Lathrop could be compelled to pay dues to support those activities which police the conduct of the profession, though it is difficult to see why. Corporation directors, who have a fiduciary relation to their companies, are not required to belong to an association of directors; they are policed by the statutes and the common law of the states.

The reasons advanced in support of Wisconsin's integration order are chimerical at best. When placed against the reasons for countermanding it, they dissolve altogether. The malady of compulsory payment to an organization which engages in political expression contrary to the belief of the member is not quite the disease of *Gobitis*[72] by which school children, Jehovah's Witnesses, were forced to say aloud the pledge of allegiance in spite of their religious convictions. When the Supreme Court overruled itself three years later,[73] it said that the state could not force an unwilling participant to avow a position contrary to his religious beliefs. It is possible here to argue that Lathrop is not "supporting" the association in that sense. He merely pays dues. He can speak against the bar's political position, and will, after all, have something to say about how the money is spent since he is a member of the association. That support of the bar is passive, however, does not make it any less objectionable. Though Lathrop is not required to agree with the association's views or recite a vow supporting its political philosophy, his forced contribution to a cause with which he disagrees is still support. For it is not true that he is merely paying dues; money is subsidizing views disagreeable to him. Could a Catholic who supports birth control be compelled to pay dues to a Catholic organization lobbying against

---

[71] See Note, "Unconstitutional Conditions," 73 *Harv. L. Rev.* 1595 (1960).
[72] Minersville School District v. Gobitis, 310 U.S. 586 (1940).
[73] West Virginia State Board of Educ. v. Barnette, 319 U.S. 624 (1943).

birth control, simply because the state has an interest in hearing the "Catholic view"? Could a doctor who disagreed be forced by law to contribute to a fund which was used by the AMA to lobby against Medicare, again on the ground that the state had an interest in organized medicine's views? Nor should the substitution of political beliefs for religious beliefs divert the thrust of the argument. Here, as in the Jehovah's Witnesses' case, the freedom which Lathrop asserts does not collide with rights claimed by any other person.

That Lathrop can involve himself in the internal affairs of the state bar matters little. Lathrop is a lawyer, not a politician. It does not save the day to justify the dues by giving the man a fighting chance to persuade his colleagues to vote his way. The wrong of taking his money is not righted by allowing him to do something he does not want to do. The choice between spending time away from his law practice or suffering in silence as his bar goes down a path he cannot follow is by any test too harsh when weighed against a not-insubstantial right to earn a living.

Yet the Supreme Court permitted it all. The Court did not endorse the policy of the integrated bar; the discussion preceding is not so much to say the Court was necessarily wrong as to demonstrate just how far the Court is willing to go in its abdication of the economic due process doctrine. For this was not an economic regulation of the state legislature — it was a decree with political overtones by a state court granting substantial power to an association of attorneys to regulate themselves.

The Court's decision to let the integrated bar stand has important political and economic effects. First, it gives the bar association a megaphone aimed at the state legislature and puts a select group of men at the mouthpiece. By amplifying the majority viewpoint it weakens the minority dissent correspondingly. Lathrop must try far harder to persuade the public or the legislature that he is right since he must overcome a well-heeled prestigious group. If there is little reason to believe the individual lawyer would speak his mind to the public and be heard, there is less reason to believe he will be heard once an integrated bar is formed. Rather than facing chaos and seeking to impose order, he must confront an organized opposition; that task is far more onerous. Second, requiring a dissenting practitioner to join an association places other restraints on him. Whenever the association has a good deal of say over the individual's ethical and professional life, he is under at least some pressure to remain in the favor of his professional leaders. Such pressure may well force curtailment of dissent.

5

So regulation has become freedom: The people are free from hazards to health and welfare when the professionals are regulated, and the professionals are free from the people when they control the regulations and define what health and welfare are. The professions may consistently be regulated, but professional associations may not be.

It is possible, on the other hand, that this kind of freedom may move to the model of Orwell. From *Lathrop*, Justice Douglas stingingly dissented that "the pattern of this legislation is regimentation. . . . The regimentation appears in humble form today. . . . Once we approve this measure, we sanction a device where men and women in almost any profession or calling can be at least partially regimented behind causes which they oppose. . . . We practically give *carte blanche* to any legislature to put at least professional people into goose-stepping brigades."[74] That Justice Douglas may be partially responsible for the Court's position by forcefully advocating withdrawal from substantive due process since his accession to the Court in 1939 is not entirely beside the point. Though constitutionality should not be confused with wisdom, it often is and it may well be necessary for the Court once more to reconcile the two.

[74] *Lathrop, supra* note 58 at 882-4.

12
The Abdication of Responsibility

They ask me what right I have as a biologist to speak about these complicated issues [of war and peace]. I have the right of an American citizen.
— Dr. GEORGE WALD, *The New York Times Magazine* (August 17, 1969)

1

Under the onslaught of professional claims, the public is rapidly abdicating its responsibility to solve community problems. The responsibility for solution—as well as the blame for origin—is shifted to the expert. Nowhere is the abdication or responsibility more evident than in the belief that Chief Justice Earl Warren should have been impeached and the Supreme Court blamed for crime in the streets and other more imagined ills. If only the Court would allow this confession or that to be used in trial, if only the Court would not handcuff the police, say Court opponents, rape, rioting, and murder would quickly be reduced. Some crimes are removed enough from the peaceful citizen's impulses and thinking that it seems only natural to blame its increase on the agency which is supposed to deal with it. That ninety per cent of criminal convictions in some jurisdictions are obtained by guilty pleas subsequent to the Court's major rulings on use of confessions and other

207

evidence does not seem to be a controlling consideration.[1] It is easier to blame one's intractable problems on others. But not until people come to see the root causes of their problems and make determined legislative efforts to overcome them will anything remotely resembling solutions come to pass.[2]

The general abdication of responsibility extends from the highest councils of government to the most mundane decisions of the common citizen. Because they are supposed to have a special competence, experts are given power over their respective realms by Presidents and desperate commoners alike. Thus President Nixon has given to the American Bar Association a veto power over appointments to all federal courts except the Supreme Court. That this delegation would be unconstitutional were it formalized was considered irrelevant to the heartfelt necessity of insuring appointments be ratified by those who know best. If the policy is adhered to, the federal judiciary will shortly become the worse for it and the next President will repudiate the idea, reasserting his constitutional mandate to appoint judges with the consent of the Senate.[3] But the President's abdication of constitutional and political re-

[1] Statistics for 89 selected United States District Courts for the fiscal year ended June 30, 1968, show that of a total of 25,674 convictions, 22,055, or 88 per cent, resulted from guilty pleas. An additional 6,169 defendants were not convicted (nearly 5,000 cases dismissed and 1,000 acquittals). Figures from *1968 Annual Report of the Director of the Administrative Office of the United States Courts,* Table D4, p. 261.

[2] Responsibility is abdicated in many other ways. A common religious abdication is the insistence that children should say early morning prayers in public school. The family has apparently so far disintegrated that breakfast time no longer suffices, or exists. The Supreme Court's decision in such cases as School District of Abington v. Schempp, 374 U.S. 203 (1963) that prayers in public schools are unconstitutional has brought national protests and widespread defiance and disobedience. See, *e.g., The New York Times,* November 23, 1969, p. 74. Of course, many who disobey no doubt do so less because they want their children to pray and more because they want to protest what they consider a misguided decision. He who ponders why the younger generation protests the way it does might consider that youth is greatly imitative.

[3] The sense of the exception for Supreme Court appointments is consistent with that of the general policy: There is none.

sponsibility is neither more nor less ludicrous than the client of a
lawyer I know who was advising her on an impending separation
and divorce from her husband. She called the lawyer's office one
morning in despair, blaming attorney and husband all at once:
"Now see what's happened," she told the attorney, "I don't even
have any milk in the refrigerator this morning."

Two other examples of the refusal to accept responsibility for
understanding the law are noteworthy. Senator Mike Mansfield
during the course of debate on legislation affecting the contro-
versial Subversive Activities Control Board in 1967 said that "I,
frankly, am not qualified to discuss the constitutional aspects of
a bill of this nature, because I do not feel that I have the requisite legal training," a candid though regrettable admission on
the part of the Senate Majority Leader.[3a] Less immediately important, though no less astonishing, was the admission of newspaper
columnist Joseph Alsop in discussing Yale Law School Professor
Alexander M. Bickel's "attack" on the Supreme Court: "This
reporter [Alsop said] is wholly unqualified to discuss, much less
to pass upon, the complex and profound constitutional issues that
Bickel has raised. They were already being raised, before his
retirement from the court, by Justice Felix Frankfurter. They
are now being raised, in certain specific cases, by Justice Hugo
Black. That is all a reporter can properly say about the issues
themselves." That is a noteworthy statement because it indicates
the depth of the mystery law conveys to the ordinary mind: Alsop
regularly pontificates on the merits of far more complex issues
of military and foreign policy with great nonchalance. The issues
of segregation and reapportionment, which Bickel thinks the Court
wrongly handled, are not beyond the intellectual capacity of most
other reporters, and the discussion of constitutional issues in the
press seems improper only because there is not enough of it.[3b]

[3a] *Congressional Record,* October 18, 1967, p. 14957.
[3b] For Alsop's column, see *The Washington Post,* December 3, 1969, p. A15.
The column is worth reading in its entirety since it represents the most
thorough possible misunderstanding of the debate over judicial method

Responsibility is abdicated when it comes to planning highways, public parks, and the environment at large. The waste of natural resources and the spoilage of water, air, and countryside has proceeded apace because the citizen has either lost interest or considered the resulting havoc beyond his proper sphere of interests; after all, there are highway engineers, city planners, lumberers, and chemical manufacturers who know all about those things.

An interesting delegation of responsibility is that of "grief therapy" assumed by the mortician. Because he deals with death, he assumes he is competent to establish public policy relating to all facets of death. He has invented for the purpose a therapy whose operative feature is the catharsis that ostensibly comes from viewing the cadaver in an open casket. Perfecting the catharsis is the necessity of making the corpse look good; this calls for embalming and cosmetic therapy, services so morbid and arcane they can draw a high price. There is no evidence that open viewing is based on any of America's principal religions; it is a secular "custom" developed by the industry and unknown in Europe, where there does not seem to be the rate of emotional depression following funerals that the open-casket grief therapy theory would predict.[4]

Morticians may accept the responsibility of relieving the grief of mourning relatives, but the American Medical Association has gone one farther: It has assumed the obligation of deciding—or at least fixing methods to decide—when the deceased is dead. In the wake of controversy over organ transplant operations, the AMA has adopted guidelines for physicians to follow in order to confirm that the organ donor is dead. The definition of death itself is being debated extensively: Is a man dead whose heart has stopped

and Bickel's place in it. Alsop claims that Bickel's Oliver Wendell Holmes lectures at Harvard Law School prove that the political "left" is beginning to turn against Warren Court. But Bickel is not noted as a judicial liberal and his position predates the 1969 lectures; Alsop apparently is unaware of Bickel's previous writings; e.g., The Least Dangerous Branch (1962). No doubt Alsop speaks truly for himself that he is unqualified to write on the subject but the assertion that no reporter could is wholly false.
[4] Jessica Mitford, The American Way of Death (1963), pp. 90–5.

beating or is only he dead whose brain functions have terminated? The question is interesting, but the current debate assumes that doctors must be the arbitrating agency. And as a practical matter they are, because most state laws are framed to permit public officials and private physicians to declare the moment of death according to "accepted medical standards." Vast questions of public policy are involved, however, in any attempt to fix the moment of death. The public legislature seems the one agency singularly appropriate for a resolution of the issue. In this sense, death is a public, not a medical, question.[5]

It is not merely the public at large which has abdicated its fundamental responsibilities. Professionals are laymen themselves when they confront the disciplines of other professions; experts are no exception to the rule that the decision should be for others. Sanity and mental competence, for example, are legal concepts that have been absorbed by the medical profession. Although judges and juries in some states nominally have the authority to pass on the question whether a particular defendant is insane, in fact it is almost universally assumed that medical witnesses are so absolutely essential to the sanity hearing that their answers—when they are in agreement—are dispositive. Legislatures draft civil commitment statutes in terms of the "medical model" of mental disease, without considering what may often be more relevant but non-medical criteria.

The old test of criminal responsibility—whether a person knew the difference between right and wrong[6]—has increasingly been rejected by American courts and legislatures in favor of a psychiatric model—whether a person is suffering from a mental disease or defect.[7] The change is more than one of nomenclature. Knowledge of the difference between right and wrong may not be a medically sound test whether a person is mentally ill. But it was perhaps a reasonable test for the legal issue: whether a person should be

---

[5] See Louis Lasagna, *Life, Death and the Doctor* (1968), pp. 237 ff.
[6] M'Naghten's Case, 10 Clark & Finelly 200, 1 C & K 130 (1843).
[7] Durham v. United States, 214 F. 2d 862 (D.C. Cir. 1954).

punished for an anti-social act. The importation of a psychiatric test merely subverts the legal issue. The right-wrong test is said to be "irrelevant" to the judicial process but it appears that the only irrelevancy is that the right-wrong test will not permit psychiatrists to testify in their own jargon, the failure to distinguish right from wrong not becoming recognized as a legitimate psychiatric malady.

To require mental illness as a criterion may lead to bizarre results. Dallas Williams, convicted in the District of Columbia seven times for assault with a deadly weapon and once for manslaughter, was released from jail in 1960 following the expiration of his last sentence. Two psychiatrists, at a hearing to determine whether Williams should be committed to a mental institution, testified that "at the present time [he] shows no evidence of active mental illness . . . he is potentially dangerous to others and if released is likely to repeat his patterns of criminal behavior, and might commit homicide."[8] He was released from confinement and within months succeeded in cold-bloodedly killing two men. (He was thereupon convicted and jailed, where he remains.) The instinctive reflex that blames the "permissive" District of Columbia courts should be stilled long enough to reflect on the fact that the District criminal code, enacted by men with no reputation for liberality or permissiveness, requires not only that the probability of danger to others be established but also that the potential incarceree be suffering from "mental illness" before the courts can send a man to a mental institution. The court-castigator would not find congenial the remaining argument for incarceration—that anyone criminally inclined is necessarily "sick."[9]

---

[8] Quoted by Professor Alan M. Dershowitz in an address at the Harvard Law School Sesquecentennial Celebration, September 23, 1967.

[9] For the judicial record of the Williams cases, see Willams v. United States, 250 F. 2d 19 (D. D. Cir. 1957); In re Williams, 157 F. Supp. 871 (D. D. C. 1958); Williams v. Overholser, 162 F. Supp. 514 (D. D. C. 1958); Williams v. Overholser, 259 F. 2d 175 (D. C. Cir. 1958); In re Williams, 165 F. Supp. 879 (D. D. C. 1958); Williams v. District of Columbia, 147 A. 2d 773 (Mun. Ct. App. 1959); Williams v. United States, 312 F. 2d 862 (D. C. Cir. 1962), cert. den. 374 U.S. 841 (1963).

The disposition of the Williams case contrasts with that of Mrs. Catherine Lake, suffering from what the staff of St. Elizabeth's Hospital in Washington, D.C., categorized as "chronic brain syndrome, with arteriosclerosis." Found wandering around the city streets, she was confined to the hospital because though otherwise harmless she was held to constitute a danger to herself. Since the requisite "mental illness" was present, confinement was legal and ordered. At the trial considering her petition for release, it was established that she had rational periods and periods of mental confusion; she preferred her home to St. Elizabeth's. Her petition was denied.

The net is that legislators have abdicated their public responsibility to decide what conduct and attitudes justify confinement under these circumstances. "It would seem beyond dispute that the question of which harms do, and which do not, justify incarceration is a legal—indeed a political—decision, to be made not by experts, but by the constitutionally authorized agents of the people."[10] Yet these agents in concert with deluded lawyers have been led to believe that certain restrictions on the liberty of citizens are medical problems.[11]

[10] Dershowitz, *supra* note 8.

[11] See Jay Katz, Joseph Goldstein, Alan M. Dershowitz, eds., *Psychoanalysis, Psychiatry and Law* (1967), pp. 526–566. A recent attempt to substitute medical for political judgment is Dr. Karl Menninger's *The Crime of Punishment* (1968). in which the noted psychiatrist argues that the present system of criminal justice is so unscientific it should be scrapped in favor of the psychiatric establishment. Although he advocates ignoring the reasons why an accused committed the crime—problems of the mind are for psychiatrists after the jury convicts, he says—he does not go so far as to suggest that psychiatrists should decide what acts should be made crimes. The public does not generally suppose criminal acts are to be totally divorced from the intent of the actor, and obviously even Dr. Menninger does not suppose that a policeman who opens fire on a suspect is automatically to be convicted of murder, with his sentence later to be decided by a prison psychiatrist (and set low if it proves that the policeman really did shoot in self-defense). For a concise and trenchant analysis of the pitfalls in Dr. Menninger's assumptions, logic, and conclusions, see Jeffrie G. Murphy, "Criminal Punishment and Psychiatric Fallacies," 4 *L. and Soc. Rev.* 111 (1969).

Those who are willing to grant that in some spheres the experts should fix public policy would do well to consider where an inexorable consistency in their position would lead them. If doctors are to be policy-makers in the realm of public health, and lawyers to determine what legal services should be available to the individual in society, then in what realm will we grant policy-making power to economists? to sociologists? and (the implication suggests the horror) to political scientists? Are these questions just a semantic paradox? Political scientists, because they are "students" of politics, have never claimed to be directors of public bodies and are therefore not to be feared as experts who would assert rule-making power, it will be argued. Suppose they did so claim, however?[12] Doctors are "students" of disease and lawyers of legal doctrines, but their medical or legal training does not alone equip them to make the value judgments our conventional wisdom places within the province of the people. The paradox, if any there be, lies in the failure to distinguish among the many different uses to which we put the terms "health" and "law." The judgment that

[12] The claim has been advanced. Traditionally, academic associations have been scientific study groups. Today there are indications of change: the American Political Science Association, for instance, is in the midst of crisis. Two action groups, the Caucus for a New Political Science and the Black Caucus, are attempting to gain control in order to move the Association from its refusal in the past to take public stands on disputed issues. The Black Caucus stated during an Association election campaign that "as a group of persons claiming expertise on matters which are political," the Association should take "affirmative actions" to eliminate "white racism" as a political force in the United States." The Caucus for a New Political Science has a list of measures it believes the APSA should adopt, many of which indicate a belief that because their members are "political" scientists they must be in the forefront of demands for social justice. Thus, "political scientists should be the first to insist on democratic control by students and faculty in shaping departmental and university policies." If there is new life thus being breathed there is also unease that the Association will become merely another contentious and shrill voice in the political arena — with serious problems in store if political scientists begin to claim the expertise for themselves among the public that their name has always implied. (Quotations from campaign statements mailed to the APSA membership, October, 1969).

a particular man has tuberculosis is not at all the same as the judgment that the quality of treatment would decline were group health plans to become widespread. Nor is the judgment that the legal order depends on the public trust in lawyers necessarily consonant with the judgment that a union attorney will not be trusted by the rank and file or the public at large.

2

The public's abdication of responsibility for actions and beliefs that intimately affect it is not due solely to chronic apathy, nor to the confessed inability of laymen to understand professional mysteries. These attitudes have much to do with it. But the increasing tendency to lodge responsibility in specialized units of society is forced upon society as well. The rationale is always the "public interest." Innocent people must be protected from themselves. Just how far this public protection can go is aptly illustrated by the Velikovsky affair.

In 1950, Dr. Immanuel Velikovsky published *Worlds in Collision*, a highly unorthodox book on astronomy. Velikovsky maintained that the Earth has undergone a series of cataclysmic events which have interrupted its normal rotation, changed the length of the day and year, and reversed the direction of its polar magnetism. Examining biblical and other records of ancient civilizations, Velikovsky concluded from his exigetic approach that these events occurred within the recorded history of mankind. The Bible tells of the sun remaining in the sky for many days; South American legends, gleaned from a people on the other side of the world, tell of a period long ago in which the night did not end. Velikovsky theorized that Venus erupted from the planet Jupiter some 6,000 years ago, that the trailing meteorites and gases caused terrible devastations which might have lasted for a thousand years or more and which accounted for the biblical plagues and the parting of the Red Sea, among many other ancient legends. His observations included the speculation that Venus is a hot planet whose atmosphere is composed of gaseous hydrocarbon. At publication time, the prevailing theory held that Venus was cold and that carbon dioxide constituted the principal ingredient of its atmosphere. So revolutionary were the implications of *Worlds in Collision* that "a full accounting of this theory's consequences must revolutionize nearly every field of human knowledge, overturning principles long considered to be axiomatic, negating the work of generations of dedicated scientists, and fundamentally revising man's conceptions of his origins and fate."[13]

The American academic community greeted the publication of Velikovsky's book with uncharacteristic abuse. Most astronomers believed his theories scientifically absurd. Even before the book was published, the scientific community began to react. Four years earlier Velikovsky had approached Harlow Shapley, director of the Harvard College Observatory, to discuss whether the University might investigate Venus spectroscopically to determine the validity of the theory. After some hedging, Shapley refused, remarking: "If Dr. Velikovsky is right, the rest of us are crazy." Shapley declined to read the book and as it went to press five authorities in five different fields denounced the work in *Science News Letter*.[14] None of these authorities had read the book either. Shapley wrote the Macmillan Company, Velikovsky's publisher: "It will be interesting a year from now to hear from you as to whether or not the reputation of the Macmillan Company is damaged by the publication of *Worlds in Collision*." Gordon Atwater, curator of Hayden Planetarium in New York and chairman of the department of astronomy of the American Museum of Natural History, had commended its publication to Macmillan. He now pre-

13 The discussion herein is based on Eric Larrabee, "Scientists in Collision: Was Velikovsky Right?" *Harper's*, August 1963; Ralph E. Juergens, "Minds in Chaos: A Recital of the Velikovsky Story," *The Amer. Behavioral Scientist*, September 1963; both excerpted in *Current*, February 1964. These articles have been collected in Alfred de Grazia, ed., *The Velikovsky Affair* (1966).

14 See *Science News Letter*, vol. 57, February 25, 1950; see also issues of March 25, 1950 and April 15, 1950.

pared a defense of the book and was fired from both his positions. Another favorable reviewer found his *New York Herald Tribune* article dropped; substituted for it was an attack by Otto Struve, director of the Yerkes Observatory in Chicago University and former president of the American Astronomical Society. He said "it is not a book of science and it cannot be dealt with in scientific terms."

Nor was it. At the peak of the book's financial success (it climbed to the top of the bestseller lists and remained there for twenty weeks as a result of the controversy), Macmillan's president called Velikovsky into his office to tell him that professors in some large universities had threatened a Macmillan textbook boycott unless the publishing house ceased publication of *Worlds in Collision*. The book was transferred to Doubleday and Company, which had no textbook department. One letter cited by Macmillan's president was from Michigan astronomer Dean B. McLaughlin who protested that Velikovsky's book was a pack of lies and that he had not and never would read it. Shortly after the transfer was consummated, the Macmillan editor responsible for contracting the book, a twenty-five-year employee of the company, was fired.

Twelve years later, in December 1962, the U.S. satellite Mariner II passed Venus and discovered that the planet's surface was very hot, as Velikovsky had predicted—more than 800°C., not −25°C., as current theory had held. The probe found, moreover, that the atmosphere was "shrouded in hydrocarbon clouds at least fifteen miles thick." Other fundamental Velikovsky predictions have proved true since that time also; *e.g.*, the "Van Allen radiation belts, the extremely high electro-magnetic potential of the sun, the possibility that the Earth's petroleum deposits are of extra-terrestrial origin, and the correct dating of Central American and Egyptian records and events."

A number of astronomers had thus borne out the dictum that professional organizations prohibit "any but the science and art that were current in the generation that is passing away. This reluctance to admit the new knowledge or the new processes is seen at its worst when what is knocking at the door is some revolution which would shift the boundaries of the profession, transfer some of its service to another set of practitioners, or consign to the scrapheap some of the processes by which its members have gained a living."[15]

This is not to argue that Dr. Velikovsky has been scientifically vindicated. But it is to suggest that even astronomers, surely among the most other-worldly of our professionals, are not above attempting a little censorship in the name of the public interest.[16]

The Velikovsky affair can perhaps be dismissed as an example of an irrational but legal boycott. Isolated examples of a refusal to permit opinions to be bruted about can congeal into operational doctrine, however. The firing of a scientist-administrator who refused to sneer at a renegade may seem trivial. So may the impact of a single hospital's refusal to hire a doctor whose non-medical (and even medical) opinions are suspect. When such examples are repeated many times it seems less and less like the case of an institution merely exercising its freedom to protect the public. Like the workers who had no need of the "freedom" to contract their services for a twelve or fourteen hour day, eventually institutional "freedom" will take on a cast of suppression. Not merely the individual, but the society, must suffer.

3

Dr. Louis Lasagna, a noted physician and essayist, has criticized the philosophy that scientists should remain aloof from social problems as "short-sighted and parochial." "Clarification," he says, "is needed in the minds of both the scientific and lay publics as to the importance of remaining a citizen despite one's professional call-

---

[15] Sidney and Beatrice Webb, "The Control of Industry," Special Supplement, *The New Statesmen*, April 21, 28, 1917, p. 47.
[16] The furor has long since died down and Dr. Velikovsky is back in print with *Worlds in Collision* and *Earth In Upheaval*.

ing."[17] It is also vital for experts to become citizens despite their choice of the wrong professional calling. Professionals are human; they import their own values whenever they make judgments affecting the public.

To argue that we should each be more responsible for our own lives is not to demand that we go back to the land and grow our own grain, thereby freeing ourselves from the vexatious necessity of relying on others for our survival. We have become too highly specialized ever to move back, even if we concluded so to regress were desirable, which I think, after some reflection, it is not. But because we cannot assume responsibility for the details of the myriad of events that shape our lives and on which the quality of our lives depends does not mean we must therefore relax our efforts to do what we can about assuming some control over the meaning of our lives. Because we cannot milk a cow does not mean we should not attempt to understand our laws. Because we remain ignorant of the process of milking the cow or pasteurizing the milk does not mean we must remain ignorant of the process by which our rights are milked. Indeed, because we need not milk a cow we have all the more time to consider those rights, and a host of other issues, as well. If the serious problems facing the nation and the world are to be successfully tackled, the public will have to assume responsibility for their solutions.

[17] Lasagna, "Doctors Out of Step," *The New Republic*, January 2, 1965, p. 15.

13
Toward Due Process (I)

The awful will of the sovereign people is not likely to be aroused because the Court has told the morticians of Winnemac that they cannot use State power to maintain a monopoly.
— ROBERT MCCLOSKEY, "Economic Due Process and the Supreme Court: An Exhumation and Reburial"

1

We seem to be at an impasse in the conduct of our public affairs. The people are not economically motivated to contest the market power of professionals; the legislatures are not politically disposed to establish necessary controls; the courts declare themselves constitutionally powerless to regulate often outrageous conduct. And the general impotence is a psychological phenomenon, the fear of expertise being sufficient to deter laymen from accepting responsibility for modern problems.

It is time to question the premises on which professionals have built their power. It is appropriate to begin with an analysis of how the courts might surmount their constitutional dilemma. Courts are presumed to listen to reason, not power. They alone, therefore, can occasionally be counted on to redress unequal balances of power. When everyone else is paralyzed, the courts have the potential ability to inject a muscle-relaxing drug into the body politic.

220

It might seem anomalous to require courts to initiate necessary political action. A standard judicial refrain is that the more readily courts find constitutional fault with legislation, the more rapidly the legislatures will abdicate their responsibility to scrutinize the bills that come before them. But it is no contradiction now to suggest that the courts must act, because the responsibility was abdicated long ago. A spendthrift heir may be denied his legacy on the ground that he would quickly go through it and then starve; but when he is starving it is less convincing that further withholding will increase the value of the lesson.

2

For more than thirty years the Supreme Court has sculpted a doctrine that puts legislative ahead of judicial wisdom in economic affairs. The monument to a theory is not yet complete and no one should complain about a few rough edges or unsmooth contours. Until the mid-sixties, however, the doctrine rested on a flimsy base.

The regulation of the economy and the exercise of the police power in the interests of health, safety, and welfare were firmly lodged in the legislature: "The forum for the correction of ill-considered legislation is a responsive legislature."[1] In one phrase or another, the Court has steadily insisted that relief from onerous legislation must be sought at the source. The premise on which the courts' abandonment of economic due process rests—that legislatures are responsive to the people—is another matter. When it became evident that the wildly malapportioned state legislatures were anything but responsive, the Court chose to change the facts to suit the theory. To abandon economic due process is to require a coherent theory of representation; it is not surprising, therefore, that a major thrust of the Court's constitutional activism in the sixties was toward redressing the balance of interests represented in the various legislatures in the land.[2] The judicial response to rotten

[1] Daniel v. Family Life Ins. Co., 336 U.S. 220, 224 (1949).
[2] Beginning with Baker v. Carr, 369 U.S. 186 (1962), and Reynolds v. Sims, 377 U.S. 533 (1964).

borough legislatures is not complete; we may expect the gerry-mander to die a constitutional death sooner or later.

But the problem will remain unsolved. Geographical represen-tation alone is insufficient to make the legislature responsive to important—even compelling—interests, such as those which con-sumers might ordinarily be expected to possess. And to organize representation on an occupational basis would be so fundamental a wrench in the American political process that not only is its hap-pening so remote as to be thought inconceivable, its realization would be so unsettling as to be disastrous. The need for some type of judicial intrusion into the theory of the professional class remains.

The principal way is still judicial construction of the due pro-cess clause. For this clause has historically been determined deep enough to hold the promise of controlling arbitrary governmental action. Yet the economic due process doctrine does not seem likely to be exhumed:[3] it received too serious a blow from those who abused it to be capable of a new life at court. Practical men, who want results even at the expense of some slight wobbles in the orbit of constitutional law, must therefore look for the transmigra-tion of its soul.

We need not look very far. Due process is still very much alive among American courts; modern interpretations of the due process clause have been extensive, continuing, and they show no prospect of abating. But it is in the procedural and political realm that they have flourished. So great have been the number of due process cases in recent years that it would be folly to attempt to recite their history here.[4] Suffice it to say that in decision after decision the Supreme Court has extended the right of individuals in innum-erable areas by viewing the constitutional guarantee of due process as a substantive limitation on both federal and state gov-

[3] Robert McCloskey, "Economic Due Process and the Supreme Court: An Exhumation and Reburial," 1962 *Sup. Ct. Rev.* 34, 53.
[4] For a capsule view, see my *Understanding Our Constitution* (1969), pp. 131–228.

ernments' power to play loosely and unfairly with the American people.

The line of decisions between the accepted principle of political due process and the rejected one of economic due process has been extremely uneven. As Professor McCloskey rightly asks: "Is it easier for the Court to appraise a law empowering a board of censors to ban an 'immoral movie'[5] than a law empowering a real estate board to deny a license unless the applicant is of 'good moral character'? The two standards would seem to be equally vague and the possibility of arbitrary administrative action would seem to be as menacing in one situation as in the other. Is it plainly easier to balance New Hampshire's need to get information against Paul Sweezy's right to withhold it[6] than it is to balance South Carolina's need to stamp out the funeral insurance business against the right of an agent of the Family Security Life Insurance Company to make a living selling such insurance?[7] The 'public need' in both cases was all but invisible. Is it easier to see that the state corporate registration law in *NAACP v. Alabama*[8] was being used to facilitate private reprisals against Association members than it is to see that state boards of plumbers, barbers, and morticians sometimes use their publicly granted powers to protect the private financial interests of present guild members to the disadvantage of non-members?"[9]

---

[5] Kingsley International Pictures Corp. v. Regents, 360 U.S. 684 (1959).

[6] Sweezy v. New Hampshire, 354 U.S. 234 (1957). The New Hampshire legislature authorized the state Attorney General to determine whether there were "subversive persons' in the state. Sweezy refused to answer a question concerning the contents of a lecture he gave at the State University or to divulge any information he might have had about the Progressive Party and its membership. Sweezy did answer questions concerning membership in the Communist Party, denying affiliation. He objected to answering certain questions, he said, because he did not think them relevant to the investigation and thought the First Amendment placed limits on the kind of investigation being conducted. He was held in contempt for refusal to answer. The Supreme Court reversed.

[7] Daniel v. Family Life Ins. Co., 336 U.S. 220 (1949).

[8] 357 U.S. 449 (1958).

[9] McCloskey, *supra* note 3, pp. 52–3.

In fact, the line of decision is not merely uneven; it is broken. The Supreme Court itself has begun to reject, in Justice Frankfurter's phrase, the "pre-Victorian" notion that political and economic interests are separable. The case that shows the way is the one we have encountered earlier—*United Mine Workers v. Illinois State Bar.*[10] It will be recalled that the Illinois Supreme Court held that a salaried union attorney who represented members in injury and death cases before state industrial commission proceedings was engaged in unlawful practice of law. The case was appealed. The Mine Workers won an important and novel victory in the Supreme Court, which held that the state could not constitutionally prohibit the union plan. Union members, said the Court, have a constitutional right to come together to hire attorneys to protect their rights under state law.

The reason may seem artificial and in a sense it was, but two previous cases had set the direction in which the Court was moving. In *NAACP v. Button*[11] the Court had held that Virginia could not prohibit the National Association for the Advancement of Colored People from soliciting state residents to use NAACP attorneys to initiate civil rights lawsuits. Though such conduct clearly violated Virginia's ethical precepts against stirring up lawsuits, the Court discerned an important constitution right in danger of abridgment: The First Amendment, guaranteeing the freedom of speech and assembly, precludes a state from denying to a group of people the ability to make known to the members of their minority that effective legal means were available to secure their rights.

Shortly thereafter, Virginia's canons were violated anew, but this time by a union in a manner palpably unrelated to civil rights. The Brotherhood of Railroad Trainmen established a Department of Legal Counsel to recommend local attorneys for personal injury litigation. The attorneys were not salaried but they paid a portion of their fees to the union. The state bar sued to enjoin the Brotherhood from carrying on this unauthorized practice of law and from

10 389 U.S. 217 (1967).
11 371 U.S. 415 (1963).

soliciting legal business. The Supreme Court approved the Brotherhood program. Again the First Amendment was invoked: Workers were banding together to discuss their rights under the federal Safety Appliance and Federal Employers Liability Acts. "A state could not," wrote Justice Black for the Court, "by invoking the power to regulate the professional conduct of attorneys, infringe in any way the right of individuals and the public to be fairly represented in lawsuits authorized by Congress to effectuate a basic interest . . . for [laymen] to associate together to help one another to preserve and enforce rights granted them under federal laws cannot be condemned as a threat to legal ethics."[12]

From these decisions, *United Mine Workers* naturally sprang. Citizens have as much right to come together to discuss and protect their rights under state laws as federal, even when a salaried attorney represents members and even when the rights concerned are economic rather than political.

Justice Harlan vigorously dissented. In discussing the central problem of fees, he pointed out that under the Illinois Workman's Compensation Act the state industrial commission "shall have the power to determine the reasonableness and fix the amount of any fee or compensation charged by any person, including attorneys." Commented Justice Harlan: "Thus there would now appear to be no reasonable grounds for fearing that union members will be subjected to excessive legal fees."[13] He thereby missed the principal contention: The mine workers supposed that they could so arrange their affairs to avoid fees altogether. In this supposition they were ultimately correct.

But from the standpoint of economic due process decisions, Justice Harlan was correct in believing precedent dictated dissent. The majority pulled a switch on him which left him blinking. "The state," he said, "was entitled to conclude that, removed from ready contact with his client, insulated from interference by his actual

---

[12] Brotherhood of Railroad Trainmen v. Virginia ex rel. Virginia State Bar, 377 U.S. 1, 7 (1964).

[13] *United Mine Workers, supra* note 10 at 229.

employer, paid a salary independent of the results achieved, faced with a very heavy caseload, and very possibly with other activities competing for his time, the attorney will be tempted to place undue emphasis upon quick disposition of each case."[14] In other words, this was not a political suppression at all; the state has the constitutional power to regulate professional practice in the interests of public welfare.

To this the majority did not accede. Justice Black dismissed the state's interest in welfare regulation rather perfunctorily: "There was absolutely no indication that the theoretically imaginable divergence between the interests of the union and member ever actually arose in the context of a particular lawsuit: Indeed, in the present case the Illinois Supreme Court itself described the possibility of conflicting interests as, at most conceivabl[e]."[15] Justice Harlan retorted: "The proper question is not whether this particular plan in fact caused any harm. It is instead, settled, that in the absence of any dominant opposing interest a state may enforce prophylactic measures reasonably calculated to ward off foreseeable abuses and that the fact that a specific activity has not yet produced any undesirable consequences will not exempt it from regulation."[16] But this was now a dissent. A dominant opposing interest had been found and with it the Court was back in the business of passing on the reasonableness of state economic legislation.[17]

To be sure, the Court did not admit that so it decided; the decision was strictly tied to political rights. Yet the conclusion is unavoidable. The case indicates that the Court found itself in a hole, escape from which was necessary but difficult. The Court's

[14] *United Mine Workers*, at 231.
[15] *United Mine Workers*, at 224.
[16] *United Mine Workers*, at 232–3.
[17] From the standpoint of ethics, the Bar's response to this decision that it was unconstitutional to prohibit the "unethical" group practice was revealing. The new code (see note 6, p. 76), in Disciplinary Rule 2–103(D), continues to prohibit coöperation with group practitioners, with certain exceptions, such as legal aid offices and lawyer referral services. The Code permits

persistent refusal to recognize the substantive due process argument in the economic field has led to a nationwide system of economic fiefdoms, creating pockets of modern feudalism. *Lee Optical Co. v. Williamson*[18] and many other cases made it impossible to jump up from the hole into which the Court, by then, had already slid. Only when the state could not ever be thought to have acted reasonably in creating economic legislation would the Court strike it down. The wonder of politics is that there is always someone who can find political decisions reasonable. So in *United Mine Workers* the Court had to reach onto the political arm of the substantive due process doctrine to lift itself out of its constitutional hole. And the political arm is a powerful one, for it quite readily presumes state legislative action suspect when political rights are endangered.

3

That the Supreme Court has begun to recognize the problem of excessive professional power by no means assures its sudden de-

lawyers to associate with other group plans "but only in those instances and to the extent that controlling constitutional interpretation at the time of the rendition of the services *requires* the allowance of such legal service activities" (emphasis added). This lawyerlike circumlocution would seem to mean that a lawyer could coöperate with a union or other plan only *after* a court had said not only that the plan was legally permissible but that it would be unconstitutional not to permit it. This kind of language is calculated to deter lawyers from participating in order to *contest* the constitutionality of this very prohibition. A strict adherence to the Rule would stifle development of group practice, evidently (in view of the debate) what the ABA majority had in mind. And the Bar goes one step farther: Rule 2-103(D) attempts to delineate cases in which it would be unethical to participate even though the Supreme Court had said it would be unconstitutional to apply Rule 2-103(D). A more fundamentally disingenuous and self-defeating rule is difficult to imagine. A fight by the Bar's Special Committee on Availability of Legal Services, a relatively progressive group, to amend the rule failed. As usual, the explanation for the rule was couched in mindless language: Without Rule 2-103(D), said the chairman of the ABA Section of General Practice, "the layman will run the practice, and not the lawyers." See 55 *ABAJ* 970, 971 (1969).
[18] See p. 194f.

mise. It will immediately be objected that to return to substantive economic due process is to return to *Lochner* and all assorted ills of judges who presume knowledge and theory superior to the people's. This objection misses the point. *Lochner* should always have been a curiosity, for its nub was the ringing protection it gave to the workingman in a suit brought by someone else. Courts would do well to follow the rule they there overlooked: When a private litigant claims he is suing to protect the interests of someone else, he's lying. More importantly, it should be recognized that the argument that a due process revival spells *Lochner* "assumes that the case for or against the validity in 1905 of a statute the purpose of which was to obtain safer working conditions for bakery workers is substantially identical to the arguments pro and con a statute in the 1950's fixing the price to be charged for cleaning a suit of clothes or cutting a head of hair."[19]

Still, it is neither unreasonable nor unwise to insist on some limitation of the Court's power to overturn economic legislation on the ground that it offends due process. That is to say, a more carefully articulated premise must be sought. It will not have escaped the reader that state courts have, on occasion, overcome the contemporary reluctance to declare licensing schemes unconstitutional. A description of some of these cases will provide a clue.

The California Supreme Court has struck down a minimum price system in the dry cleaning industry.[20] New Jersey has decided, through its supreme court, that its legislature went too far in prohibiting dentists from leasing, rather than buying, dental equipment.[21] The North Carolina court found objectionable a statute that, by defining such practice to be exclusively within the province of optometrists, prohibited opticians from replacing broken lenses without a prescription.[22] State laws regulating barber

[19] John A. C. Hetherington, "State Economic Regulation and Substantive Due Process of Law," 53 *Nw. U. L. Rev.* 226, 250, (1958).

[20] State Board of Dry Cleaners v. Thrift-D-Lux Cleaners, Inc., 40 Cal. 2d 436, 254 P. 2d 29 (1953).

[21] Taber v. State, 135 N.J.L. 255, 51 A. 2d 250 (Sup. Ct. 1947).

[22] Palmer v. Smith, 229 N.C. 612, 51 S.E. 2d 8 (1948).

shops' prices have been invalidated by at least seven state supreme courts.[23] The Illinois Supreme Court struck down parts of the plumbing code,[24] while North Carolina voided the tile laying scheme.[25]

A series of decisions in several states held licensing of photographers to be violative of due process. The provisions of these licensing laws should be familiar. The Arizona law, for example, established in 1939 a board of five members, each of whom had to have been a practicing photographer in Arizona for at least five years. The board was authorized to examine applicants and to license "such as qualify as to competency, ability, and integrity." The board could take testimony "as to technical qualifications or the business record of the applicant, and . . . may, at its discretion, for sufficient reason, grant or withhold a license to practice." As usual, those who already owned cameras when the act was passed could continue the professional practice without benefit of examination or payment of fee. When presented with the constitutionality of the statute, the state supreme court became rather exercised. Quoted at some length is a sampling of the court's remarks in voiding it:

"The act in question does not pretend to regulate the practice of photography in the interests of the business or the public but, rather, in the interests of those professional photographers who are fortunate enough to obtain a license . . . . The business or profession of taking photographs of people, animals, and things does not need regulation. It is one of the innocent, usual occupations in which everybody who so wishes may indulge as a pastime or a hobby or a vocation, without harm or injury to anybody, or to the

---

[23] Edwards v. State Board, 72 Ariz. 108, 231 P. 2d 450 (1951); State Board v. Cloud, 220 Ind. 552, 44 N.E. 2d 972 (1942); Christian v. La Forge, 194 Ore. 450, 242 P. 2d 797 (1952); Cincinnati v. Correll, 141 Ohio 535, 49 N.E. 2d 412 (1943); Revne v. Trade Commission, 113 Utah 155, 192 P. 2d 563 (1948); Noble v. Davis, 204 Ark. 156, 161 S.W. 2d 189 (1942); State v. Greeson, 174 Tenn. 178, 124 S.W. 2d 253 (1939).
[24] See p. 29. People v. Brown, 407 Ill. 565, 95 N.E. 2d 888 (1951).
[25] Roller v. Alden, 245 N.C. 516, 96 S.E. 2d 851 (1957).

general welfare, or the public health and morals, or the peace, safety and comfort of the people. It needs no policing.

"Some of the things accomplished by the act are: (1) a complete internal control of the practice of photography by the interested members of that business or profession through admissions thereto with little else relating to regulation; (2) it selects one owner of property and authorizes him to sell in Arizona and prohibits others from selling in Arizona the same kind and quality of property, honestly and lawfully acquired.

"The business or profession of making photographs is not inherently dangerous to society but is an entirely innocent occupation. If there be those engaged in it who make false representations as to the finish, quality, or price of their product, it is not different in that respect from other lines of business. All businesses have their cheats, whose crimes are cared for by the general laws. Photography is not supposed to be an unhealthy or insanitary business needing medical supervision. It will not prosper the community or other lines of business or trade to limit the number of those who may engage in the business. It cannot harm those who pursue it nor anyone else, but may benefit its votaries in both health and finances."[26]

The language resembles *Lochner,* but the result is manifestly different; the bakers' law was for the protection of bakers, the photographers' for the public, and the voiding of the latter does not require the former to fall. Most state courts overruled photographic licensing rather early in the general trend toward professional licensing.[27] Although photographic guilds have practically disappeared, photographic licensing has not. Some states license

---

[26] Buehman v. Bechtel, 57 Ariz. 363, 114 P. 2d 327, 367, 376, 372 (1941).
[27] Florida: Sullivan v. DeCerb, 156 Fla. 496, 23 So. 2d 571 (1945); Georgia: Bramley v. State, 187 Ga. 826, 2 S.E. 2d 647 (1937); North Dakota: State v. Cromwell, 72 N.D. 565, 9 N.W. 2d 914 (1943); Virginia: Moore v. Sutton, 185 Va. 481, 39 S.E. 2d 348 (1946); Tennessee: Wright v. Wiles, 173 Tenn. 334, 117 S.W. 2d 736 (1938); Hawaii: Territory v. Kraft, 33 Hawaii 697, (1937); Montana: State v. Gleason, 128 Mont. 485, 277 P. 2d 530 (1954); North Carolina: State v. Ballance, 229 N.C. 764, 51 S.E. 2d 731

itinerant photographers, requiring not merely financial security but also evidence of good moral character.[28]

The photography cases have been the basis for decisions involving other licensing systems as well. The Oklahoma Watchmaking Act of 1945 went under on this authority. The state board sued to enjoin Wood from "practicing watchmaking" because he never obtained a license from the Oklahoma Board of Examiners in Watchmaking. It was charged that his practice injured "persons lawfully engaged in watchmaking, rendering them insecure in their property, and thus [constituted] a public nuisance [and] that the conduct of the defendant would endanger the health and safety of others."[29]

From these cases a principle may be discerned, or at least constructed. That is that legislative schemes for which less economically and politically restrictive alternatives are feasible should be voided as violations of due process.[30] If the fear of itinerant photographers is simply that they might abscond with the funds of bilked customers, bonding is appropriate. If the fear is that dry cleaning establishments will be fire hazards, periodic inspection is in order. It is important to point out, however, that the less restrictive alternative test does not mean that the courts can water down legislative policy. The test does not prescribe a finding of unconstitutionality every time the courts see an alternative way of accomplishing *some* of the legislative goals. Legislation should not fall under the test unless there is a feasible method of carrying out the entire body of regulatory purposes, exclusive, of course, of the purpose to limit the freedom to practice for limitation's sake.

(1949) (The decision by the then state supreme court Justice Sam Ervin overruled a previous court decision only a few years old, State v. Lawrence, 213 N.C. 674, 197 S.E. 586 [1938]; it was this case to which Justice Fortas alluded at hearings when questioned by Senator Ervin about a certain penchant of the Supreme Court to overrule prior decisions).

[28] See, *e.g.*, Maine (licensing by Secretary of State): Maine Rev. Stat. Ann. 32-2955.

[29] State ex rel. Whetsel v. Wood, 207 Okla. 193, 248 P. 2d 612 (1952).

[30] Guy L. Struve, "The Less-Restrictive-Alternative Principle and Economic Due Process," 80 *Harv. L. Rev.* 1463 (1967).

The fear in *United Mine Workers v. Illinois State Bar* was that the salaried attorney might not follow through in his fiduciary capacity with the utmost perspicacity. The courts retain the power to discipline a lawyer who renders ineffective assistance, just as they are empowered to question the actions of an independent attorney. A prohibition against employment of an attorney to represent union members, therefore, is constitutionally unacceptable.

The less restrictive alternative test is not an easy one to apply. Whenever the question is how best to effect social purposes through legislation, reasonable men are bound to differ, even those of the same partisan persuasion. It may well be that much of what now exists in the form of licensing legislation and statutory definitions of unauthorized practice will continue to exist even with a rigorous application of the principle. It is doubtful, for instance, that any court could ever—or should—be persuaded that physicians should not be required to attend school and pass an examination before practicing medicine. Something more than the less restrictive alternative principle will be required, therefore, if we are to protect the public and professionals from the power that the professional associations gain as a side effect of their licensed and regulated status.

4

The problem of controlling the professional organization is but a special case of a more general problem. "Private groups" take actions daily which affect outsiders, yet only certain people are said to possess the legitimate power to control or shape these actions. When they are not socially beneficial (as defined by those who feel aggrieved), the actions of private groups irritate, harrass, and even oppress. In part we may so understand the waves of unrest with which university campuses are beset, on which the 1968 Democratic Convention was wrecked, which spark destruction of glass and files at a chemical company office building. To varying degrees, all are "private" groups—that is, groups which affect many who have no control over them. Violence has consciously been used as a reaction to a felt misuse of power.

The appropriate response is not a countering display of public power. It is rather to accept the growing evidence that the line of demarcation between private and public sectors has become blurred and even obliterated in recent years. The fearsome "military-industrial complex" conjures up the image and the thesis is vigorously demonstrated in the case of the "techno-structure."[31] So, too, the line is blurred in the case of the professional estate. Where the state ends and the "private" association begins is increasingly difficult to determine.

The consequences of this blurring are immediately apparent: More and more activity will be seen as promoted and directed by the state. There is small difference between an organ of the government and a supposedly private company retained by the government, or delegated the authority, to do the same task. In many instances, the only difference in fact is the nimble hypocrisy by which the government avoids its constitutional obligations to the citizenry. A "private" company or association can discriminate on the basis of race, for instance; the government cannot. If, therefore, private action has become state action, courts will require private conduct to conform to the fundamental constitutional precepts of due process and equal protection.

The doctrine of "state action" is a wedge for the injection of federal constitutional standards into "sovereign state" programs. The intervention of federal power in the regulation of the professions would spell the end of the last real bastion of absolute "states rights"—it is an anomaly that it has lasted so long.

In the political realm the Supreme Court long ago came to recognize the power private entities wielded over the lives of citizens. In a series of voting rights cases from 1927 to 1953, the Court expanded the concept of "state action" to reach and control racially exclusionary practices. When Texas enacted the White Primary

---

31 John Kenneth Galbraith, *The New Industrial State* (1967), pp. 60 ff.

Law, permitting whites only to vote in the Democratic primary, the Court saw in it an (extremely effective) attempt to abridge the voting rights of Negroes, protected by the Fifteenth Amendment. That the law was concerned with the primary within a party mattered not at all. Who won the Democratic primary won the election. Texas responded by repealing the White Primary Law and enacting a more subtle variant; to the executive committees of the parties was given the power to decide who would be entitled to vote. The parties were "private," after all; they could refuse members, Texas erroneously reasoned. The Court struck it down; the executive committees became agents of the state when they exercised such a function. For a third time the law was changed, now to permit the entire statewide membership of the Democratic Party to decide whether Negroes could enroll and vote in its primary. The Court at first permitted it; then three years later, in 1944, reversed itself, deciding that the contrivances of a political party, be they by decision of committee or the entire membership, converted the party into an instrumentality of the state. The fifth Texas test went still farther. The Jaybird Democratic Association was a local party officially unaffiliated with the state party. It ran a pre-primary primary for candidates within the county in which it was established; for sixty years the winner invariably went on to win the primary and the general election in November. Yet the Jaybirds did not operate under state primary laws, used no state funds, and did not require state voting machines. Negroes were excluded. The Court held in 1953 that the Jaybird operation, too, constituted state action.[32]

Similarly, the Court has held that a town entirely owned by a private corporation cannot deny the First Amendment right of a lady to distribute religious literature on the company streets, because in performing municipal functions the company itself

---

[32] The cases are Nixon v. Herndon, 273 U.S. 536 (1927); Nixon v. Condon, 286 U.. 73 (1932); Grovey v. Townsend, 295 U.S. 45 (1935); Smith v. Allwright, 321 U.S. 649 (1944); Terry v. Adams, 345 U.S. 461 (1953).

becomes an agent of the state.[33] In a series of very recent cases, the Supreme Court has found the state lurking in many hitherto unsuspected regions — in ostensibly private restaurants,[34] in small parks,[35] and even in the actions of that cherished American institution, the avenging posse of private vigilantes.[36] The fusion of state and private authorities in a working partnership has been discovered and the state labeled the dominant party, subjecting the entire plan to the restrictions of the Constitution. The courts have not been so ready to find this same fusion of state and profession, though the comparison is obvious, once noted. In some few instances that probably portend the spread of the "state action" doctrine, however, the courts have begun to think.

The case of the North Carolina dentists shows the beginning of the realization that racial restrictions on minority practitioners can be subjected to judicial attack. In 1958 the Dental Society by law elected all six members of the Board of Dental Examiners. The Society was also required to nominate one member of the North Carolina Medical Care Commission and to appoint one member of the Mental Health Council from among Society members. When Dr. Hawkins filed suit, the state legislature quickly changed the rules. Members of the Board who were not candidates to succeed themselves were declared a Board of Elections; any dentists may be nominated by petition filed with the Board and signed by at least ten dentists; the electorate was broadened to encompass all licensed dentists of the state. In three subsequent elections, to fill three, two, and two vacancies, all seven elected

---

[33] Marsh v. Alabama, 326 U.S. 501 (1946).

[34] Burton v. Wilmington Parking Authority, 365 U.S. 715 (1961) (The state leased a parking facility to private persons who operated a segregated restaurant out of part of it).

[35] Evans v. Newton, 382 U.S. 292 (1966) (1911 will left private park to white people of Macon, Ga., to be operated by city; fearing it could not continue the segregation, Macon attempted to turn the park over to private hands but the Court ruled the park was a public instrumentality in any event).

[36] United States v. Guest, 383 U.S. 745 (1966); United States v. Price, 383 U.S. 787 (1966).

not surprisingly were members of the Society. In 1963 the Medical Care Commission and Mental Health sections were changed; the Governor could henceforth appoint members following a recommendation from the Dental Society, among others. During argument before the appellate court in Dr. Hawkins' case, the Society attorney seemed to agree that these statutory provisions might taint the claim of the professional association that it was unrelated to the state. He told the court that the law could be taken care of at the next session of the North Carolina legislature. It was. But despite — or perhaps because of — the cutting of the Society's ties with other state machinery, the United States Court of Appeals for the Forth Circuit found the requisite "state action"; Dr. Hawkins was entitled to admission.[37] At the time of the decision there were 1529 licensed dentists in North Carolina of whom approximately 100 were black. The Dental Society had 1214 members, none of them black.

The racial problem extends as well to professionals who will not deal with minorities. A New Jersey barber who refused to cut the hair of a black patron found his licensed status thrown in his face by the New Jersey Supreme Court. The barber had argued that he was not subject to the state's public accommodation and antidiscrimination laws because barbering is the performance of a "personal service" outside the scope of those laws. Pouring acid on his own case, he argued further that the "unusual texture and quality" of the Negroes' hair was beyond his competence to cut. The court dismissed his contentions: Barbers hold a "special status" as licensed practitioners in New Jersey. Since they do, they can neither plead their own incompetence nor any inherent right to deal with certain people only. Status implies obligations.[38]

State action need not be confined to racial issues. The fact that professions are regulated in the public interest should be sufficient to subject professional associations to constitutional requirements

[37] Hawkins v. North Carolina Dental Society, 355 F. 2d 718 (4th Cir. 1966).
[38] Sellers v. Philip's Barbershop, 46 N.J. 340, 217 A. 2d 121 (1966). See *The New York Times*, February 22, 1966, p. 1.

where the organization presumes to speak or act for the public in any way. This is not a widely accepted doctrine; but it has a toehold in our jurisprudence through the case of the diligent doctor. Unlike attorney Lathrop, Dr. Falcone didn't want to get out of an association; he wanted to get in. He was about to become a full member of the Middlesex County (New Jersey) Medical Society when it was discovered that seven months of his medical training had been spent at a school not approved by the AMA, contravening an unwritten Society rule. He was dropped. Unfortunately, Society membership was prerequisite for affiliation with the county hospitals, according to an unwritten hospital rule. (Had the hospital accepted Dr. Falcone, the medical society might well have cancelled its accreditation.) He lost his job and went to court.

Noting the reluctance of courts to interfere with the internal affairs of private associations,[39] the New Jersey Supreme Court nevertheless ordered Dr. Falcone reinstated. The court was impressed with the fact that he was licensed to practice medicine and surgery in New Jersey. If the Society had shown that in spite of the fact that he was licensed, Dr. Falcone was otherwise incompetent, that he somehow fooled the state medical licensing board, it might have won the suit. For the court did not presume to pass judgment on the Society's assessment of the technical competence of individual doctors. But the Society did not contest Falcone's competence, except on the ground that he had briefly attended an unaccredited school. The denial of membership on this ground alone was held unconstitutionally arbitrary since the legislature had already determined that the schools which he had attended were of sufficient caliber to assure competence. Because membership in the Society was an economic necessity, the court viewed its monopoly position as a "fiduciary power" to be exercised in the advancement of both the medical and public interest.[40]

---

[39] See note 56, p. 199.
[40] Falcone v. Middlesex County Medical Society, 34 N.J. 582, 170 A. 2d 791 (1961).

This is a rare case. Of the decision the editors of the prestigious and austere *Harvard Law Review* noted that it "is virtually unprecedented."[41] Yet it really did not go very far; if the
medical society had had the power to set school standards for the
state, Falcone's entire case would have been undercut.

In still another way, the state action doctrine can be activated
by courts to serve the commonweal. Most professional associations
in disregard of the democratic virtues they usually espouse, combine their investigatory, prosecutorial, and adjudicative functions
when they discipline an errant member. A Federal District Court
in Florida has found serious fault with the practice of that state
dental board's proceedings. At a hearing to determine whether a
dentist had engaged in unprofessional behavior, the adjudicator
of fact had discussed the case with the investigator prior to the
hearing. The prosecutor acted also as the legal advisor to the
adjudicator, which meant that he ruled on motions made by the
accused's attorney and actually ruled on certain of his own
motions. As legal adviser, the prosecuting attorney attended what
were, in effect, the "jury sessions." These practices were held to
be unconstitutional.[42] Yet these practices are all too common
among state agencies and the discipline committees of professional
associations alike.

It is open to courts to fashion a general rule of associations:
The fact of licensing should be enough to transform the profession
into an instrumentality of the state; the private professional association should not be allowed to deny its public character,[43]
whether or not it has regulatory power. Only the blind could
deny state action when the association has some statutory role in
the licensing of the profession or in its regulation. It takes merely
the glassy-eyed to overlook the significance of the association in

[41] Note, "Judicially Compelled Admission to Medical Societies: The *Falcone*
Case," 75 *Harv. L. Rev.* 1186 (1962).
[42] Mack v. Florida State Board of Dentistry, 296 F. Supp. 1259 (D.C. Fla.
1969).
[43] *Cf.* Note, "Exclusion from Private Associations," 74 *Yale L. J.* 1313, 1319
(1965).

any event — for regardless of the formal degree of control the association may have over any state board, the tie between them today is so great there should be a judicial presumption of incest. As yet there has been no hurried judicial rush toward this policy. The New York State Psychological Association "proclaim[ed] itself the voice of all New York State psychologists and claim[ed] to be the organ through which the psychologist could have a voice in regulation of the profession,"[44] but the state court evidently did not believe this piece of puffery and pretension and could find no basis for assuming state action.[45]

5

Implicit in the foregoing discussion is the unfashionable assumption that there is a "right to work." It has long been recognized, it will be argued, that the state may legitimately regulate conduct which has an impact on others. No one has an "absolute" right to do anything in a democracy of checks and balances, and surely there is nothing intrinsically fundamental about the nature of work that its different manifestations may not be subjected to reasonable regulations.

Indeed, the argument would be persuasive except that its usual exposition contains a serious defect. For it is usually asserted that there can be no absolute right to work because for every right there are responsibilities which must be met. The state may impose conditions on the rights it grants, it is widely assumed. There is danger here: Rights and responsibilities are alliteratives but not correlatives. To require every one with a claimed right to perform responsibly is to reduce the right to a metaphysical dimension. "Responsible" is a word of wide applicability, susceptible of many interpretations. If the right to vote were con-

---

44 *Supra* note 43, at 1318–19.
45 Salter v. New York State Psychological Ass'n, 14 N.Y. 2d 100, 198 N.E. 2d 250 (1964). Psychologists in New York are certified — a psychologist must have a Ph.D. in the field and meet standards set by the state. The association works closely with the State Advisory Council in formulating rules of ethics, among other things.

ditioned on its responsible use — *i.e.*, the support of responsible candidates — there would be no right to vote. Similarly the right to practice law or other professions should not be conditioned on the political beliefs of the would-be attorney or other professional; when his opinions come within the frame of relevant scrutiny before a license is to be issued, the "right" to practice becomes a mere privilege which can be suspended at will. And so the basic assumption has changed: In the attempt to prevent the dangers of incompetent practice, the "right to work" has been encumbered with numerous questionable conditions.

It need not be so: Rights and responsibilities need not be contraposed. We should not judge the possible consequences of the exercise of a right to ascertain whether it must be controlled. The freedom of speech is not dependent — or should not be — on what the consequences of the speech will be.[46]

The short of it is that responsibility should be imposed only on power. Insofar as people possess power to injure others they are held by law to standards of care; in other words, to a responsible exercise of their power. Professionals are no exception and it may be that the licensing of professionals is a better guarantee of responsibility — of curbing the power of the quack to injure — than litigating malpractice claims case by case.

The difference between correlating rights and responsibilities and responsibility and power is not only theoretical.[47] The abridgment of individual constitutional rights is more difficult to maintain when responsibility is viewed as a limitation on power

---

[46] Subject to certain narrow exceptions, libel and slander of the ordinary citizen are not protected by the First Amendment, but they are difficult kinds of cases for plaintiffs to win, and libel of persons in public life is becoming an increasingly narrow legal concept. False or palpably misleading business advertising is not protected, and neither is obscenity, but obscenity has almost disappeared as a legal concept.

[47] "Rights" and "responsibilities" usually go hand in terminological hand in part because they are alliteratives and Anglo-American law has been favorably disposed toward rhythmic phrases. See David Mellinkoff, *The Language of the Law* (1963), pp. 42 ff. Historically, the reason for their conjunction may be this: The medieval serf obtained "rights" to physical pro-

rather than rights, because the limitation will be scrutinized more carefully for its relevance to the power feared. Moreover, the ability of professional associations to dominate the lives of individual practitioners can be considerably weakened if responsibility is seen as a necessary correlative of power. The organizations have been insisting that since they are merely private clubs they may act as they see fit. Insofar as they exercise power affecting the public, however, their actions may be legislatively required to be responsible. The legislature need not fear the legal argument, in other words, that it must keep its nose out of their business. The legislature may impose regulations that cut deep into the traditional power and prerogatives of professional associations.

Worriers may find it dangerous to advocate public regulation of private associations. Though governmental control of business enterprise is now fully accepted in practice, it is still an American custom to debate its wisdom and to seem on the defensive whenever new controls are advocated. It surely will be the case here that dissent will focus on the natural illegitimacy of government's intruding into private spheres.

History provides a substantial answer. The earliest form of judicial process came from within the private organization itself. The medieval Church applied its own canon law, the local manors their land and tort law, and local ports their interpretation of the international law of the sea and maritime. But private power requires as much control as public power. To apply rules equally, the body of common law slowly developed. This was public power, though it took centuries to develop and become legitimated. Private laws — customs and traditions — were consolidated in a

tection and to till his land in return for his obligation to support his lord. In the theory, there was an original contract. A correlation between right and responsibility inhered in a society organized on a hierarchical basis in which it was assumed that the sons inherited the contractual rights and duties of the fathers. In a modern democracy, however, the presumption does not hold; when all people are presumed legally equal, there is no necessary connection among the ultimate rights of all individuals. The right of an individual to speak his mind need not depend on a responsible use of it because all other individuals have an equal freedom of speech.

system of public jurisprudence because their impact on an increasingly expanding public required evenhanded administration by judges outside the circles of special interests. So today, as regulations concerning occupational status increasingly affect the public, public law must inevitably take charge.

R. H. Tawney reports that the English budget of 1909 created a sensation because the newly-imposed land taxation involved the sweeping doctrine that property was not an absolute right, that it "may be accompanied by special obligations," a doctrine which implied not uncertainly that property was conditional.[48] In time, law and new philosophy practically extinguished the old belief.

It is similarly required of us that we draw anew the line between public and private in order to impose responsibilities on those who exercise power over the public through their control of the professions. Private power as well as public power must be contained. We do not abridge (say) the AMA's "right" to shape legislation; let it publish journals and lobby against appointments and laws. But this right does not extend to controlling the professional lives of its members.

Application of the state action doctrine to professional associations will of course call for judicial intrusion into the organizational activity. The groups cannot be expected to welcome it, but a body which regulates its members' activities with respect to the outside world should not justifiably expect to be free from regulation itself. If any object that judicial intervention could cut into the associations' lobbying strength (because they can no longer maintain a solid front by virtue of their untrammeled stranglehold over the professions), the answer must be that this strength was unlawfully gained; there is no right to compel people to lobby for laws they do not want.

6

The ultimate question is whether the dangers feared from

[48] R. H. Tawney, *The Acquisitive Society* (Harvest ed., 1948), p. 22.

incompetence and negligence outweigh the value of living in a society which permits human relationships to flourish free from prior regulation by a state official or his private delegate. Until the recent past the answer has been that freedom is worth the price. If increasing complexity increases the cost, we ought still to be willing to bear it.

The ultimate answer lies with an indignant public speaking through an alerted legislature. Because the relief sought is often far smaller in amount than the cost of litigation, it is not likely that the problem can be solved on a piecemeal basis in the courts. But it is important to realize that courts have played a large role in the development of undue process, that they are not constitutionally required to, and that a strategic reversal can do much to educate and arouse the sleepy, unconcerned public to action.

The Supreme Court's major political due process and equal protection decisions — civil rights, reapportionment, criminal justice — may be considered as grounded on a political understanding of the "republican form of government" which the Constitution adjures the federal government (including the Court) to respect and maintain within and among the states: Important competing interests must be allowed the chance to organize into majorities within legislative bodies.[49] If they are not, decisions affecting the unrepresented lack the requisite due process.[50]

The interests in question in each of the areas bruted about since the 1950's — blacks, the disfranchised urban populations, and the criminal suspect — were not accorded the due process that should be theirs as a class: Laws were enacted by unrepresentative bodies — or assumed by even less representative executive agencies — and the political system would not otherwise permit change. When the injunction of *Munn* v. *Illinois* becomes unworkable —

---

[49] Though not usually discussed in these terms and constitutional dogma at present might not support this view, but see Dowling, "The Methods of Mr. Justice Stone in Constitutional Cases," 41 *Col. L. Rev.* 1160 (1941).

[50] See South Carolina v. Bramwell Bros., 303 U.S. 177 (1937), in which Justice Stone for a unanimous Court discussed the effect of representation on constitutional decision-making under the commerce clause.

when, that is, the people cannot find a remedy at the polls for abuse of legislative power because the legislation complained of itself hinders the development of countervailing political power — the Court must act to repair the balance of power between important competing interests. So with occupational licensing and professional power over fellow practitioners: Legislatures are politically unable to withstand the producer onslaught. In order to redress the balance between expert and layman, it is necessary for the Supreme Court to embark on at least a limited judicial revolution in yet another area: The power of producers must be balanced by setting limits on its exercise. The Court cannot order consumer groups into being, or demand their representation in the legislature, but it can bring consumer power onto the same field as producer power by restricting the scope of the latter.

This chapter has suggested some ways in which the Court might begin to enunciate a constitutional policy. But constitutionality is not the beginning of wisdom; it is merely its precondition. Without seeds, even fortified soil is forever barren; courts may tinker with constitution but it is up to legislatures to act.

14
Toward Due Process (II)

It is not necessary to think of occupational boards as selfish, venal, or arrogant in order to think of them as inept, inefficient, and costly.
— WALTER GELLHORN, *Individual Freedom and Governmental Restraints*

1

Judicial remedies are not social solutions. Courts may order a medical society to admit a physician; they can never succeed by ukase in establishing professional friendships or viable relationships between hospital and suspected physician. The hospital which would not extend staff privileges to Dr. Falcone without medical society membership, granted him "courtesy privileges" after the court order and society admission, but these privileges did not permit him to engage in surgery.[1] More general policy than that which the judicial process is capable of formulating is required.

The first step is simple: Delicense most occupations. This is not as radical a step as it may sound. A brief examination of dozens of licensing laws quickly reveals that there are significant exceptions in each of them. Architects must be licensed; but there are numerous kinds of structures which may be designed and constructed by non-licensed "architects." Similarly, there are exemption clauses in many other licensing laws, depending on the size

[1] Note, "Judicially Compelled Admission to Medical Societies: The *Falcone* Case," 75 *Harv. L. Rev.* 1186, 1196, n. 84 (1962).

245

of the project, its cost, its nature. Where such exceptions exist, it is a difference in degree only to broaden them further.

Moreover, licensing is always proclaimed to be in the interest of public health and welfare. Rarely are the statutes distinguished according to their separate purposes. At least six different kinds of licensed activity emerge from the cases presented: (1) activity which if negligently performed may lead to death or serious bodily injury (*i.e.*, inherently dangerous injury); (2) activity which may result in deprivation of legal rights; (3) activity resulting in defective craftsmanship of an objective nature (*e.g.*, watchmaking); (4) activity resulting in defective craftsmanship of a subjective nature (*e.g.*, photography); (5) activity by those who receive money in advance or those who do not have a fixed place of business; and (6) activity involving a fiduciary trust the breach of which can lead to serious psychological or economic injury. Not all of the prospective dangers presented by these types of activity necessarily warrant licensing.

Few will deny that regulation of some activities by licensing is necessary.[2] But it by no means follows that most professions should be regulated. The original justification for licensing was that performance of some occupations without due regard for professional standards of technical competence could result in death, serious bodily injury, catastrophic destruction, or a deprivation of legal rights. Thus the medical, engineering, and legal professions require licensing. Common law, after-the-fact remedies are inadequate; prior restraint is necessary to protect the public.

Performance of most occupations does not raise the standard dangers, however. There are methods of control other than licensing which will forestall injury, and there are remedies which by all tests of history and law are adequate to compensate when injury does occur. Greatly expanded state inspection programs to insure that health and safety standards are met in a score of

---

[2] For the argument against all forms of occupational licensing, see Milton Friedman, *Capitalism and Freedom* (1962), Chapter 7.

industries would probably be more than adequate substitutes for licensing. Indeed, inspection is a growing necessity now, despite licensing. Were legislatures to authorize private and public treble damage suits for breach of ordinary warranties and to permit recovery of attorney's fees by the winning side, pocketbook injuries could be repaired. To be sure, such sanctions are not perfect; they will not always deter, and they will not always give adequate compensation for harm. But the alternative, regulation, is worse in most instances. Licensing by no means guarantees the abolition of negligence, and the same imperfect sanctions and remedies must be brought into play when a licensee causes harm as when an unlicensed practitioner does so.

Moreover, an alternative to prior licensing is licensing "by operation of law." Professor Gellhorn suggests that upon registration a license would be automatically issued to the applicant. Criminal sanctions would be necessary for failure to register. Then, "provision could be made for a decree of suspension or revocation upon a finding, after suitable judicial proceedings, that the licensee had misrepresented his skill or training, had demonstrated his incompetence, or had engaged in dishonorable conduct relevant to his occupation."[3]

It has occasionally been suggested that no profession should be licensed. "The medical profession is often cited as a case where social costs are greater than private costs. It is usually said that 'incompetent' practitioners may diagnose a disease incorrectly and thus start an epidemic. To complete the argument, it is necessary to contend that this is more likely or more damaging than the possibility that, if the expensive medical practitioner is made unavailable, the consumer will neglect to consult a physician at all, thus starting an epidemic."[4] The argument that those who cannot afford high-priced care should be able to purchase cheaper care from a less competent physician is unhappily based on the

---

[3] Walter Gellhorn, *Individual Freedom and Governmental Restraints* (1956), p. 150.

[4] Moore, "The Purpose of Licensing," 4 *J. of L. and Econ.* 93, 110 (1961).

notion that medical care is like a television set or any other product in the market. "Insofar as he harms only his patient, that is simply a question of voluntary contract and exchange between his patient and his physician," Professor Milton Friedman argues.[5] In this theory, the distribution of medical care – like the distribution of justice, presumably – rests on the ability to pay. But it is late in the day to propose the sadly-worn phrase "voluntary contract"; not only does it presuppose adequacy of remedy, it requires equality of bargaining power between patient and doctor, a condition that simply does not obtain in modern society. The alternative to "cheap" care is the development of a host of trained sub- or para-professionals who can do more efficiently the jobs now being done by highly specialized practitioners.

The case against licensing is untenable if it is made against all licensing. No one would call for abolition of federal licensing and testing of airplane pilots, because everyone fears objects which unaccountably drop from the sky. Airline safety is a national goal, and we would not want an incompetent pilot flying, even if some passengers were fool enough to go aloft with him. Is there any reason for a distinction in the case of doctors or lawyers, if we view health and justice as a national resource? But if we do count these national as well as purely personal resources, we must be prepared to overcome the narrow parochialism of the organized professions.

2

The commonly suggested alternative to licensing is certification and registration. By that is meant simply that only those meeting requisite standards set by a state agency could use the particular title – e.g., architect, psychologist – or refer to themselves as "certified." Others could engage in the occupation but would not be able to call themselves by the professional name or to represent to the public that they are certified. It is said that certification and registration would perform essentially the same functions as

[5] Friedman, *supra* note 2, p. 147.

licensing: A way to supply the public with information about standards would be achieved and fraud would be prevented.[6]

Registration and certification, as opposed to licensing, are premised on a hopeful theory of the American character: Just tell the average man the facts and he will choose his course wisely. Tell the sufferer what is in the patent medicine (the basis of the Pure Food and Drugs Act of 1906) and he will choose that which will cure him. Unfortunately, "the facts" are most often meaningless because they give no guide to action. Certification may be a plausible political alternative in those situations in which licensing is unnecessary but delicensing cannot be immediately obtained. But it is doubtful that certification could protect the public from those quacks who have historically not been tolerated, nor would it be conducive to the development of health or justice as national resources.

The general economic theory of certification and licensing is that the costs incurred by consumers in their search for the highest quality service are too high to be met when the service in question is specialized. We live in a producer society and people have neither the time nor the background to consume intelligently. When the cost of consumer search rises above the cost of registration, certification, or licensing, the time to impose these controls is at hand.[7]

Evaluating costs is extremely difficult, however. Opponents of licensing point out that certification is cheaper than the costs of consumer search in highly specialized fields such as medicine, because the layman cannot be expected to spend his time going from office to office trying vainly to judge the quality of service. And, the argument goes, certification is less costly than licensing because certification does not prevent the uncertified from practicing, thus preserving freedom of choice and allowing those who do not want highly specialized care the possibility of going to cheap doctors, lawyers, or others. It has already been remarked

[6] See Moore, *supra* note 4, pp. 104–5, for this proposition.
[7] Moore, p. 105.

that the alternative to high-priced professionals is the development of sub-professionals for less specialized tasks.[8]

There is another flaw in the consumer-search argument preferring certification to licensing. It ignores the vast educational expense in preparing the public to understand the meaning of certified competence. If the cost of consumer search is high without any certification, it may not be appreciably lowered at this stage in our history by allowing anyone to practice medicine but requiring any who do to say they were certified by a particular board as A–1, B–6, or H–17. And inevitably the certification system would be extended to the requirements of specialization within each profession. Professionals would have to be given separate ratings and jurisdictional disputes would proliferate, requiring agencies to decide what (say) the certified ophthalmologist would be competent to do.[9] The fact is that certification to meet the

[8] These exist in a few occupations; in some states, for example, nurses are to be distinguished from registered nurses and accountants from certified public accounts. Those who are neither registered nor certified can do some jobs but not all.

[9] See Kronen v. Pacific Coast Society of Orthodontists, 237 Cal. App. 2d 289, 46 Cal. Rptr. 808 (Cal. App. 1965), cert. denied, 384 U.S. 905 (1966), in which a licensed California dentist was not admitted to membership in the Pacific Coast Society of Orthodontists, without belonging to which he could not become a member of the American Association of Orthodontists, membership in which in turn was prerequisite for certification by the American Board of Orthodontists, without which he could not, under the American Dental Association's code of ethics, announce to the public that he was limiting his practice to orthodontics (i.e., specializing). California had no provision in law requiring separate licensing of orthodontists. In other words, Dr. Kronen could legally practice orthodontics, but he would be acting unethically to tell anyone about it. The court held that it was a private affair and given its reasons, the Coast Society had not acted arbitrarily. This doctrine has now been significantly altered by the California Supreme Court in a case rejecting the notion that courts cannot intervene in private membership cases unless the rejection jeopardizes property or contractual rights or substantially deprives the applicant of the opportunity to make a living. Pinsker v. Pacific Coast Society of Orthodontists, 81 Cal. Rptr. 623, 460 P. 2d 495 (1969). Although Kronen was distinguished on the facts and hence not overruled, the Pinsker case makes substantial economic disadvantage a sufficient criterion for judicial intrusion.

cost of consumer search has not been used and the cost of converting from conventional licensing might be prohibitive.

3

Regardless of where the line is drawn among the alternatives — freedom to practice without licensing, or certification, or full-scale licensing — a more serious problem remains. The malpractice remedies proclaimed by the self-regulators as superior to the judicial remedies they posit as alternatives are often illusory. If a small loss is involved, going to court in the first place is too expensive; lawyers have seen to that. Once in court, it is next to impossible to proceed. In medical malpractice suits, ethical doctors will not testify against their fellows; doctors have seen to that. The ethics committee, local judicial council, or other administrative board of the professional organization is supposed to be the efficient mechanism for hearing complaints brought by aggrieved consumers. But if they do not act as outright protective devices for their fellows by smothering the case, they are hardly as effective as courts: the angry client must present his own case, and he is usually incompetent to do so. Moreover, when the professional associations do sometimes act, it is often with the kind of terrifying speed and lack of respect to the rights of individual practitioners that courts (in theory at least) exist to protect. Whether or not they are clothed with enough public power to warrant their decision-makers to claim the title of judge, agencies which exist to hear and settle disputes such as we are considering are similar and share defects; the virtues that the more unofficial bodies possess do not make up for the vices they automatically assume.

It is time to take the professional at his word: The essence of ethics is the attempt to avoid not merely the impropriety but the appearance of impropriety. The conflict of interest is everywhere abhorred even if the conflict does not materialize into the harm imagined. Accordingly, power to prescribe ethics and to monitor professional performance must be removed from the hands of the experts.

Because regulation of some professions is necessary does not imply that the profession itself should do the regulating, nor does it imply that anything beyond bare technical competence of the professional should be judged by the regulators. Dr. Falcone would have lost his job in New Jersey had it been up to the professionals to admit him to practice. Apprentice plumbers in Illinois were left to the mercy of their masters, who were also their competitors. Photographers in Arizona, North Carolina, and other states could be denied the chance to earn a livelihood for reasons not remotely related to any dangers to the public inherent in their occupation. If control is required, the regulatory power must be dispersed to public agencies.

The removal of all regulatory power from private associations will be objected to; professionals will assert their hoary belief that only they can regulate, administer, and test. This belief must finally be rejected. As Professor Gellhorn points out: "Government is surely as serious and complicated a profession (or art or trade) as, say, chiropody, manicuring, or horseshoeing."[10] As management becomes a distinct profession itself, doctors, lawyers, barbers, morticians, architects, and all other experts should lose their claim to competence. The virtue of consistency, professionals may conclude, is treacherous. "Accordingly, there is no more reason to imagine that a horseshoer can be a good bureaucrat than to imagine that a bureaucrat can be a good horseshoer."[11] By the time the horseshoer or any other specialist learns bureaucracy and administration, we may doubt whether he is or ever will again be a horseshoer.

Ideally, one public agency ought to perform whatever regulatory tasks are necessary in the occupational field. A uniform licensing law ought to be enacted for all professions in the state in lieu of private proscriptions. The National Conference of Commissioners on Uniform State Laws should draft a model Uniform Professional Licensing Act, the provisions to vary to accommodate

10 Gellhorn, *supra* note 3, p. 143.
11 Gellhorn, p. 143.

only substantial differences among the professions (*e.g.*, contingent fees might be permissible for lawyers under certain circumstances but not for doctors).[12] The legislature should declare the standards or delegate to the agency the declaratory power. One standard that would seem tolerably clear is that the professional should be divorced from an interest in products — like drugs — which may be necessary as a result of his services. The attorney-general or other state officials should be empowered to bring an alleged violator before the courts or public board, so that the public will be represented at the hearing and so that the public will have to justify the revocation through their appointed representatives, not through a private body speaking for the profession. Agency members should be appointed by the governor and not be representative of any profession. Ties between professional associations and the state agency should be severed; private groups should not be given the power to name or nominate members of the state agency. Whatever technical experts are necessary to prepare exams or interpret particular testimony for the agency should be hired as part of a permanent technical agency staff. Testing, too, is now a profession, and there is nothing in medical or legal or engineering theory that makes these professionals experts also in testing.[13]

12 One such suggested code is extremely weak-kneed. "A Model Professional and Occupational Licensing Act," 5 *Harv. J. Legis.* 67 (1967), does nothing more than to codify the prevailing sentiment, with some minor reforms. Thus, § 404 gives the licensing board power to approve the license and to revoke it if the licensee ". . . has come within any of the special grounds established by that particular profession, trade, or occupation as set forth in this Act" (p. 77). But the Act enumerates no special grounds. And, of course, special grounds neutralize any uniformity otherwise obtained.

13 *Cf.* Louis Lasagna, *Life, Death and the Doctor* (1968), p. 57: "One professional attempt to maintain medical standards is in the area of licensing. From their beginning, however, state boards of medical examiners have been handicapped by the fact that they are made up of political appointees of either the party or the medical group in power, rather than experts in the various subjects covered by the examinations. In some states it is specifically required that board members cannot belong to faculties of medical schools. In addition, these boards often have disciplinary and administrative functions that overshadow the duty of giving examinations."

The judicial, prosecutorial, and rule-making functions of the agency should be formally separated. It is no answer to say that a public agency would be subject to all the infirmities and problems of administrative and bureaucratic procedures; private regulatory agencies are subject to those infirmities and more.

The objection that these tasks are beyond the competence of laymen is untenable. No doubt there are many laymen who could not pursue effective careers as judges, legislators, or executives, but that is not to say that public officials should be chosen from a cadre of specially-trained experts. Although judges will not pass on the ethics of physicians because they currently respect the boundaries of a sister profession, their refusal to review professional standards other than those of lawyers is disingenuous; courts undertake difficulties far more complex than that every day. No one has ever suggested that decisions in antitrust cases should be reserved for economists.

4

A host of other possible controls on professional power can be mentioned in passing. The concept of interstate commerce can be easily broadened to bring professional services within the sphere of antitrust. Traditionally, the professions have been held to be outside interstate commerce, and thus beyond the power of Congress to regulate on a national scale. But it is apparent that there are many laws and customs which have been developed to hinder the development of multi-state practices. The professional characterization of their practices as "noncommercial" should not bar the application of federal power to control obvious interstate commercial aspects of professional practice. State legislatures are equally capable of enacting broad state antitrust legislation that could effectively reach professionals.

A commonly discussed solution to consumer problems is a Department of Consumer Affairs, at the federal cabinet level, to act as a counterweight to producer-oriented agencies. The danger of such a concept, if it be given rule-making power, is that like the other agencies, it might be captured by those it is empowered to regulate.[14] There is another problem. To be politically viable, there would have to be an organized consumer interest to support it; a large-scale public organization needs an organized constituency to drive and sustain it. But the Department of Consumer Affairs is proposed for the very reason that there is no such organized constituency.

The possibility of building such an organization is not completely beyond hope, however. In principle, the consumer coöperative can effectively oppose highly organized producer interests. Burial societies have been able to force funeral prices down. Group-employed attorneys can represent member clients at much lower costs than can privately retained counsel. Group practice of medicine is an increasingly common way of providing many medical services at reasonable prices. The government must encourage the development of these sources of countervailing power. A truly invaluable contribution to the commonweal which management consultants and others should be called on to make is an innovative way by which diffuse interests within the general public can be effectively organized.

It is occasionally suggested that professional associations would become more public-service oriented if two-party systems could be established within them. But the probability of establishing an organized opposition within a professional association is not high; professionals are specialists, not politicians; the philosophic interest to be served probably cannot be made competitive; the cost in time and money of establishing a party system would be enormous. This is not to say that if competition to serve the public interest were developed it would be undesirable. It is simply unlikely. The National Lawyers Guild, for instance, which was created more than thirty years ago to do battle against the status quo philosophy of the American Bar Association, has not

[14] See Louis Kohlmeier, *The Regulators: Watchdog Agencies and the Public Interest* (1969).

been able to compete seriously against the ABA; its experience suggests the futility of relying on movements from within the ranks of professionals to change the direction of their organized interests.

5

It will be duly noted that the legislative controls here suggested are far from definitive.[15]   Detailed solutions are absent not only because it is easier in the abstract to ask questions than to provide answers.   Pervasive public problems of the sort considered in this book are also the type that are peculiarly susceptible to solution by many minds.   Committees are useful political devices for just these problems.   A public discussion must begin.

For such a discussion to be sustained, however, the psychological burden under which the layman labors must be lifted.   Constitutional decisions may spark political change, but a public which does not believe itself capable of understanding the issues at stake will not hold on to political gains for long.   The public must therefore be educated, and to this subject we must now turn.

[15] And politically difficult to enact. At the 1951 Governors Conference, alarm at the growth of occupational licensing was expressed. Since that time the problem has been for the most part ignored. In September 1965, I wrote the fifty governors, soliciting their opinions on the gravity of the problem. Within a month, twenty-seven responded. Of these only seven expressed any concern. One was a nationally prominent Southern Governor who had been elected many times by his constituency; he suggested the power of occupational groups by requesting anonymity. Said he: "May I say that we are having increasing difficulties in this field. New boards and commissions are being created all the time. Always they are created under the guise of protection of the public and improved service to the public. All too often the law specifies that the board appointments must be made from a list submitted by the members of this particular occupation or profession, and all too often through these recommendations the profession can control the agency. Many of these agencies are rapidly developing into protection facilities for the members of this particular profession or occupation, principally to keep down competition, serve as a price-fixing facility, and all too often the interest of the public is becoming secondary."

15

The Failure of Education

To promote the study of the classics — the product of a pagan culture — as the essential education of the ruling classes of a self-consciously Christian nation might be thought a difficult intellectual exercise, especially considering the subject-matter of some of the most admired Roman authors.

> — W. J. READER, *Professional Men: The Rise of the Professional Classes in Nineteenth Century England*

1

During early post-colonial days, professionals were widely distrusted in America. The many "lawyers" who helped draft the Constitution were in fact really only educated laymen. The tradition of the British profession made His Majesty's Counselors prone to verbalisms and technical niceties which would have choked a new country. Yet because of the distrust, a legal order flourished. This was not a paradox: "The American Revolution could be framed in legal language because that language spoke for the literate community."[1]

In 1777, Ezra Stiles, President of Yale University, proposed a chair in law — not to train lawyers but to teach laymen. "The Professorship of Law," he said, "is equally important with that

[1] Daniel J. Boorstin, *The Americans: The Colonial Experience* (1958), p. 205.

257

of Medicine; not indeed towards educating Lawyers or Barristers, but for forming civilians [citizens]. Fewer than a quarter perhaps of the young gentlemen educated at College, enter into either of the learned professions of Divinity, Law, or Physic: The greater part of them after finishing the academic Course return home, mix in with the body of the public, and enter upon Commerce or the cultivation of their Estates. And yet perhaps the most of them in the Course of their Lifes are called forth by their country. . . . How Happy for a community to abound with men well instituted in the Knowledge of their Rights & Liberties. . . . It is scarce possible to enslave a Republic of Civilians, well instructed in their laws, Rights & Liberties."[2]

One hundred ninety-two years later, Yale had changed. Stiles' eminent current successor, Kingman Brewster, Jr., had occasion in 1968 to reflect on the course of Yale's undergraduate education when he instituted the University's de-ROTC-ification program. In explaining why students in the Reserve Officers Training Corps would no longer receive academic credit for their military courses, Mr. Brewster emphasized that the liberal arts college was not endowed to impart vocational training. Yet Yale's non-specialist educational approach only partially bears scrutiny. It is all too easy at Yale — or any other liberal arts college — to get only the very narrowest education: He who plans to be a doctor, scientist, philosopher, English teacher, or lawyer can easily slip into a comfortably arcane major which insulates him from the objective of a liberal course of study. If Yale fears professional courses, it should not seriously condone and encourage majors in mathematics, economics, French, and biology, to name only a few. For that matter, Yale should not condone "majors." To downgrade the study of "professional" subjects is inconsistent with the approach of virtually all universities in requiring undergraduates to possess a specialized training before they can study most disciplines at a graduate level. It makes little sense to distinguish "mil-

2 Boorstin, pp. 204–5.

itary science" from architecture or engineering on the ground that the one is a vocational subject and the others not.[3]

There is a traditional distinction between subjects the mastery of which can lead to careers in liberal arts teaching and subjects the study of which can lead to "professional practice." Concededly, the French teacher does not practice the same kind of profession the lawyer does. There is also a traditional distinction between the academic graduate school and the professional school. But it is a historical distinction only. It is becoming increasingly clear that the lawyer ignores the social sciences at his peril, and that the social scientist can ignore law only if he cares not how irrelevant his eventual studies become. Yet the formal distinctions between professional and academic subjects remain at the undergraduate level.

The "real world" that students have lately complained so bitterly about missing in their studies is very largely defined by professionals who operate in it. What lawyers, doctors, the military, businessmen, politicians, social workers, and others do is the relevant concern. Though there are courses in economics and politics that consider theories of economic and political behavior, and even occasionally a course on law as a social process, almost never are these considered in their professional aspect. The retail marketing strategies of the businessman are relegated to business schools, and the methods of the lawyer in the adversary system to the law schools. The reasons for and effect of bureaucracy in

[3] To be sure, "military science" as taught was a far less sophisticated discipline than many other courses of study. Obviously military drill is not the same as mathematical drill. And ROTC and NROTC were the only subjects taught by professors whom the University could not hire, assess, or fire. But it does not thereby follow that the study of military techniques is any less deserving of credit (under appropriate circumstances) than laboratory techniques. It should be noted that Harvard University has begun a philosophic reappraisal of its entire curriculum. Said Dean Ernest May, "there exists need for considering the appropriateness of . . . training and experience in one or more of the arts; . . in social or political action; and vocational training." Quoted in *The New York Times*, December 21, 1969, p. IV–4.

the political, military, and business communities is a matter for schools of public administration. The liberal arts college almost completely ignores professionalism as a general phenomenon. Surely that is not because there is nothing of interest, merit, or significance to study.

More likely, the curricular lack is due to the fear that a course about professions is a course for (or to make) professionals. It need not be so. The colleges think it desirable for students to study the economic process even though they do not plan to become economists. Similarly, students are requested to study science though they do not wish to be scientists; English, though they shudder at the thought of teaching literature; a language, though they will never be interpreters and the world to which they will someday travel will speak to them in English.[4] On this theory, students ought also to study technology, warfare, and even medicine, which in the immediate years to come will provide the community with such political and social questions as the redefining of death, the artificial extension of human life, the control of expanding populations, the conquest of genetic diseases and of genetics itself. The impact of modern knowledge on the concerns of the individual has not lessened the need to "form civilians" in the sense of Ezra Stiles, but it has broadened the scope of the inquiry necessary to that task.

The desire for a "liberal education" can create a serious mental block toward the professions. Although the occasional course exists, the undergraduate typically can graduate successfully from Yale or any other college without a whiff of understanding about

---

[4] The Yale course catalogue (p. 5, 1968–1969 edition) states that "mastery of a foreign language increases subtlety of mind and sharpens sensitivity to the use and meaning of words in one's own language." This recalls the logic of physicians in arguing that group practice leads to medical deterioration: Heavy reliance for proof is placed on the assertion. A foreign language may be desirable for its own sake, or because it is a necessary tool, but if it sharpens one's sensitivity it is only to make one sensitive to the fact that the English Department does not offer a solid course in its own language that would do directly what it is claimed the foreign language does indirectly or by osmosis.

legal process, medicine, accounting, professional business management, the press and its functions, governmental and business bureaucracy, technology, and, of course, the military. This failure, multiplied across the country's colleges, helps create a nation of liberally-educated quacks.

In the areas circumscribed by the professions lie the protein whose lack in their educational diets students characterize as the lack of "relevancy." How can the student today who is concerned about problems of the poor, the sick, about urban ills, and the military-industrial complex feel liberally-educated when he does not have even a glimpse at the work and processes of the most important professions? Aside from the mundane consideration of learning how to cure social ills, the graduate cannot even claim an understanding of what is going on around him. The difference between the undirected undergraduate radical who lashes out wildly at the "Establishment," mouthing words like "participatory democracy" without having the foggiest notion of what it means or how to put it in practice and the more restrained young lawyers who are litigating on the side of the poor and disadvantaged not without effect is a testament not only to the failure of "liberal education" but also to the novel thesis that the American political and legal theory might even work, if put to the practice. Professionalism should be recognized as a dominant trend in American life; the college must respond to it by creating courses about professionalism and the professions — not so students can specialize but precisely so that they need not fear specializing later when they enter a profession or an academically narrow subject in graduate school.

One group today is concerned about this lack: black students. The insistent demand for a Black Studies program is largely a demand for a professional course that will enable its graduates to solve very pressing, concrete, and individual problems. (Even the demand for courses such as Swahili, not useful in themselves, may be understood as a way of creating group cohesiveness necessary for building a community among professionals to enable them to seek the solution of common problems.[5] True black studies courses — the kind likely to be acceptable to militant blacks — would seem as out of place at Yale and other colleges as ROTC training for credit. But there is an adequate, integrated solution and that is to establish a core of courses which deal in part with professionalism and professional issues and which would be taught to large segments of the undergraduate body. Whether the "adversary system" protects the rights of the American people is as worthy of debate in the undergraduate curriculum as it is in the law schools where it theoretically, but not practically, is carried on. When Yale teaches five times as many Latin courses as those dealing with urban problems, it is time to question whether the liberal arts college understands, much less meets, its own professional obligation.

The need, let it be stated again, is to teach the public how to evaluate the deeds and statements of professionals. So ingrained does the system of specialization become that each prefers to let the other alone. Without a factual basis or a psychological inclination to criticize, the student (hence society) is impotent to question what a large and increasing segment of the population is up to. We need tools and means by which we can comprehend the claims of experts and puncture their pretensions. One beginning would be a course on expertise; not easily put together, but a delight to learn and teach, it would embody, at minimum, case studies of claims and statements by many experts with whom the student has had no formal contact whatsoever — the professionals here under review, as well as numerous other experts from academia, business, and government. Another course should deal with the extent and limits of modern knowledge — not a course in outworn epistemologies but a study of our current limits, interests, and speculations.

[5] This explains why the demand for Black Studies carries with it an insistence in many quarters that black teachers and students only participate in Black courses. The law student would not study his subject in a class whose teacher was a doctor and his classmates all historians. See Dunbar, "The Black Studies Thing," *The New York Times Magazine*, April 6, 1969, p. 25.

We may expect such an approach to be resisted. Mrs. Esther Peterson, when she was Special Assistant to the President for Consumer Affairs, proposed a course for high school and junior high school students on consumer economics. Business response was sharp. Grey Advertising, Inc., a large New York firm, cited the "perilous potentials" of her proposal: "There is grave danger," said Grey, "in the kind of economic education which the 'consumer protectors' favor, education which begins with the premise that business is a big bad wolf, ready to devour its own customers. . . . We must protect the people's right to know, but we must protest against *tainted* knowledge. We must prevent the take-over of the schooling of youth in economics by those who have no faith in our economic system."[6] Of course, no statement by Mrs. Peterson that she had proposed the course just because she had faith in the economic system and understood that the system called for consumer knowledge would ever dissuade producers who fear any criticism. The blind may live in the dark, but if an operation enabled them to see again, they might ask for the lights to be turned on. Those who were not where they belonged would object.

There is still another reason to require such education in the schools. To single out only one current problem, that of "law and order": the Supreme Court has decided certain cases requiring police to warn defendants of their rights because the schools have utterly failed to educate citizens to an awareness of these rights. A vocal element (currently known somewhat sarcastically as "the silent majority") has condemned these decisions for impeding "law and order." But decisions such as *Miranda v. Arizona* would not have been necessary but for the schools' failure to teach the public what the Court has now required police to tell them. To be sure, the defendants in *Miranda* may not have been the types to profit from whatever their teachers taught. But the failure is national and has affected all strata of society. Stu-

[6] *The New York Times*, August 5, 1965, p. 45 (emphasis added).

dents at Yale University, when questioned by agents of the FBI concerning possible draft violations, proved themselves profoundly ignorant of their rights at the time of interrogation.[7] No doubt the lay reader, if he stopped now to wonder what rights he could avail himself of were he ever questioned or arrested, would be equally incapable of answering. The impact of the legal system on the individual must be taught in elementary and secondary schools, as well as college. Teachers must be trained to the task and materials developed for the curriculum. Otherwise "law and order" will scarcely be possible.

Ultimately, we come down to the need for a generalist approach to undergraduate education. Only the specialist is trained today; those few men and women who become generalists do so only by the expenditure of enormous energy to overcome their particular parochial training. Our entire educational system today is effective in blocking the development of generalists — the bias is nearly absolute. Yet unless the literate public can be educated to see beyond the boundaries of each of its specialist groups, society stands a fair chance of collapsing when the day arrives that every man is his own specialist and no one is capable of effective communication with anyone else because of it.

2

The Academy's failure is not limited to the lack of teaching. The task of studying the means and goals of the professionals has been largely abrogated by the academics as well. This is another reason for the closed nature of the professions and of the associations' power to enforce their separate cultures.

Much of the expert proclamations are *ex cathedra*. They can be spotted immediately by noting that they contain neither supporting data or argument. Professionals say "our expert advice is that (medicare; abolition of the fault basis of automobile accident

---

[7] "A Postscript to the Miranda Project: Interrogation of Draft Protestors," 77 *Yale L. J.* 300, 312–318 (1967).

liability; land reform) is no damn good." But *no good for whom?* and *why?* are questions they prefer not to be asked.

To a large extent, they are questions not asked by academics. It is remarkable that with the burgeoning social sciences have come no major analyses of the nature and effectiveness of professional ethics, for instance. There have been occasional studies,[8] but they are not consistent parts of an institutionalized inquiry. The academic social scientists have defaulted, perhaps, because they have decided the professions are beneath them. Scientists, after all, are seekers after truth; professionals are after something else again. A small group of sociologists who express an interest in the sociology of the professions usually have a too-narrow focus: The practical political and economic consequences of their sociological data do not interest them.

There are consistent critics of professionals, of course, and they should not go without mention. The academic professional — the professor of law or medicine — is often so critical that he is widely regarded with suspicion by the practicing branch. By contrast, the professional academic is often far less critical of the subject he studies. This difference is perhaps to be attributed to the fact that the academic professional can, if he wishes, practice the profession about which he teaches and very often is teaching because practice is not satisfying enough. The professional academic, on the other hand, usually does not have a profession outside the academic world, or at least, has not practiced one; he more readily identifies with the subject of his discipline, and though he may occasionally despise those who people his discipline there is at the same time also a love for their doings in the abstract. But the problem with academic professionals is simply that they are specialists: Their very criticism is apt to be couched in specialist

---

[8] See, *e.g.*, Clyde L. King, ed., "The Ethics of the Professions and of Business," 101 *The Annals* (1922); Benson Y. Landis, "Ethical Standards and Professional Conduct," 297 *The Annals* (1955); James C. Charlesworth, "Ethics in America: Norms and Deviations," 363 *The Annals* (1966).

language that is not readily intelligible to the lay public and to be circulated in journals not readily accessible to them.

Social science is not a developed science, nor is it even a single science. Like physics hundreds of years ago, when mechanics was differentiated from the study of heat, and that from light, social science today is a collective term for a host of seemingly different inquiries: political science, economics, sociology, anthropology, psychology, and (usually) history. In nearly every popular magazine article on current social problems, the author comments in a tone combining exasperation and surprise that we can land men on the moon but we cannot define mental illness, clean up slums, eradicate poverty or hunger. There may be reason for exasperation but there surely should be no surprise: An economy is more complex than the organization of the universe, and man has come far later to a study of himself than the world around him. Yet the attempt of academics to find solutions is hindered to the degree that academic separations are insisted upon. The failure of the social scientist to incorporate the world of the professions in his discipline is at least as serious as his failure to study whole social problems.

3

Counted among the failures of education must be the dismal role played by the press and broadcast media in reporting professional doings. A public that has graduated from its schools must rely on the popular press for most accounts of the way in which the world changes. Lacking a theory of the professions, the press has defaulted in its job of reporting pertinent news. Even *The New York Times* is content for the most part to report annual meetings of the American Bar and Medical Associations as the doings of these professions, and very often the professional aspect is lost in the mist surrounding declamations on law or medicine. Television and radio give signs only occasionally of ever having heard of such institutions as the Supreme Court; and such of the times that its decisions are reported must suffice for reporting the profession. Although those newspapers which abstract the Court's decisions duly digested *United Mine Workers v. Illinois State Bar,* there has been no attempt to follow up the decision to see whether private group legal services have been increased as a result. There has been an even more appalling failure of the press to report such little-known phenomena as the virtually complete adoption of the Uniform Commercial Code throughout the United States. In drafting and lobbying stages for more than a quarter century, the Code took effect in the forty-ninth state, Mississippi, in April, 1968. Only Louisiana remains a holdout. The press has been silent; even *Business Week Magazine* has never once reported on the subject. Yet the Code, which has given a decade of law students nightly headaches, has had a decided effect on the commercial practices of the nation and on the consumer as well; its impact and the defects in commercial relations and creditor–debtor affairs are worthy at least of mention.

Of course, in a world surfeited with hard news and dominated by war, crime, and public malfeasance, much must go unreported for lack of a theory of importance and lack of the necessary expertise to report it. The press, too, has failed to demand generalists capable of reporting specialist doings to a public very much in need of enlightenment.

The time has come for the press to realize the importance of professions, to investigate them, and to report them as a whole, not as successions of delegates gathered at convention sites in grand hotels. The time has come for the great liberal arts schools to recognize the professions in their undergraduate curricula, not as technical courses, but as a great part of social, political, economic, and institutional history. And the time has come for graduate students in search of dissertation topics to seize on the professions and write their histories, but law not by lawyers and medicine not by doctors. Independent minds must gather up the raw materials for processing. There is a vast, as yet untapped field, ripe for mining. The rewards could be incalculable.

16
The Future of the Professions

The Bureau of Reclamation is a dam building machine which will keep building dams as long as there is running water in a stream in the United States. At the same time, it lacks a broader outlook which might consider the values that dams destroy. Professionals, in short, can be counted on to do their job but not necessarily to define their job.

     — CHARLES REICH, *"The Law of the Planned Society"*

We have no intention of displacing technicians, of making decisions whose validity rests on professional knowledge and experience which is not ours. However, the decision of the kind of development we want in our river basins and communities is a value judgment which should properly be made by citizens rather than engineers and technicians.

     — League of Women Voters, on the potential thermal pollution of the Connecticut River

1

The past is rarely a sure guide to the future. What we take for granted today was often singularly not the case during the centuries when the professions were being formed. It may seem astonishing that doctors could ever have been universally held in low repute, yet as late as the mid-1800's, doctors in some areas

268

of British life were sneered at. In the British armed forces, the surgeon was considered beneath a gentleman in dignity and forbidden decorations and honors paid other officers and denied a commission in the Navy until 1843. Engineers were also scoffed at: They came from the lower classes, beginning their careers in smithies and other shops; initially they concerned themselves with handcrafts; they made little use of scientific methods; and they were manual workers for whom a study of the classics would obviously not be a profitable endeavor. Yet the same culture regularly supposed the military to be a "profession of arms," despite the appalling lack of training, manner of promotion, and the questionable character of the men accepted for service. Commissions in the British Army were regularly purchased until late in the nineteenth century and the thought that a professional education would be helpful to the army officer was regularly derided until British disaster during the Crimean War forced a reappraisal.[1] In this country, it did not seem strange for a legal writer to take the defensive in writing on the importance of the profession: "Divinity, medicine, arms are perhaps the most important of what are usually called the professions; but those who know that the profession of law has always furnished the most zealous assertors and defenders of liberty in this and other countries, cannot believe it far behind the others in utility."[2]

The shift in prestige and quality of professional performance since the 1800's has been marked. We should not be fooled by the values of our times into believing the present like the past, and immutable. The priesthood today is not widely regarded as the road to riches; any positive assertion that it should be is likely to strike us as inconsistent with the work involved. Few defend as part and parcel of the clerical profession the organizing

[1] W. J. Reader, *Professional Men: The Rise of the Professional Classes in Nineteenth Century England* (1966), pp. 65, 70-1, and see Chapter 8.

[2] Daniel H. Calhoun, *Professional Lives in America: Structure and Aspiration 1750–1850* (1965), quoted at p. 199, n. 4; from *Atlantic Magazine*, I (1824).

evangelist to whom fundamentalists send large quantities of cash. One hundred fifty years ago, however, the English clergy found the robes of God highly profitable and rationalized this fact as necessary to the established religion.   One British commentator, discussing the parliamentary patronage which secured jobs for the well-born, noted that "it tempts parents of good families and fortunes to educate younger sons for the church . . . who . . . may, by their manners and rank, raise the whole profession in the esteem and respect of the public.   Church benefices may thus be considered a fund for the provision of the younger sons of our gentry and nobles; and in this point of view, it cannot surely be a matter of complaint to any of the higher and middle classes in the community, that the clergy enjoy a large portion of the riches of the state."[3]

The roles of many professionals have changed. Modern science and technology have split the great professions into scores of specialties unknown to their predecessors.   Modern industries have created still more professionals.   Yet the past is not all buried with the men who lived it: There is a professional image which lingers on.   One part of this image is that the professional is a fiercely independent practitioner whose very independence is essential to the interests of his client or patient; a corollary of the image is that he does not work for organizations.   Superimposed on the independent image of the experts is the gloss that the government should not regulate or otherwise participate in the doings of the professionals.   Still another part of the image is that professionals need not work in their self-interest (as businessmen are supposed to act) in order to achieve the public interest, even though both businessmen and experts are paid for what they do.

The image persists from habit and repetition but it no longer accurately portrays the professions.   Recent studies have shown, for instance, that at least in urban settings where the pressure of competition may be great, the individual doctor or lawyer is

[3] Quoted in Reader, *supra* note 1, p. 14.

forced to become a specialist in rather menial fields: Lawyers do errands, rather than law; doctors fill out insurance reports and treat industrial accidents at the laborers' places of work.[4] Commenting on the discovery that independent doctors and lawyers seem to become hacks and "choreboys of their clients," Professor Hughes notes that "we are at a paradox of modern professional freedom. The effective freedom to choose one's special line of work, to have access to the appropriate clients and equipment, to engage in that converse with eager and competent colleagues which will sharpen one's knowledge and skill, to organize one's time and effort so as to gain that end, and even freedom from pressure to conform to the client's individual or collective customs and opinions seem, in many lines of work, to be much greater for those professionals who have employers and work inside complicated and even bureaucratic organizations than for those who, according to the traditional concept, are in independent practice."[5]

Working for large organizations does not automaticaly mean that the quality of service will be low. We have passed the time when medicine and most other professionals can be supported by private financing and when practitioners can work alone. The brightest young law graduates go to work for large firms; and doctors for clinics and hospitals.[5a] Those who spurn private practice find themselves not as private practitioners in the ghettos but as employees of private or public agencies. Increasingly, the young professional, too, is becoming an organization man.

That professionals are independent of government is so obviously fallacious as to require no new recitations of evidence to dispute it. Governmental power is exercised to keep professionals

---

[4] See the studies by Jerome E. Carlin, "The Lawyer as Individual Practitioner: A Study in the Professions" (1959) and Joe L. Spaeth, "Industrial Medicine: A Low-Status Branch of the Profession," (1958), cited in Everett C. Hughes, "The Professions in Society," 26 *Canadian J. of Econ. and Poli. Sci.* 54 (1960).

[5] Hughes, *supra* note 4, p. 61.

[5a] It has been noted of late that increasing numbers of bright law graduates are "bypassing" the Wall Street and other law firms. See, *The New York*

in line, and that it is called "self-regulation" does not deny that public power is invoked in the process. It is perhaps not quite as clear that government participates in the professional process in many other ways as well. Large industrial concerns today generate their own source of investment capital from earnings, but the largest companies depend on the federal government as purchaser and contractor. Most large industries depend on the government for research and development assistance of many kinds; ties between the professions and government are inevitable. Medicine, for instance, is rapidly developing a need for large investment in capital resources: Laboratories, machinery and tools of all sorts are multiplying only less rapidly than the need. To establish adequate facilities and to put medicine in a position equal to that occupied by large manufacturers, massive federal aid is no doubt required.

As the bond between government and the professions hardens, the claim that professionals achieve the public interest through an antiseptic market system loses merit. Physicians have long argued and continue to insist that the most efficient method to develop and maintain quality health services and medical care is to let the private physician alone: The classic profit system (with an ethical additive) would take care of this industry just as the market took care of everything else. Dr. Morris Fishbein, long the editor of *JAMA*, has said that "state medicine," by which he meant state payment to doctors who treat in a clinic a particular part of dis-

---

Times, November 19, 1969, p. 29, and *Time*, December 12, 1969, both of which note that probably none of the editors of the *Harvard Law Review* will go into private practice upon graduation in 1970. No doubt many new kinds of jobs are attracting public-spirited young lawyers, but as the editors of the *Harvard Law Review* themselves commented, they are accepting one-year jobs as judicial clerks or going traveling or onto further schooling: "It would probably be more enlightening to know what former editors are doing two or three years after graduation . . . the occasional contacts we have had . . . provide some basis for an admittedly intuitive feeling that many more former editors find their way into private practice than statements like that which appeared in *Time*." "With the Editors," 83 *Harv. L. Rev.* vii (1970).

ease, such as tonsils or influenza, "is unthinkable. . . . It is the death of initiative, of humanity, of science."[6] His perfervid style should not detract from the faith many doctors place in what he says. When it was pointed out that many people cannot afford high medical costs, the physicians were quick to respond, though sometimes morosely, how beneficient their pricing system really was — and is: poor patients, they said, don't pay nearly as much as rich ones. The latter subsidize the former.[7] It is a wonder, if this be the truth, that there has been no spontaneous revolt by the wealthy against this highly peculiar manifestation of free enterprise. Imagine General Motors ranging their prices for Cadillacs from $20,000 to nothing, depending on the prospective buyers' income level. And if the rich are to subsidize the poor, it is difficult to see that the redistribution of wealth by doctors is to be preferred to that carried on by the federal government.

The image no longer squares with reality. The professions have so far been unable to insist that the public see what was not there because until relatively recently the professional quackery did not do any great social harm. Of medical quackery, Dr. Fishbein has written that "homeopathy owed its initial success to the fact that it prescribed small doses of remedies in vast quantities of water, and so did not interfere with the natural tendency of the body to recover. On this tendency — the *vis medicatrix naturae* — all of the cults of history have floated their frail vessels."[8] So with the professions. When society was simpler, the pretenses of the professions did not interfere with the ability of society to benefit from

---

[6] Morris Fishbein, *The New Medical Follies* (1927), p. 233.

[7] Occasionally the doctor will suggest his acceptance of the Robin Hood system is begruding at best. Thus one hospital administrator has said: "The doctors on the active staff here carry a very heavy load of charitable work. This, of course, is part of the code, but at times it gets very arduous. . . . There are a lot of low-income people who like to live like the upper group and who contract for better medical services than they can afford." Quoted in Hall, "The Stages of a Medical Career," 53 *Am. J. of Sociology* 327 (1948).

[8] Fishbein, *supra* note 6, p. 140.

what the professionals had to offer. We should no longer be so sanguine about this possibility. The professions can no longer support themselves with the shibboleths of a simpler time when the general practitioner knew most of what there was to know and did most of what could be done. Like the rest of the industrial sector, professional services require capital and coordination.

2

To adapt successfully to the future, the licensed professions must recognize a public right to their services. Already a significant number of citizens reject the notion that essential services need go only to those who can pay for them. The transformation of the consumers' interest in the professional service from a market orientation to a right—from contract to status—corresponds directly to the transformation of the producer's interest already effected.[9] Professionals depend on status to achieve their ends. It is neither radical nor shocking to suggest that consumers must increasingly rely on status to balance the ends sought.

The development has begun. In 1962 the Supreme Court recognized the constitutional right of the criminal suspect to be defended by a qualified attorney, regardless of the suspect's income or wealth. The indigent are entitled to court-appointed counsel.[10] The right to professional services must be broadly extended, and the rights must not be limited by conventional definitions. The status to which the consumer must become entitled, in other words, is not to be limited to a circumscribed right to a particular service. For the power that stems from the professional status runs deep and the new status of consumers must be equally rooted. Thus, not only should the "right to work" be more expansively understood, the right of schools and other institutions to accreditation should be understood to depend on more than the say-so of private institutions. Similarly, the student's right to the academic degree,

9 See Chapter 3.
10 Gideon v. Wainwright, 373 U.S. 335 (1963).

or to the requisite training, should be recognized and protected.[11]

That consumers should have rights and that these rights should be protected by an understanding that they are vested rather than contractual is an easily resisted notion. Opposition will be kin to the detesters of government handouts: No one has a right to welfare, it will be contended. You get what you pay for; you deserve what you earn. But self-help is an attitude which many people do not have. They do not because it was never engendered in them. When they are adults we blame them while sympathizing with their children, of whom we say, "How can we expect them to live a decent life? They are not educated to it." We believe it evil to lessen the incentive to self help and we believe we do lessen it when we provide free social services. We tolerate the providing of these services by the government because we are not without compassion and because we fear the revolution. We rationalize the welfare check.

We need not. The social system which defeats the incentives to self help by denying them to the child must learn to encourage them. This calls for action, not chit chat. The self-help attitude is not a natural instinct in a complex society, though the comfortable thought that it is might be. A society which prefers to remain vital must be prepared to keep its constituent members vital: Health, legal rights, education, a decent environment (including housing), and job opportunity (including the opportunity to become professionals) need not be purchasable commodities.

3

The time for heresy is overdue: The expert is the wrong person to define his job or to evaluate how well it is performed. If the

[11] See, e.g., In the Matter of Howard G. Carr v. St. John's University, 17 App. Div. 2d 632, 331 N.Y.S. 2d 410 (1962), in which the court agreed that the Catholic institution could refuse a degree to a student who had been married in a civil ceremony, thus violating a university rule, even though he had finished all course work and graduation was only three months away. See

definition and evaluation are to avoid inevitable bias, they must be carried out by public institutions.

As our civilization matures, more and more problems require professional solutions. At one time even law and medicine seemed mere trades. The management of business enterprises and the government bureaucracy scarcely required any training. Yet as the matters with which certain practitioners dealt hardened into a complex of related issues, professionals emerged to handle them. In time, law, medicine, engineering, architecture, accounting, and dozens of others congealed. We can expect as yet ill-defined current problems to be fitted into a professional framework in the future. Population expansion, environmental pollution, collapsing cities, overcrowded living spaces and archaic transportation will some day soon have recognized professionals attending them.

The serious question is whether such professionals as city planners will assert themselves as haughtily as their more established brethren. Will they so cow the public by impressive displays of knowledge that the public will be deterred from criticizing their "solutions" to "professional problems"? It would be unfortunate. As Harold J. Laski has aptly said: "The expert, in fact, simply by reason of his immersion in a routine, tends to lack flexibility of mind once he approaches the margins of his special theme. He is incapable of rapid adaptation to novel situations. He unduly discounts experience which does not tally with his own. He is hostile to views which are not set out in terms he has been accustomed to handle. No man is so adept at realizing difficulties within the field that he knows; but, also, few are so incapable of meeting situations outside that field."[12] It follows that experts must be held in check.

If we are to hold them in check, we must realize the vital necessity to organize others for the preservation of our own individual-

also Webster Jr. College v. Mid States Association of Colleges and Secondary Schools, Inc., 302 F. Supp. 459 (1969), which held that an accrediting association cannot refuse to accredit a college merely because it is not a non-profit institution.

[12] Harold J. Laski, *The Limitations of the Expert* (1931), pp. 6–7.

ity. We must know that the equation is complex and shifting, calling for many types of organizations, now one type seeming most prominent, and now another. We must cast aside the false dichotomy that our integrity and freedom will be preserved by either the private association or the government alone. We need private associational power and we need public governmental power, and whatever the mix, at the same time.

We must be frank to recognize the qualitatively different kinds of possible solutions to the problem of undue process. We can seek institutional measures to correct or check abuses that spring from the professionals' undiluted exercise of their power. We do this because we believe that the probability of changing "human nature" is low, at least at present. On the other hand, many problems are caused by human motivations and aspirations which can be redirected—from one generation to the next, if not in particular individuals. Clearly we must seek both institutional and psychological changes: institutional because psychological changes are never complete and never immediate; psychological because institutional changes are not deep or persistent and stand daily in danger of corruption.

The time may not be far distant, as man measures time, when the preoccupation of philosophers who theorized about the quality of life and its ultimate meaning will become the occupation of the average person. If we look beyond the threat of famine, nuclear holocaust, and other planetary mishaps, we can see a people —at least in this country—who in their surfeit of leisure will contemplate ultimates and absolutes.

Specialists will not be the best judges of those ultimates, nor will the combination of special interests identify the public interest. No theory of expertise has been sufficiently developed and tested to permit experts to be the arbiters of our moral values. But someone must have the power to resolve public issues. "In a world imperatively needing organization the risk of granting power in some forms is inevitable."[13] The risk that democratic regulation will lead to total regulation must be borne. The Constitution does not guarantee its own success, nor could it. The continued existence of a democracy depends in the end on the responsibility of its people; that responsibility cannot be imposed upon the person by government, whether public or private. The advocate cannot be tossed into jail in a democracy for his irresponsible advocacy; he may destroy the nation by the power of his persuasion, but that is the risk of life itself. The risk can be reduced by shucking off the parochialism of our past. Our success is not guaranteed for we are only at a beginning, but that is no cause for pessimism.

[13] Jaffe, "Law Making by Private Groups," 51 *Harv. L. Rev.* 201, 251 (1937).

Epilogue: A Word of Warning

All professions are conspiracies against the laity.
— GEORGE BERNARD SHAW, Preface to *The Doctor's Dilemma*

Divers professions and many vocations subsist and are grounded only upon public abuses and popular errors.
— MONTAIGNE, *Essays II*

1

Except for the writer who hopes for revolution on whatever terms he can command, no author can honestly expect his readers to agree with all opinions expressed through the course of a book. In this case, however, agreement or disagreement is quite beside the point. For the heart of the argument here is not what the substantive resolution of the issues will be but in what manner that resolution is to be brought about—whether important public issues are to be resolved by all of us or by experts in private groups.

Of course, a strongly held position may provoke attention as well as pause, dissent as well as happy agreement. It can also lead to outright dismissal. Most would view this a misfortune. I would. I do not wish to be accused of saying merely that each profession is a monopoly and monopolies must be broken to size, thus to be dismissed on the grounds of ignorance, rancor, or even

279

lack of elemental patriotism.[1] I have not said that professionals should not be regulated, that they are incompetent, that we can do without them, that courts should overturn all licensing legislation, or that legislatures are the willing tools of corrupt legislatures. I have not said that the professions now control us, nor have I said that professionals are capable of deep passion only when the interest at stake is their own. I have not said all professionals subscribe to the theory of the professional class. I would not be happy to see a crusade to abolish the professions, citing this as its source. I give no such cause and promise no celebrated revolution. What I do say is that enough professionals, strategically located in management and other roles, do adhere to the theory to force the economic, political, and social consequences described. I hope to have persuaded the reader that undue process is a problem larger than the affixing of convenient labels to it would make it seem.

None of the foregoing is to argue that the professional associations do not occasionally, or often, do good works. The American Bar Association, for instance, is developing new standards for disciplining errant lawyers; the special committee is headed by retired Supreme Court Justice Tom C. Clark. Another panel, headed by the highly respected and liberal retired Chief Justice of the California Supreme Court, Roger J. Traynor, is preparing a new code of judicial ethics. The ABA came out in 1969 against the noxious Murphy Amendment, which would have permitted governors to veto expenditures of funds for lawsuits brought by the Office of Economic Opportunity (OEO)-sponsored legal aid program that is effectively challenging numerous laws restricting the poor and underprivileged. And it is probably unfair to say that the ABA opposed it because lawyers do not approve of governmental power to veto lawsuits, since private attorneys did not stand to gain from any lack of competition the Murphy Amendment would have induced. The poor did not — and will not —

[1] As was Jessica Mitford, by the funeral industry, shortly after *The American Way of Death* was published. See David Finn, "The Businessman and his Critics," *Saturday Review*, September 12, 1964, p. 60.

go to private attorneys. So, too, the AMA and other organizations do quietly pursue the public interest in some areas. But that is beside the point here, because professional associations do not so limit their activities.

Another line of attack on the present argument is possible. When Professor Galbraith attempted to demonstrate that the growth of the big corporation has been away from the market toward a planning regime, that antitrust has proved a charade behind which large firms hide, and that the nexus between private industry and the state has increased organically as a result, he was met with a curious rejoinder. A panel of three distinguished economists disputed Galbraith's thesis before a joint session of the Senate Subcommittee on Retailing, Distribution and Marketing Practices and the Subcommittee on Monopoly of the Select Committee on Small Business. The economists testified in essence that the facts showed the large companies were guilty of abysmal planning, that small, competitive firms were more innovative and, therefore, that a market system is to be preferred. The argument, that big companies are seeking — and finding — means to escape the market, is thus met with the objection that we are the worse for it.[2]

In much the same way it is possible to criticize the thrust of this book: examples can be produced to show that professionals can act truly in the interests of the client and that this is more desirable than examples cited herein. I agree. But that is simply

[2] The testimony is reprinted in 1 *Antitrust L. and Econ. Rev.* 11 (1967). Much of the dispute concentrated on a rather narrow point: whether Professor Galbraith, because he saw an escape mechanism, thereby advocated it. Contradictions in the various discussions trace ultimately to this point and could have been avoided, since the argument for more incisive regulation than antitrust hinges on whether a market system can in fact be restored or whether the capture of governmental power to implement economic plans will proceed apace. This has nothing to do with whether Professor Galbraith enjoys the process or thinks it desirable (though the belief is desirability does have very much to do with whether or not it is thought undesirable to break up large firms).

to say that if self-regulation worked it would be a good thing. Theories are always good in theory.

That self-regulation does not fail more than fifty percent or even twenty-five percent of the time does not prove self-regulation is an acceptable device if exclusively relied upon, though it does suggest it is a useful one. I do not advocate that responsible members of the professions become morally lax because some members are so already. But I have asserted throughout that a significant number of professional practitioners are not deterred by "self-regulation," that the system of self-regulation is not conducive to such deterrence, and that a "significant number" may be numerically or relatively small and yet be enough to call sharply into question the traditional means of controlling professional behavior.

In this sense the argument in this book is far from radical and in fact is rather conservative, for it presumes that the professional service is necessary and vital. But that professionals are invaluable members of a modern society does not mean we need credit their claim that the public is protected by self-regulation. We may believe in the desirability of self-regulation without believing that it often occurs or that when it does it regulates what it ought. And if it does not, some other form of control is necessary to protect the public and at the same time to guard against an intellectual debasement of the place of the modern profession.

This book has not assayed the technical problems of any particular profession.[3] Much professional reform is still undeniably necessary. The quality of law schools, for instance, varies greatly, from

---

[3] Nor has this book pretended to include all professions. Education has been neglected entirely, in part because the intimate relationship of teacher and state makes it a very special case. Nevertheless, just as doctors claim as a corporate group to possess the necessary expertise to decide issues of social policy and medicine, so teachers also claim a peculiar competence: in their corporate status as an academic "faculty" they presume to know better than anyone else about the process of education. This is a claim we rarely dispute but which we might find increasingly useful to doubt. The biologist, English critic, and professor of history—in committee—do not necessarily possess the last word in academic policy, though they often have the final one. Engineering, too, has been ignored, in part because the more

the diploma mills which fool their students into thinking they know something to the great institutions whose professors can trick their students into thinking they know nothing. All these schools may create "lawyers" who may never go into law at all, but their paths are far apart. And while the best schools have had their share of questionable practitioners, it is far more likely that a large number of shady lawyers who give the profession a bad name come from the lower spectrum of law schools. Because they have not been able to join prestigious law firms or accept responsible government positions, some of these lawyers gravitate to that kind of practice in which it is easy to give bad advice to ignorant people.

At the same time, it is well to remember that simply because there is a congeries of tasks which we call a "profession," problems of practice do not automatically follow from the quality of training or the motives of practitioners. Autopsies at the public morgue, diet clinics, care for the criminally insane, performance of abortions, and conduct of army physicals are all part of the large world of medicine. Collecting debts, drafting federal statutes, evicting tenants who are unable to pay rents to a slumlord who refuses to repair his apartments, and negotiating contracts are all a part of the legal profession. In each case, the practitioner is a "doctor" or a "lawyer." A profession is not intrinsically bad or inefficient because some of its practitioners are coarse, undereducated, or corrupt; it would remain in disrepute if all practitioners were angels so long as conditions permit its members legally to perform certain tasks. If it were illegal for landlords to collect rent unless they performed their obligations, landlord lawyers would not hurt the professional image. In most states there are no such laws. Yet many landlord lawyers are good lawyers: They are proficient in their work, ethical toward clients and other lawyers, respectful in court.[4]

than one hundred professional societies that exist at the national level alone have tended to fragment the profession, making it a special case also. Many other occupations are left out as well, not because they are unimportant but because all of life cannot be put in a single book.

[4] *Cf.* Everett C. Hughes, *Men and Their Work* (1958), p. 71: "The very

Many other problems will remain because we are predisposed to discount things as the partial basis of human suffering. We do not regulate guns because they only shoot; people kill. So with drugs. To be sure, a person is at fault if he is foolish enough to believe fradulent drug claims; obviously a person is at fault when he makes the claim. But we cannot therefore dispense with pharmaceutical regulation. The cost of medical quackery is estimated at greater than $2 billion annually, more than all research spent on disease,[5] and that estimate does not include the pain and suffering of and later costs to patients who will need more treatment because they did not seek reputable help early. But the public regulatory agencies which now have sufficient legal power to take action are hampered by the failure of legislatures to fund sufficient enforcement programs. The failure to fund is not merely the lack of money; a fraction of the annual waste of private dollars on quackery could finance a handsome enforcement enterprise.

It is also well to remember that the power of professional organizations is there to be used; the question is, by whom? As the pressure of work increases, professionals tend to ignore their national and even local organizations.[6] By 1960, ninety per cent of practicing physicians, but only thirty-five per cent of non-practicing physicians' were members of the AMA.[7] The result is comparable

demand for highly scrupulous and respectable lawyers depends in various ways upon the availability of less scrupulous people to attend to the less respectable problems of even the best people."

[5] James Harvey Young, *The Medical Messiahs* (1967), p. vii.

[6] "If your main interest in life is the helical structure of DNA or if you practice in a sanctuary where private fees only supplement your basic salary, it seems a waste of time to attend local medical society meetings where the socioeconomic problems of medicine are a main interest. Ignored is the fact that these problems are vital to the profession and to the country, that they become mundane only when left to the unopposed deliberations of a mundane minority." John Gordon Freyman, "A Doctor Prescribes for the AMA," *Harper's*, August, 1965, p. 79.

[7] See Elton Rayack, *Professional Power and American Medicine: The Economics of the American Medical Association* (1967), Chapter 1.

to what might happen should a sizable segment of the professional and educated population decide no longer to play a role in the United States Government or to what is happening in state governments for that very reason. It is unfortunate that powerful organizations are a part of every professional's responsibility—for doubtless the professional would rather spend his time at his job than at organization meetings and politics. But critics must be educated to their responsibility: To deplore and then ignore the AMA is to let it get away with the very acts critics despise. The only solution to the abuse of power is its taming by capture.

Much more is involved in the processes and problems of the professional class. An interdependent society necessarily implies that everything has some effect on all else; some remote and some direct. Although this book has not dealt with the organization of state legislatures, their universal failure to enforce their programs, their general failure to attract good minds to the problems worth solving, the absence of non-partisan legislative research and reference centers, the abysmal procedures used in recruitment of judges and other important state officials, the effect of government by legislative committee and the seniority system, and the woeful inadequacy of education generally—these, and far too many other factors to list here, are crucial to the problem at hand.[8] The solution is not an end but a process and it will require changes across the board.

But the fact that many other institutions and beliefs are poorly organized and outmoded should not make us condemn as futile attempts to attack the problem on a piecemeal basis. That many automobile accidents are caused by poorly-trained drivers is no reason to conclude that driver training courses are the only answer. So with the organization of the professions.

[8] One large repository of private law-making power only briefly alluded to throughout is the national and state trade associations. Though the trade codes of New Deal days were short-lived, trade associations gained in power because of the National Industrial Recovery Act, and they exercise that power still. See Walton H. Hamilton, *The Politics of Industry* (1957).

We must attempt to live the principles we espouse. To the believer in democracy, there is no surprise in learning that extension of the franchise in the South has helped improve minority conditions. So, also, our belief that law can channel change and settle disputes peacefully must be put to the test by bringing representation to the poor who have heretofore been victimized by highly questionable and sometimes illegal practices of landlords and merchants. The belief that professionals must adhere to high standards to serve effectively must be enforced by broad public policy, not a narrow private one.

Still another word of warning is necessary. A public debate, prompted by Vice President Agnew's denunciation of the press, calls to mind the danger of wrapping complex problems in simple slogans.

Mr. Agnew has spoken out against the "unelected elite" that controls the press. The Vice President's slogan is not particularly apt, since the entire private sector of the economy and of all the professions are made up of "unelected elites." We evidently believe that to carry out some jobs people who are not publicly elected or even appointed are required. This, lest the Vice President has forgotten, is called "free enterprise."

Of course, Mr. Agnew has foresworn public control of the press; governmental censorship is to have no role in his unformed plan to make the press more "responsible" (*i.e.*, less subjective — one man's media, it seems, is another's poison). The hint is fairly plain, therefore, that the press should govern itself. Here the lessons of this book suggest that a self-regulating press, organized in a manner similar to that by which other professions regulate themselves, is just as dangerous as public regulation and in the end would amount to the same thing.

This is not the first time that a philosophy has been enshrined in a slogan to sidestep the hard questions and the important issues. "Responsibility" is a general proposition, which does not of itself decide the concrete case. The requirement for public responsibility of doctors and lawyers and beauticians need not —

and should not — carry over to journalists simply because they might also be classed as professionals. That a member of the National Commission on the Causes and Prevention of Violence has publicly proposed the licensing of journalists is disturbing, apart from the dubious constitutionality of the proposal.[9] For a free press has an independent and critically necessary value. If bias is an inevitable cost of freedom, we must be prepared to bear it.

There is, unfortunately, a growing belief that the correlative of the right of the free press is its responsible exercise. In denying a motion to enjoin newspapers and television from reporting stories concerning alleged American atrocities and massacres in Vietnam because of an impending military trial, the Court of Military Appeals said that the right of the "responsible press" to publish is not questioned.[10] Because the court implies that "irresponsible" reporting could be enjoined, it blatantly and alarmingly has misread the First Amendment, which does not make responsibility a prerequisite for freedom.

Yet the simple-minded thought is spread about even by the press itself. No stranger to coining slogans, the press has long argued against erosion of its charter in the First Amendment by proclaiming the "right of the people to know." If followed to its logical end, this would spell the end of freedom, for if the public does not get the information that someone in the government or elsewhere presumes the public should know, the response would be for sanctions against the press to force it to open its pages. It is not a long step from that to editing stories which are "misleading" or "not properly informative." And that is censorship. The apocalyptic vision that there be dissenting prefaces to the Bible, that the last fifty pages of every book be reserved for reply, and that the second section of every newspaper be held

[9] The suggestion came from Dr. Walter Menninger, a psychiatrist. He views his proposal simply as a means of weeding out the "totally inept." See *The New York Times*, February 5, 1970, p. 26.

[10] United States v. Calley, 19 U.S.C.M.A. 96, 97, 41 C.M.R. 96, 97 (1969).

open for the "opposition" may seem absurd, and so it is, but serious lawyers, among others, have come close to advocating it.[11]

The answer to press responsibility is not to be found in government or self-regulation. It is to be found, even if it is difficult to accomplish, in the individual education of journalists to the need for reporting news in which individual preferences are held to a minimum. But these preferences (or "biases") will never be eliminated, not only because value-free machines will never become reporters, but also and more importantly because readers will always insist on finding dark and sinister motivation in the journalist who reports news that is sad, unsettling, or mad. Likewise, the public needs an education in the relevant.

2

Though there is much to be done, the first fluttering steps of progress have already been taken. I close on a note of hope. So complete did the hold on professional associations by traditionally-oriented practitioners seem to be that in Chapter 1 I doubted that the social concern of students would quickly focus on the power of these organizations. Since those words were written young physicians and students did just that: A protest was staged inside the 1969 AMA Convention in New York City. To the resolution of the South Carolina delegation proclaiming "that the AMA endorses the concept that medical care is a marketable service made available by a dedicated medical profession to everyone regardless of economic status, and that it is not a right guaranteed by government," and the resolution asking for agreement with the ABA to limit use of malpractice suits, the leader of a number of dissidents who picketed the convention was allowed two minutes to speak. Calling the AMA the "American Murderers Association," he burned his membership card. The attack was not immediately

[11] See, e.g., Jerome A. Barron, "Access to the Press — A First Amendment Right," 80 *Harv. L. Rev.* 1641 (1967).

productive, except for its evoking from one older delegate the response: "Let's kill the bastards," proving that self-righteous doctors, no less than those who uphold political principles, often lead the call to physical slaughter.[12] But protests are symbolic and progress depends on hard and often anonymous work. The disaffected have challenged society; it is time to realize that society has issued its own challenge, and that "freedom" and "justice" are not achieved by crying for them.

[12] *The Washington Post,* July 16, 1969, p. 2. Law students, too have decided private practice is not necessarily conducive to social justice. To date, they have concentrated on picketing law firms, however, not bar associations, though not without results: many firms across the country have suddenly found an interest in clients too poor to pay. See, *e.g., The Washington Post,* December 22, 1969, p. A2.

Acknowledgments

This book derives from an undergraduate thesis that was begun in January, 1964. During the succeeding six years, many people came to my aid, and I gratefully acknowledge where possible their assistance.

In 1964 it was incumbent upon me to write a thesis at Yale University for the undergraduate major in Politics and Economics. Very early in that year my father, J. Ben Lieberman, suggested I look into the activities of private groups to see whether they could create public policy. It was not difficult to discover that most political scientists assumed that pressure groups influenced public policy by lobbying but not by capturing the power of government itself. Professional groups of the type discussed throughout this book were almost entirely ignored, even by my own teachers, Professors Robert A. Dahl and Charles E. Lindblom, who declared in their path-breaking book *Politics, Economics, and Welfare* (1953) that "the future of freedom in the West, and certainly in the United States, is inescapably bound up with the future of the four main hierarchical organizations through which so many of our most vital decisions are made — in short, the business corporation, the government bureaucracy, the trade union, and the political party" (p. xxii).

290

The thesis was completed in the spring and I am glad to acknowledge that the criticism given it by my readers, Professors William G. Foltz and William Lee Miller, was sufficient to result in only a tenuous relation between that work and this. I also gratefully acknowledge the help of my then colleagues — i.e., students — from whose conversations the issues were sharpened: Sherman T. Brewer, Jr., Thomas R. Vischi, and, especially, Sherwin Goldman (then at Yale Law School), who instructed me in due process before my time.

That summer and the following year at Harvard Law School I rewrote the thesis and was indebted to George Schatzki, then a teaching fellow at the law school, for the interest he took in the work. During the next summer I had the opportunity to meet the then Attorney General, Nicholas deB. Katzenbach, and in a very brief conversation he indicated that he did not see much of a threat in the actions of professional groups. (Medicare had passed Congress the week before.) The conversation acted as a spur; I wrote the fifty Governors shortly thereafter to solicit their views. As noted, twenty-seven responded in a short time, and six or seven even acknowledged a problem; but the views of all those who responded were helpful indeed.

I began to rewrite again. In particular I wrote a short article on *Lathrop v. Donahue* under the auspices of the Second Year Writing Program at the law school and had the good fortune to be guided by Professor Paul A. Freund and by Robert A. Warden, then a third year editor of the *Harvard Law Review*. The article, under the title "Rule by Experts: The Rise of Undue Process," appeared in 3 *Harvard Legal Commentary* 182 (1966).

Meanwhile I began to work on other books and this one was laid aside, though clippings from *The New York Times* and desultory reading continued. In December, 1968, Edward R. Burlingame, then editor-in-chief of Walker and Company, agreed to publish the book — and work began in earnest. Sometimes a rule not to mention or thank one's editors or publishers is invoked but that is a silly rule, for a book is almost never the product of one mind, and an editor is an important shaper of the final product. I am grateful for the enthusiasm Ed Burlingame showed and for his help, and for the same enthusiasm and help of the book's editor, James K. Page, Jr., Walker's current editor-in-chief.

For his willingness to read the entire book in manuscript form, I am deeply grateful to Adolph A. Berle.

I must thank also many others who have helped these past six years: my parents, who have seen me through the entire project in innumerable ways; for their forbearance, my parents-in-law, who must have been a little suspicious when I excused myself of late "to go work on footnotes"; Esther and Harry Plotkin, whose hospitality to my family and me during the past year was largely responsible for the book's being finished on time; Jon M. Van Dyke, who read the entire manuscript, and Robert M. Keating, who read parts of it, and both of whom through discussion helped clarify many issues; Sandor Frankel, for counsel on many points; Dr. Barry Berlin, Dr. David Grodsky, Coleman S. Hicks, Bernard M. Imber, Dr. Heiman G. Lieberman, Dr. Leonard G. Rhodes, John H. Stassen; and my wife, who aided in too many ways to enumerate. Of course any errors of fact or judgment are attributable solely to me.

My debt to scholars, their books, and their articles should be apparent from the material cited in footnotes throughout. At the same time, it should be clear that the subject matter is not one that has been affected by an overwhelming scholarly interest. More than forty years ago, Sir Alexander Carr-Saunders said that the "story of the evolution of the professions is an unwritten chapter in the social history of the last two centuries."[1] His statement still

[1] Sir Alexander Carr-Saunders, "Professions, Their Organization and Place in Society" (The Herbert Spencer Lecture, Oxford, 1928)

stands today. In collaboration with P.A. Wilson, he published *The Professions* in 1933, but that was only a beginning pertaining to Great Britain and is now dated. Only a handful of other books has charted the field. *A Guide to the Study of the United States of America,* a bibliographic compilation by the Library of Congress in 1960, contains not a single index reference to the professions or professionalism. If this book serves to awaken a theoretical as well as a public interest, it will have served its purpose.

J. K. L.

Washington, D.C.
January, 1970

Index

Freyman, John Gordon, 284
Friedman, Lawrence, 49, 185
Friedman, Milton, 153, 247, 248
frog dealers, 15
fruit dealers, 16-7
funeral board, 24
funeral directors, see morticians
funeral industry, investigation
    of, 4
funeral prices, 81
funeral societies, 153-4
funerals, annual number of, 156
fur dealers, 17

Galbraith, John Kenneth, 10,
    42, 59, 81, 152-3, 155, 160,
    167, 175, 223, 281
Galdstone, Iago, 35
garage operators, 17
Garceau, Oliver, 107-8
Garfield, James A., 49
Garrison v. Louisiana, 127
Gellhorn, Walter, 2, 3, 19-20,
    30, 245
General Motors Corporation, 273
general will, 41
generally accepted accounting
    principles, 121
Georgia, photographers, 2, 30, 230
Gideon v. Wainwright, 274
Gilb, Corinne Lathrop, 3
Gimbel Brothers, 176
Goddard, Sam, 138
Goesaert v. Cleary, 194
Goldstein, Joseph, 213
Goode, William J., 35, 54, 60
Goodman, Linda, 66
government, capture of by
    private group, 8
grading, lumber, 107
Graham, Howard J., 9
Grammer, Stella, 39
Grant, Ulysses S., 49
grass cutters, licensing of, 17

Greenwood, Ernest, 56, 119
Grey Advertising, Inc., 263
grief therapy, 210-11
grievance committees, 108-9,
    see also specific committees
grocers (ca. 1600), 43
Group Health Association, 76-8,
    119
*Group Health Cooperative of
Puget Sound v. King County
    Medical Society,* 26
group power, belief in, 8
group practice, 223-6
    of lawyers, 73-6
Grovey v. Townsend, 234
guide dog trainers, 16
guild system, 3
guilds, 37-42, 155, 172-3
    return to, 199-200
Hale, Robert L., 198
Hamilton, Walton H., 285
Hammer v. Dagenhart, 187
Hamrick, J. Nathaniel, 16
Hanft, Frank, 16
Harlan, John Marshall, 100-1,
    109, 201, 225-6
Harvard College Observatory,
    216
Harvard University, 259
hatmakers, colonial, 39
hatters, 40
Hawaii v. Kraft, 230
Hawaii
    lawyers, 126-7
    photographers, 230
Hawkins, Dr. Reginald A., 103-
    4, 168, 235-6
*Hawkins v. North Carolina
    Dental Society,* 27, 103, 168,
    199, 235-6
Hayakawa, S. I., 52
Health Insurance Plan of
    Greater New York (HIP),
    119-20